Teaching Reading in Early England

*"Reading — the Key to Grammar." From Gregory
Reisch's* Margarita Philosophica *(Heidelberg, 1486)*

Teaching Reading in Early England

W J Frank Davies MA

*Senior Lecturer in Education, The School of Education,
University of Southampton*

 Pitman Publishing

First published 1973

Sir Isaac Pitman and Sons Ltd
Pitman House, Parker Street, Kingsway, London WC2B 5PB
PO Box 46038, Banda Street, Nairobi, Kenya
Sir Isaac Pitman (Aust) Pty Ltd
Pitman House, 158 Bouverie Street, Carlton, Victoria 3053, Australia
Pitman Publishing Corporation
6 East 43rd Street, New York, NY 10017, USA
Sir Isaac Pitman (Canada) Ltd
495 Wellington Street West, Toronto 135, Canada
The Copp Clark Publishing Company
517 Wellington Street West, Toronto 135, Canada

ISBN 0 273 00029 2

Text set in 11/12pt. IBM Baskerville, printed by photolithography, and bound in Great Britain at the Pitman Press, Bath

G4683:15

Preface

Before World War II the scientific study of the skill of reading was mostly confined to a few notable pioneers in the United States. By most parents and indeed by many teachers, particularly those instructing the higher grades, the ability to read was regarded as something that "just happened." As Holbrook Jackson wrote, "the ease with which so many acquire it proves it to be one of mankind's most natural endowments."

Since then the picture has radically changed. Hardly a week now passes without an educationist receiving catalogues advertising all sorts of pedagogic works and research studies that are concerned almost wholly with this one field. For example, one recent commercial bulletin listed books dealing with such topics as the psychological bases of reading ability, the prediction of reading achievement, formulae of readability, techniques of remediation and the potential of programmed learning through the medium of electronic devices.

Yet, despite this upsurge in professional fervour and expertise and in public awareness of its significance in education, one aspect of reading, the story of its evolution in England, has been largely ignored. In fact, only three works, and all American, have been devoted entirely to its study. Moreover, the pre-1612 period has been grievously neglected. One unpublished thesis that ranges generally over the whole span of its history provides merely a brief synopsis of what was supposed to have happened in the centuries of pre-American history. Another work dismisses the whole of the pre-1612 period in some thirty pages, half of which are devoted to the Greeks and Romans, before hurrying ahead to the American share of the story, and the third book takes up its theme at the beginning of the seventeenth century. Many articles and books, it is true, have dealt competently with the origins of the alphabet but an integrated study of reading practice and the teaching of reading in England between classical times and the early seventeenth century has not previously been produced.

This is strange, for this was a formative period in which the seeds of many of our modern methods and attitudes were sown. For instance, we should discover that the kinaesthetic, linguistic shape-of-the-letter and phonic techniques might not be as new as their twentieth-century adherents claim; or that spelling reform and the use of a modified code for the teaching of reading were lively issues many centuries before the Initial Teaching Alphabet made its bow. Or, in view of the current confusion about the most suitable age at which a child can be successfully introduced to formal reading, we might well ask in this respect if sufficient heed has been paid to the remarks of Quintilian in classical times or the various arguments that were being powerfully voiced by our sixteenth-century English teachers of reading.

This book tells the story of how the Britons and later the English, exposed to classical and Christian influences, were introduced to the alphabet and so to reading, why and where and by whom our ancestors were taught to read, by what methods and with what basic devices they were instructed, to what extent they could enjoy the skill once it had been acquired and how many failed or were slow to master the process. It is not a historical disquisition for the pedant. It is an examination of the teaching of the skill of reading in England up to 1612, with the essentials of reading techniques and implements as the dominant element throughout. An endeavour has therefore been made to relate the historical aspects of the teaching of reading to modern practice but, to prevent the material from becoming too pedagogically technical for the non-educationist, an abundance of interesting circumstance and picturesque story has been provided to enliven the theme. Further, as the teaching of reading tends to fall into a number of different specialisms, the material has been arranged on a thematic basis. Even so, one still has to roam over other relevant areas, such as the contribution of the Church to the encouragement of reading, the development of the primer, catechism and other instructional books, the art of reading aloud, the place of corporal punishment, the progress of the vernacular Bible, the importance of reading as a means of saving one's neck, the availability of books for the potential reader and sample content of children's supplementary readers at various stages of the period.

No attempt has been made to examine the teaching of reading at higher, critical or aesthetic levels. For this book, reading skill has been limited to such sufficiency of competence as would enable an ordinary person of that period to cope with the material he might have been required to read in the course of his daily life. As the technical measurement of reading ability in terms of mental age and achievement had not yet been devised, the definition must needs be left vague.

The study goes no farther than 1612 for three reasons. With the publication of the Authorized Version of the Bible in 1611 a long period of strenuous native endeavour for the provision of the Bible in the vernacular came to a neat official end. Further, the publication of John Brinsley's *Ludus Literarius* in 1612 set the seal on what had been previously advocated by Elizabethan educationists as exclusive practice in the teaching of reading. Above all, the story of the teaching of reading in subsequent centuries has already been adequately told elsewhere.

In these days of Black Papers on education, inquiries into the training of teachers, allegations about deteriorating standards of literacy, suspicion about contemporary progressive methods and informal attitudes, and an official investigation into reading, one might question how far we have really advanced in reading instruction since the days of Elizabeth I. This book therefore may be quite revealing.

Note. Where necessary, quotations in period English have been slightly edited or rendered in Modern English to facilitate reading. The titles of books have been similarly modernized.

The author would like to thank Mr John Allen and his colleagues of the Teaching Media Centre, University of Southampton, for their assistance in the production of some of the illustrations.

The School of Education,   W. J. Frank Davies
University of Southampton

Contents

Illustrations

1 The Arrival of the Alphabet

To the peoples on the continent of Europe in early times knowledge of neighbouring Britain must have been as hazy as the mists that seemed to swirl around the islands for most of the year. Herodotus (c. 480–425 B.C.) mentioned "the Cassiterides from which tin comes to us," a name which has been traditionally identified with Cornwall, but he added that he knew nothing about them. Aristotle (c. 384–322 B.C.) baldly affirmed that "beyond the Pillars of Hercules the ocean flows round the earth, and in it are islands called British." Strabo, the Greek geographer (c. 64 B.C.– A.D. 19), included in his work a short description of Britain which is said to have been based on that of Pytheas who visited here about 320 B.C.

Legend, however, insists that in these early centuries the Phoenicians, a race of intrepid seamen, had busily exploited British natural resources such as the tin of Cornwall, the lead of Somerset and the iron of the Weald and the Forest of Dean. If this were true, then one might be forgiven for toying with the idea that as part of their commercial exchanges the Phoenicians might have introduced the Britons to the alphabet which we now know the Phoenicians already possessed. Yet, though they had pushed their trading stations as far west as Cadiz, "there is no evidence whatever that the Phoenicians came as far north as the Isles of Scilly or the southwest of England. . . . Here again it is not *impossible* that the

Phoenicians should have ventured so far to the north: we can say that after plenty of excavation in England and Scilly it is a fact that no trace of them has been found nor a trace of any culture even remotely resembling theirs."[1] Any romantic vision of a literacy transported to Britain by them can be dismissed.

The search for the origins of English literacy through the introduction of an alphabet must be directed elsewhere.

The Druids and Greek Letters

As time went on, the passage from Europe to Britain was found to be not unduly hazardous at certain times of the year. Consequently, when Julius Caesar first reconnoitred Britain in 55 B.C., he encountered inhabitants who had not been entirely isolated from the main stream of life on the Continent. Not only had migrations been taking place but one powerful tribe, the Belgae, had crossed over from Gaul hardly more than a generation earlier. Though resettled in Britain, such tribes proudly retained the tribal names borne by the rest of their group on the Continent and continued other social and cultural links with them.

In his *Gallic War* (V. 14) Caesar referred to "the people who live in Kent, a wholly maritime district," as being "easily the most civilized, not differing much from the way of life among the Gauls." Diodorus Siculus too (*c.* 40 B.C.), in *The Library of History* (V. 22), remarked that the Britons were "especially friendly to neighbours and have assumed a civilized way of life, as a result of their contacts with traders from other peoples." In view of such statements as these, one might safely suppose that some of the more privileged Britons were already enjoying the skills of literacy. Among them were the Druids.

Again in his *Gallic War* (VI. 13, 14) Caesar described the way of life of this priestly sect in their home in Southern Gaul. The Druids "are concerned with sacred matters. They look after the public and private sacrifices and expound points of religion. A large number of young men gather around them for the purposes of education, and they hold the Druids in great esteem. . . . Many come to them for such instruction of their own accord or are sent there by their parents and relatives. Once there, they are said to learn off by heart a great number of verses, and some pursue this training for twenty years. They do not consider it proper to commit these particular subjects to writing, although for most other affairs, both of a public and private nature, they use Greek letters. To my mind, they adopted that practice for two reasons: because they do not want their system of instruction to become a matter of common knowledge or because they are afraid that their students, by putting their trust in writing, would become less enthusiastic about the value of memorization. It often happens that when a person begins to place reliance on writing, he grows slack about the necessity of learning a thing thoroughly for the purposes of memorization."

The first direct reference to the presence of the Druids in Britain concerned the slaughter of their fanatical followers in Anglesey in A.D. 59 but Caesar plainly states in this same passage: "Their system is thought to have been founded in Britain and conveyed from there to Gaul. Nowadays if people wish to learn more about its nature, they generally travel to Britain to find out about it." Thus, with the known close contacts between the tribal groups of Gaul and Britain, one can also assume that the Druids of Britain were using the Greek alphabet some time before the invasion of Julius Caesar.

Unfortunately, apart from Caesar's account and a fairly recent discovery of a hoard of objects which probably belonged to them,[2] evidence about them is flimsy. Supposed archaeological evidence, such as the Coligny Calendar of the first century A.D., which would point further to literacy, has been dismissed. Still, Caesar's confident assertion leaves one in little doubt that they fully appreciated the implications of the Greek letters they were using. The Latin word, *rationibus*, which Caesar used in the original, also embraces "business undertakings" and its usage might signify a knowledge of sophisticated accounting in commerce.

An interesting question therefore arises. If the Greeks did not have close dealings with the Druids of Britain in these early centuries, how did they come to learn Greek letters? To seek an explanation, one must revert to the Phoenicians.

Origin of the Western Alphabets

The Phoenicians were a branch of the Semitic peoples who occupied the narrow coastal strip between the mountains of the Lebanon and the Mediterranean Sea. They had also established a settlement on the coast of Egypt where they met a system of writing which the Egyptians themselves had devised as early as 3000 B.C. to give permanent form to the sounds of their own speech. The Phoenicians were a shrewd commercial people and were not slow in recognizing the practical potentialities of the

Egyptian invention. They realized that by its use the Egyptians, no longer restricted by factors of time and space, had immeasurably enlarged the power and extent of their communication. Moreover, their accumulated experience and knowledge could be permanently stored and effectively handed on to others. The Phoenicians set about modifying the hundred or so marks of the Egyptian system to suit the sounds of their own language. They decided that twenty-two were sufficient for the purpose. As Phoenician was a branch of the Semitic group of languages and all its member languages, such as Early Hebrew, were closely and compactly related, the earliest symbols of Phoenician and Early Hebrew were remarkably akin.

The original Egyptian code was probably a syllabary, that is, with a set of symbols standing for vocables or breaths rather than individual letters. This was also the style of the Phoenician version which therefore seems to us today to consist wholly of consonants without vowels. Though the vowels were not represented as separate individual letters, this does not mean that there were no vocalic values. These were also included in the consonantal or syllabic combinations. A hint too that the Phoenician alphabet had a pictographic origin can be detected in the names they gave to their characters, e.g. *aleph*, "ox"; *beth*, "house"; *gimel*, "camel," etc. These names were also used in other Semitic alphabets and the original letter-shapes probably bore a close resemblance to the outline of the basic objects themselves.

The nearest neighbours to the Phoenicians in the Eastern Mediterranean were the Greeks. Not surprisingly the Greeks borrowed from their trading rivals an alphabetic system that would afford facility and sense of permanence to their own language. With traditional legendary embellishment Cadmus of Thebes has been honoured with the supposed borrowing (*c.* 1500 B.C.), but most scholars date its appearance some five hundred years later. The Greeks also found that they had to trim both the names and the shapes of the Phoenician letters to suit the genius of their own language. For example, *aleph* was changed to *alpha*, *beth* to *beta*, *gimel* to *gamma*, *daleth* to *delta*, etc. Further, instead of discarding the Phoenician symbols for sounds that were not found in their own language, the Greeks applied them to sounds which were characteristic of Greek. Some of the discarded Phoenician consonantal symbols, for example, were used for Greek vowels. With the introduction of seven such Greek vocalic symbols, α, ϵ, η, ι, υ, ω, o, every letter had its own name and every Greek sound was

Egyptian Ancient Hieroglyphics	Phoenician Symbol	Name	Meaning	Phonetic Value	Greek Western Symbol	Classic Symbol	Name	Etruscan	Latin 4th/3rd Cent.B.C. Symbol	Latin 4th Cent. A.D. Symbol	Modern English
🐂	Ɀ	aleph	ox–yoke	'	ΑΛ	A	alpha	⋈	AΛΛ	Ā	A
	৭	beth	house	b	ΒB	B	beta		ΒB	B	B
	𐤂	gimel	camel	g	ΛC	Γ	gamma	C	‹C	C	C
	𐤃	daleth	door	d	ΔD	Δ	delta		D	D	D
	⅄	he	?	h	ЕE	E	epsilon	Ɛ	ΕΕⅡ	E	E
ΥΥ?	ΥΥ	wau	hook, nail	w	ΥV	Υ	(digamma)	ʃ	ΛFΓ'	F · G	F / G
	ΙΖ	zayin	weapon, olive	z	I	ΙΖ	zeta	⋔			
	ΗΒ	kheth	fence	h(kh)	ΘH	H	eta	⊟	H	H	H
	⊕	teth	ball, clew?	ṭ	⊗Θ	θ	theta	θ			
	𐤆	yod	hand	y	!	I	iota	I	I	I	{ I, J }
	𐤊	kaph	open hand	k	K	K	kappa		ΚF		K
	𐤋	lamed	rod	l	L	Λ	lambda	Γ	L	L	L
	₥	mem	water	m	ΓΛ	M	mu	ʍ	MVM	M	M
	𐤍	nun	snake, fish	n	ΓV	N	nu	N	N	N	N
	𐤎	samekh	fish	s		Ξ	xi				
	O	'ain	eye	'	O	O	omikron		∩O∩	O	O
	𐤐	pe	mouth	p	ΓΠ	Π	pi	Γ	ΓP	P	P
	𐤑	ṣade	step, nose	ṣ(ts)			(san)	M			
	ϘϘ	qoph	monkey	q	ϙ		(koppa)		?Q	Q	Q
	⅂	rēsh	head	r	PR	P	rho	Ρ	RR	R	R
	W	shin	tooth	sh	ΣΞ	Σ	sigma	ϟ	ΣS	S	S
+	Χ†	tau	mark	t	T	T	tau	T	T	T	{ T, U, V, W }
						Υ	upsilon	Υ	V	V	
					ΦΦ	Φ	phi	Φ			
					Χ†	X	khi	X	X	X	X
					ΨΨ	Ψ	psi	Υ			
						Ω	omega		Υ (1st Cent. B.C.)		Y
									Z (1st Cent. B.C.)		Z

1   *Descent of the English Alphabet*
The symbols for **aleph, he** *and* **'ain** *represented breathings in the Semitic languages (e.g. Phoenician) but came to represent vowels in Greek*

separately represented. In this way the phonetic principle, one letter/one sound, was established and its advantages were manifest.

Provided the graphic symbols truly represented in uniform manner each of the different sounds of the spoken language, and all the written symbols were recorded in the same order as the speech-sounds had been uttered, a way of committing oral language to writing had been devised. On the other hand, provided a person spoke the same oral language as the writer, all he was required to do was to identify consistently the written shapes of the letters, equate them to the oral sounds which they represented and then blend them in a complete and faithful series. Using this key he was able to decode or read what was written. Basically this was the alphabetic principle that came in due course to be handed down to the English. As long as the equation of sound and letter remained consistent, on a one-to-one basis as reading teachers say, all was well. No language, however, remains static, and by the sixteenth century the historical ebb and flow of phonological vicissitude was to have serious consequences for the person trying to learn to read or spell his native language, English (see pages 144 ff.).

Another feature of the Greek code which was destined to affect the skill or performance of the person learning to read English concerned the direction sequence of the letters. In the early centuries this was usually left to the caprice of the individual writer. "Quite ephemeral reasons would influence the choice, as for example the advantage of inscribing a short epitaph vertically on a pole or horizontally on a flat stone. Thus the orientation of letters underwent local change through the whim of scribes or stonemasons, so that the same symbols were twisted about vertically or laterally."[3] The Greek symbol △ for Latin *D* could be recorded as ◁ or ▽, and ⌐ for Latin *G* as ∟ or ⌐. "While the art of writing and reading was still the privilege of the few," observed Hogben, "the need for speedy recognition was not so compelling, and the urge for standardization was weak."

The direction of sentence patterns demonstrated the same freedom. Just "as the ox ploughs," so the earliest Greek of Homeric days was written in "boustrophedon" fashion, alternating from left to right and then right to left, etc. This was a most helpful arrangement for the reading of any long inscription on a large monument some distance away or some height above but by the fifth century B.C. the Greeks had settled into a left-to-right consistency which has since remained the direction sequence of our Western European writing systems. One can only conjecture why the Greeks favoured this particular order of writing. Possibly it was a deliberate act of nationalism to distinguish their system of writing from the right-to-left mode followed by the Semites. Or it might have been that the Greeks decided to cater for the majority of people in our midst, those who are born right-eyed and right-handed and who find it easier to read from left to right.

Meanwhile the Greeks were so active in their expansionism that by the eighth century B.C. several of their settlements were firmly rooted on the coast of Sicily. By the fourth century Plato described the spread of their communities around the Mediterranean basin as resembling "frogs around a pond." One such flourishing settlement was that of Massilia, now Marseilles. This was the base from which the Greeks pushed farther into Southern Gaul up the rivers to Arles and Avignon, where they came into contact with the Druids. As the Druids were an influential group, the commercially-minded Greeks appreciated the benefit of having these native leaders sympathetic to their presence. Possibly it was at this stage that the Greeks introduced to them the Greek letters which Caesar mentioned and which they probably exported to their religious fellows in Anglesey. This alphabet was not destined to become the permanent code of Britain. The group of Greek colonizers who had taken root on Sicily must be given credit for that.

About 750 B.C. an offshoot of this settlement crossed the straits to set up a base on the mainland of Italy at Cumae, just north of modern Naples. Here their neighbours were the Etruscans, with whom the Greeks again entered into relations of both a commercial and civilizing nature. The process was repeated. The Etruscans borrowed the Greek alphabetic code but adapted it to their own linguistic circumstances. As the writing on the earliest Etruscan inscriptions bears a close resemblance to that practised by the Greeks at Delphi, this date can be roughly assigned to the seventh century B.C.

One of the modifications made by the Etruscans resulted from their realization that they had no need of the full scale of seven vowels which the Greeks used. So they discarded two of them and retained only those five which have remained familiar in our own alphabet.

In time the Etruscans handed on their version to their neighbours, the Romans. It was their modified Roman-Etruscan form of the Greek alphabet which became the principal code for the langusages of Western Europe and, with later modifications and additions, the permanent code for the written representation of English.

7

Another future difficulty for the teacher of reading in England can also be traced to this stage. When the Etruscans borrowed their code from the Greeks, for some reason or other they failed to take over the names, *alpha, beta*, etc., which the Greeks used to identify their letters. Therefore when the Romans borrowed the Etruscan version, they had to devise their own names for the letters. They hit upon the effective and seemingly innocuous device of referring to them simply by their sounds, e.g. *a*. For the consonants they used the initial letter to which was attached a convenient vowel sound, e.g. *beta* − *b* + *ee* = *bee*. But, by resorting to this short cut, they gave the impression that the name and the letter-sound were one and the same. It may have been so at the time of the original borrowing. When, however, the sounds of the letters in English began to veer away from their original Latin values but the names remained the same, confusion was unavoidable. So began the now hoary argument as to whether reading is best taught by alphabetic or phonic methods.

The Alphabet and the Foundations of English Literacy

It is impossible to estimate when the Roman alphabet was first introduced into Britain. As the process of romanization of this country was under way soon after the second invasion by Caesar in 54 B.C., it was probably in use here well before the beginning of the Christian era. In the first century B.C. the Romans were already agreeing treaties with amenable tribes, tribute was being exacted from them and several British princes, including Dubnovellaunus, were seeking protection from their native enemies by fleeing to Rome. "There is no doubt," writes one historian, "that the full diplomatic dossier would reveal a more or less continuous Roman concern in British affairs."[4] With the dispatch of Aulus Plautius and four legions to Britain by Emperor Claudius in A.D. 49 the Roman Conquest began in earnest, and by A.D. 85 most of England had been subjugated.

Fascinating though it might be, a detailed consideration of the spread of literacy through the medium of Latin in this formative period would take us too far afield from the main study of the teaching of reading. In the initial bitterness of conflict the two races might have kept themselves distinct but the advantages, military, commercial and educational, that would accrue from positive contact eventually reconciled many Britons to their Roman overlord. The extent and depth of romanization, and so the use of

Latin, varied throughout the country. In the restless north the Britons might have been hardly affected by the alien, if superior, culture. On the other hand, the more easily controlled southern region, which had been in contact with the Continent long before the invasion, would have been more markedly and rapidly affected. In the towns, where the occupying forces and the established Roman authority were in regular contact with the native, romanization was probably extensive, whereas in rural districts it might have been scattered in infrequent pockets. As the Roman Occupation wore on, evidence of a comparatively rapid spread of literacy also increases. One can, for instance, point to the remains of theatres of the first century A.D. in Colchester, St Albans and Canterbury or the literary themes such as the story of Dido or the Labours of Hercules worked into the mosaics in villas owned by British princes, such as that in Bramdean, Hampshire, or that of Cogidumnus in Chichester, Hampshire.

Unfortunately there are few literary references by way of substantiation. In his *De Defectu Oraculorum* Plutarch (A.D. 46– *c*. 120) speaks of Demetrius of Tarsus, a poet and teacher of grammar (the subject also included the study of literature), returning from Britain where he might have practised his profession. The Latin poet, Martial, in one of his epigrams puffs himself up that in A.D. 96 "Britain is said to hum my verses"; and Juvenal (born *c*. A.D. 60–70), refers to British lawyers being taught by Gaulish schoolmasters. One might infer from these that schools were already being operated by the Romans in Britain in this century.

This is certainly implied in a passage of the *Agricola* (xxi) of Tacitus, where he provides a shrewd appraisal of what was happening in Britain at that time. "In order that a people, scattered and uncivilized and therefore inclined to war, should become accustomed through comfort to peace and pleasure, he privately encouraged individuals, but at the same time he publicly assisted groups to build temples, market-places and houses. . . . Likewise he set about providing a liberal education for the sons of chiefs, as he preferred the natural ability of the Britons to the zealous endeavours of the Gauls. As a result, those who at one time used to disdain the Latin tongue now coveted its rhetoric."

There is also evidence that some of the artisan or labouring classes were able to read and write. Haverfield cites inscriptions from tiles such as *FECIT TUBUL[UM] CLEMENTINUS* or the English-translated versions of such graffiti as "Primus has made ten tiles," "Cabriabanus made this wall tile" and "Austalis goes off

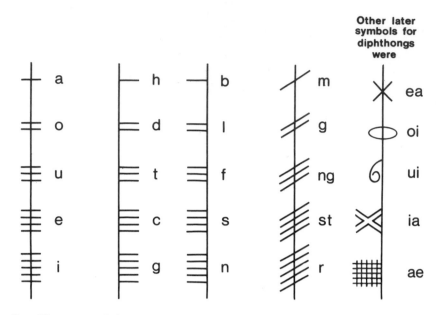

2 *Characters of the Ogam/Ogham Alphabet*

daily on his own for a fortnight" in support of his contention.[5]

The impact of the Roman Occupation can also be seen in the matter of vocabulary. Evidence has been found of some eight hundred Latin words being adopted by the three Brythonic languages, Welsh, Celtic and Breton. More specifically, several Latin words, such as *abecedarium*, *grammatica* and *littera*, all of which have a direct relationship to the skill of reading, became an integral part of the native languages. Latin was more than the language of the Roman military power. It was the universal language of the learned men of the western world, and all men who desired education had to learn to read and write it. "It would not occur to anyone to write in British, nor indeed could they know how to do so. One tends to forget that to write down in an alphabet the sounds of speech (even though it is one's own) which one has never been taught to write is a very considerable intellectual feat. In Roman Britain those who had enough education to know the alphabet had enough to know some Latin, and those who had none did not write at all."[6]

This last statement, however, is not wholly accurate, for there is evidence that some Irish Celts, Britons and Anglo-Saxons could on occasion read and write in scripts of their own native manufacture.

Runic Symbol :	ᚠ	ᚢ	ᚦ	ᚩ	ᚱ	ᚳ
Runic Name and Meaning :	feoh (money)	úr (aurochs) or wild ox	thorn (thorn)	ós (god)	rād (ride)	cen (torch)
Latin Equivalent :	f	u	th	a	r	R

	ᚷ	ᚹ	ᚻ	ᚾ	ᛁ	ᛄ
	geofu (gift)	wyn (joy)	hægl (hail)	nied (need)	īs (ice)	gear (year)
	g	w	h	n	i	j

	ᛇ	ᛈ	ᛉ
	eōh (yew) or yew bow	peorð (dance)	eolh or secg (elk or sedge)
	e	p	r

3   *Old English Runic symbols (early period)*

Native Alphabets

Ogam/Ogham
Several stones of a memorial nature have been discovered in Ireland, some with Latin and native Irish inscriptions in consort. This ogam or ogham script, as it is usually called, consisted of an alphabet of twenty letters, each letter having a prescribed number of strokes to indicate its particular identity. The consonants were represented by a number of strokes to the left or right of a middle line, and the vowels were characterized by a number of notches. The mode of its structure by strokes and notches might indicate that the code was originally devised for incision on slabs or wooden sticks. As such it might have been in use even earlier than the fourth century A.D., the date of manufacture usually ascribed to the earliest inscriptions found. Similar stone inscriptions, with parallel writings and assigned to the fifth century A.D., have been found in Wales, Devon and Cornwall. The values of the various alphabetic characters are roughly demonstrated in the diagram opposite on page 10.

Runes
When the Anglo-Saxons or English were living on the mainland of the Continent and to a lesser degree after they had migrated to

Britain in the fifth century A.D., they too used a native alphabetic code, called runes.

The origin of runes is still shrouded in mystery, though modern scholarship inclines to the view that their creation can be credited to a Germanic-speaking tribe of the second century B.C. It has been suggested that during their migrations the tribe had been in contact with a North Italic people who had developed their own system of writing and, a familiar technique, the Germanic tribe had evolved their own particular system from it. They carried this with them on their northwards migrations and about the third century A.D. they introduced it to the Scandinavians who, it is believed, handed it on to the Anglo-Saxons as yet on the Continent.

This runic system came to be known as the "furthark," a name compounded from the serial order of the first six runes, and consisted of twenty-four symbols. The angular-shaped characters did not assume any set pattern of alignment and were arranged sometimes in boustrophedon or vertical fashion, starting from the base. Sometimes the letters were separated from each other by a dot or were so fashioned as to share a common vertical stroke, e.g. ᚺᚠ for HF. Some runes were also used as a convenient form of abbreviation, e.g. ᛗ *mon*, ᛞ *daeg*.

The runes were at first probably incised on wooden staves or, according to the sixth-century Venantius Fortunatus, "painted on tablets of ash-wood. The smooth stick is just as efficient as the papyrus." Later they were also inscribed on metal objects such as the hilt or handle of a sword, or on funeral crosses of stone or the beak of an eagle or the paw of a bear.

In the beginning they might have been used for purposes of divination or for influencing the future through the casting of lots. Tacitus in his *Germania* (x) has described the practice: "They pay special attention to divination and lots. Their method of casting them is simple. They cut into small pieces a branch which they have lopped off a fruit-bearing tree. They then notch these with particular marks and pitch them at random and without care of order upon a white cloth. Next, after invoking the gods and lifting his eyes to heaven, the priest of the community if it is a public consultation, but the father of the family if it is a private affair, picks up the pieces three at a time and interprets them in accordance with the code of the marks previously notched on them." To preserve the magico-ritual secrecy, probably a knowledge of runes was confined to a select band of initiates.

In the first fine flush of Christian enthusiasm pagan practices such as this must have been distasteful but they lingered on, even if clandestinely, for a long time. For example, Bede in his *Ecclesiastical History* (IV. xxii) tells how the bonds of a prisoner, Imma, in 679 invariably fell asunder whenever his priest brother, Tunna, celebrated mass for his death, and this caused the others to inquire if he had "any loosening runes" about him. As late as 803 the Council of Clovesho was so anxious about the persistent use of runes that it expressly forbade incantations and divinations which were closely concerned with them.

Sometimes runes were used, as in the Old English poem, "The Husband's Message," to conceal a private communication: "I combine the symbols ᚻ, ᚱ, ᚹ, ᚦ, ᛃ, ᛗ to give you solemn assurance that he was there and that for the rest of his life he would keep inviolate that pledge which you two discussed so often in the days of old." Or they were used to help complicate even more the meaning of a riddle or to serve as tallies or receipts for cross-Channel trading. Occasionally their characters were inscribed on objects to denote ownership, and one coin of the time of Honorius (died *c.* 423) has the runic words *scanu modu* ("Scanu owns me"). Or they were cut into funerary stones, e.g. the Sandwich stone of the late sixth century. Later their use was almost purely sophisticated. Cynewulf, probably a Northumbrian poet of the eighth century, employed runes to conceal his name in his "Riddles," e.g. ᚻᛗᛏᛗᚹᚾᚱᚪ. The eighth-century Franks Casket and the Ruthwell Cross, a stone monument in Dumfriesshire, with its runic passages from the old English poem "The Dream of the Rood," are both magnificent examples of runes being used for decorative purposes. Otherwise, runic script was probably never used for communication on a mass scale.

Although two runic symbols, ᚦ, and ᚹ, were borrowed by the Anglo-Saxons to represent *th* and *w* in their modified Roman alphabet, the general purpose of runes was too specific and the area of usage too restricted to have made any significant contribution to the acquisition of mass literacy. For us today both ogam and runes have merely the fascination of a collector's rare items.

It is most probable that Christianity had taken root in this country early in the days of the Roman Occupation. Tertullian, for example, in his *Carmen apologeticum adversus Judaeos* (vii) says that by his own time (*c.* A.D. 200) Christianity had reached even the inaccessible parts of Britain. Origen too (*c.* A.D. 240) asks the revealing question, "When indeed did the country of Britain agree to the worship of one god before the coming of Christianity?"[7]

There are also reliable stories of Christian martyrs in St Albans as early as 284, and British bishops were supposed to have attended the Council of Arles in 314. By the fifth century Christianity was reasonably established here.

As the Christian Church was the all-important agency in the encouragement and development of mass literacy in this country, one must now begin to consider the various aspects of her contribution.

Agencies and Agents for the Teaching of Reading

2 Christian Pillars of Early Literacy

From early in her history the Christian Church had urged her clergy, both regular and secular, to pay heed to their responsibilities in the provision of reading instruction for their flock.

Irrespective of the other duties that an efficient and independent community might demand from its monks, education in and for the Christian religion was essential for all inmates of monastic organizations. In the Rule of the first such group of which we have record, that of St Pachomius at Tabennis on the bank of the Nile in 320, a familiarity with the Bible was explicitly prescribed and the importance of teaching reading strongly emphasized. If a new entrant could not read, he was to be directed to a monk or other inmate who could teach him. Further, if he did not want to learn, then the instructor could force him to write his letters and syllables. "Let there be in this monastery no one who is not willing to learn his letters or to know the Scriptures, the New Testament and the Psalms at the very least."[1] As this Rule provided the guide-lines for the monasteries later founded by St Basil (370—9), it can be assumed that this became common practice in other monastic establishments. When they grew in numbers and size, their educational facilities were not restricted to those who elected to remain for life in their service. The children of outside lay people, who were not destined to take the habit, were welcomed within their walls and shared the schooling offered to the regular members.

In the early mission field, too, education was a vital instrument of conversion and, for example, when St Patrick went to Ireland in 432, he took with him some twenty clerics to help in the task of teaching the inhabitants. It is of interest that St Patrick himself carried around with him a small book which was referred to as "The Elements" or "The Alphabet." On several occasions he was supposed to have taught the alphabet to converts, one of whom, for instance, had the name of Mochoe. He also wrote an alphabet (*"scripsit elementa"*) for Fiace and, according to the historian Nennius, he composed 365 alphabets in all. If we try to interpret this as a sparkling display of multilingualism by the great saint, we should be disappointed. In the famous eighth/ninth-century vellum codex, the *Book of Armagh*, the alternative Latin phrase used is *scripsit abigitorium*. The Irish phrase used elsewhere for this is *scribais aipgiter,* which signifies that he wrote the outline or summary of something, not necessarily a series of alphabetic letters. St Patrick's small book was probably a convenient synopsis of the Christian faith which could be used by converts in their own work of teaching or preaching. As such it could be regarded as the earliest reference to the use of a rough and ready Catechism as a basic reading primer in the British Isles (see pages 105 ff.).

So successful were the educational efforts of these pioneer missionaries that by 445 the famous school at Armagh, which was said to have as many as 7,000 students, was founded. Many others were later instituted at such places at Clonmacnoise in 541, Derry in 546 and Bangor in 552. Little is known about the nature of the actual instruction in these early Irish schools other than that they taught Celtic literature in addition to the Holy Scriptures and Latin. By the end of the sixth century Ireland was regarded as the best-educated country in Europe.

The Church on the Continent also issued directives about the provision and standards of education. For example, the Council of Vaison in South-east France, attended by twelve bishops (529), directed all supervisory priests to conduct classes for potential ordinands in their own houses and to ensure that these same ordinands would themselves in turn teach the young children of the district. Another Provincial Council of Narbonne (589) declared that no uneducated person could be ordained priest or made deacon. If by any chance such a person was already ordained and refused to learn to read, his stipend was to be stopped till he was prepared to do so.

Nor had the stream of educational endeavour in these early centuries left Britain untouched. Soon after the Pelagian troubles of the fifth century, St Germanus (*c.* 378—448) and St Lupus (*c.* 383—479) were already advising that the most effective way to eradicate heresy was through education, and both of them have been credited with the establishment of schools in this country. St Germanus is said to have had St Patrick among his pupils. Dyfrig, the Bishop of Llandaff, and Illtyd were said to have founded schools in the Wye valley and at Llantwit in Glamorgan, a school which has been traditionally supposed to have had the historian Gildas and the poet Taliesin as pupils. The Llantwit school had over 2,000 scholars, and its curriculum was concerned with the study of the Bible and other sacred writings.

Reading: a Necessity for Evangelization

By the sixth century Celtic missionaries were already engaged in the evangelization of the northern regions of Britain, and in 563 St Columba, an Irish noble, laid the foundations of the famous monastery of Iona. Yet, the momentous date in the story of Christianity in this country was 597 when Pope Gregory dispatched Augustine and his mission to England. There were now two Christianizing forces at work here, with the Celtic Church in the north and the Roman Church in the south, and a Synod was held in Whitby in 664 to arbitrate between them. Their decision in favour of the Roman rather than the Celtic mode brought this island into closer relations with the learning and thought of the more experienced mother Church on the Continent. The organization of a more determined missionary effort inevitably led to a wider spread of literacy among the native masses.

This Augustinian mission faced two immediate tasks: how to save the souls of the natives and how to ensure that, once converted, they would not lapse. Both tasks were huge. For nearly two centuries the immigrant English had remained undoubted masters in the country they had conquered and were not inclined to abandon lightly the pagan beliefs and customs of their forefathers. Now these same people had to be initiated into the doctrine of Christianity and made active participants in the corporate act of worship that was an obligatory part of it. Then there was the problem of priests. Unable to call upon sufficient numbers from her own resources on the Continent, the Church had to recruit them from the natives and train them with appropriate skills to cope with the projected conversions. Such ministers required not only a knowledge of the Holy Scriptures and a familiarity with the traditions and commentaries of the great Mother Church but also an appreciation of the conduct of the necessary act of worship.

The position was further aggravated by the fact that one language was recognized by the Church, and that was Latin. It was the language which had been taken north by the Celtic missionaries from Ireland, and it was the language of the Augustinian missionaries. The Bible, the works of the Christian Fathers and all the commentaries were written in it, and the prayers and readings were uttered and the Psalms chanted in it. Even if they had wanted to use English as the linguistic medium for the offical purposes of the early Church, the native language was neither sufficiently systematized nor broad enough to cater for the sophisticated religious or liturgical requirements that had resulted from the practice of several centuries (see page 32). Latin and Christianity were destined to proceed hand in hand. At the very least it was hoped that the priests, and possibly the masses, would be able to sing and read to a limited extent — in Latin.

Rather disappointingly, little is known about the actual agencies for the teaching of reading in the Anglo-Saxon period, and a rough picture of what was happening has to be sketched from occasional snippets of information. We know, for example, that Pope Gregory the Great who had sent the Augustinian mission to England had already set the pattern of early education for young Christians by establishing in Rome a *schola cantorum*, a song school, where the scholars were taught singing and the elements of Latin and reading to prepare them for participation in the services of the church. His example was followed in England. For instance, about 633 Paulinus, the Bishop of Rochester, had appointed James the Deacon, who was "unusually talented in singing . . . to teach the members of the Church to sing after the custom of the Romans or the people of Canterbury."[2] Another Abbot John, who died in 721, came from abroad "to teach the singers of the said monastery the order and manner of singing and reading aloud, and committing to writing all that was required throughout the whole year for the celebration of festivals. . . . He not only taught the brothers of that monastery but also those from other monasteries who cared to come to listen to him. He was often invited to teach in other places."[3]

The burden of teaching the rudiments of reading fell on the shoulders of the secular priests and monastic institutions. Herebald, later Abbot of the monastery near the mouth of the Tyne, recalled *c*. 686 that he had spent the prime of his youth among the clergy learning to read and sing.[4] Acca, the Bishop of Hagulstad, now Hexham, c. 709, also said that as a boy he had been brought up and educated by the clergy of Bosa, the Bishop of York.[5] Bede too was educated in a monastery. "At the age of seven," he wrote, "I was handed over to be educated by the most reverend Abbot Benedict and later by Ceolfrid. I gave myself wholly to the study of the Scriptures. In addition to the observance of regular discipline and the daily conduct of singing in the church, I derived constant delight from my learning, teaching and writing."[6]

Schools were also being founded in England. In 631 Sigebert of the East Angles, wishing "to copy the good institutions he had seen in France, established a school for youth to be instructed in literature. In this he was assisted by Bishop Felix who came to him from Kent and supplied him with masters and teachers after the manner of that country."[7] Others were set up at Winchester in 648, the famous one at York soon after the Synod of Whitby in 665, at Canterbury just after the arrival of Archbishop Theodore of Tarsus in 669 and at Worcester in 685.

Nothing is known about the actual instruction offered by these schools but for centuries the curriculum served the needs of the Church. Pupils were taught to sing so that they could join in the chanting and they were taught to read so that they might understand the Bible and take part in the services. They were taught arithmetic so that they could calculate the date of Easter and other festivals. Sometimes, especially if the pupils were in monastic schools, they were taught to write so that they could copy sacred works or compose commentaries on the Scriptures. In due course, with further Christian expansion, the schools themselves became more highly organized both to cope with the growing demand for education and to deal with the increasing specialization required by the curriculum. This is clear from a letter sent by Alcuin to Archbishop Eanbald II in 796 when Alcuin was in France helping Charlemagne to organize his own educational system. Alcuin suggested that separate provision should be made for those who were engaged in the study of letters, the transcribing of letters and the practice of music, and each group should have its own separate master. As no mention is made in this letter of children learning the rudiments, it may be assumed that they were outside Alcuin's scheme of things. As we shall see later (page 43), buildings distinct from the church itself came to be used for the school, and beginners were often allocated to a section away from the main or senior teaching block, usually in the house of the priest.

"Priests shall keep schools in the villages and teach small boys without fee: priests ought always to keep schools of schoolmasters in their houses and, if any of the faithful is willing to give his little ones to be educated, he ought to receive them willingly and teach them kindly."[12]

Imitation also took a practical form, and less than a century later Charlemagne's enthusiastic example was repeated in England by King Alfred. He too set up a school at court where his son, Ethelward, "was given up, under the watchful care of masters, to the pleasure of discipline of letters, in company with almost all the children of noble birth in the whole realm and even many of lower birth. And in this school books in both tongues, that is, in Latin and in Saxon, were zealously read and they had leisure for writing."[13] His children, Edward and Aelfryth, "carefully learned both the psalms and Saxon books, and especially Saxon poems, and they use books very often." So stern was Alfred in his directives that "almost all the ealdormen, reeves and thanes, who had been illiterate from childhood, took to their books, preferring to study laboriously the unaccustomed learning rather than lose their jobs."[13]

The Mediaeval Church and the Teaching of Reading

After the Norman Conquest the Church authorities continued to issue injunctions reminding the priests of their duties in the sphere of basic education. For example, Pope Gregory IX (1227–41), decreed: "Let every priest who presides over a people . . . have a man to keep school [the gloss has "for teaching the Psalter and singing"] and admonish his parishioners that they send their sons to church to learn the Faith and that the priests may chastely educate them." This was repeated in 1280, and others of similar intent were promulgated in the ensuing centuries, though it would be unprofitable to itemize them here.

Towards the end of the period under study we shall still find the Church in England urging her clerics to remember their responsibilities in the matter of teaching the members of their Christian flock to read. For example, the Convocation of Canterbury (1529) directed in some detail: "As idleness is the mother in some ways of all vices, this Holy Council commands and orders all those with cures, rectors, vicars and chantry priests [see page 39] that after divine service they shall employ themselves in study, prayer, lectures or other honest affairs or business, which becomes their profession: namely, by instructing boys in the alphabet, in reading, in singing or grammar: and on three days in the week for three, or at least two, hours a day [they] shall, in the absence of some lawful hindrance, occupy themselves in reading Holy Scriptures or some approved doctor. The ordinaries shall make diligent inquiry about this in their visitations to the end that they may severely chastise and punish lazy priests or those who spend their time badly."[14]

After the Reformation the English Church was equally circumspect. An injunction of Bishop Hugh Latimer to his Worcester diocese (1537) ordained that "everyone of you that be chantry priests do instruct and teach the children of your parish such as will come to you at the least to read English so that thereby they may the better learn how to believe, how to pray and how to live to God's pleasure."[15]

In 1577 the Bishop of Durham, Richard Barnes, instructed his parsons, vicars and curates who were not licensed to preach "to duly, painfully and freely teach the children of their several parishes and cures to read and write: and those whom they will by good and due trial find to be apt to learn, and of pregnant capacity, then they shall exhort their parents to set them to school and learning."[16] As late as 1581 Richard Mulcaster, the educationist, in his *Positions* was assuring his readers that "every parish has a minister, if no one else in the parish, who can help [with] reading and writing."

Throughout the centuries, then, the burden of teaching the local children to read lay principally on the shoulders of the priest. If he was unable to do it himself, he had to arrange for another church official or lay person to teach in his stead. The records of the late Middle Ages abound with such references, especially the Chantries Acts (1546—8).

David Edwards, the chaplain at Brecon, was required "to teach the young children resorting to the said school their ABC."[17] The priest at Kingsley, Staffordshire, was "to keep school and teach poor men's children of the said parish grammar, and to read and sing."[18] At Hereford "Sir Philip Hye, of the age of four score years, incumbent, being a right honest man indifferently learned" took "pains in keeping a school and bringing up of children."[19] At Braughing parishioners learnt their letters from two parish priests,[20] and in 1569 at Canterbury Archbishop Parker directed a school to be set up with a master appointed to teach twenty poor children to read, sing and write, with their books, pens, paper and ink being provided free.[21]

The Statutes of Sibthorpe College (1342), however, allowed for the appointment of a clerk, who was to "serve at altars, tend the lamps, sleep in the church and, if time, to teach their letters to small boys and any others of the parish for a fee agreed by him and the parents."[22] The parish clerk at Faversham in 1506 was required to "teach children to read and sing in the choir and to do service in the church as of old time he has accustomed."[23] Similarly in 1571 the Injunctions of Archbishop Edmund Grindal of York, and later of Canterbury, stated that "he [the parish clerk] must be able to read the first lesson, the Epistles, and the Psalms, with answers to the suffrages, as is used . . . and also that he endeavours himself to teach young children to read, if he be able to do so."[24] At Penryn, Cornwall, the bell-ringer John Pound "of the age of thirty years [taught] poor men's children their ABC."[25] At Launceston John Balmok was "schoolmaster there, a teacher of poor men's children their ABC"[26] and later "John Bannek, now teacher there, of the age of sixty years, chosen by the mayor."[27]

Sometimes the parson made provision by bequeathing money for the education of a parishioner. Richard Wolaston of Aldwinkle left twenty shillings to John Bett "if he will go to school, else not,"[28] while the parson at Moor Monkton left ten shillings for Roger Robinson "to find him to the school, and it to be paid as he has need upon it."[28]

Mediaeval Monasteries and the Teaching of Reading

Despite the abundance of documentary evidence which is available about monks and nuns in mediaeval times, it is remarkable how little is known about their endeavours in the field of primary education at that time. So sparse is it that it is doubtful if the mediaeval monasteries, as opposed to their Anglo-Saxon predecessors, had much of a part to play in the teaching of the elements of reading. In the early centuries the monks, deeply involved in the urgent missionary situation, had been obliged to keep schools to promote Christianization. By the Middle Ages their pre-eminent function was no longer educational.

Robert, the Earl of Leicester, was educated at Abingdon in the eleventh century and Giraldus Cambrensis at Gloucester in the twelfth, but both were men of favoured birth. Only rarely were children of the lower social ranks educated within their precincts, except for the express purposes of the monastery, as oblates or prospective novices. The monasteries opened the occasional choir school to train singers for the Lady chapel, though there were rarely more than ten in attendance at the same time.[29] They also set up their own almonry schools for that purpose. These were usually kept in the almonry at the abbey gate and were open to the poor children of the district. Again, it is questionable if the almonry schools introduced them to the rudiments of reading in this later period. The provision of one such school in 1520 expressly stated that no scholar would be accepted unless he could read and sing in the chapel and was ten years of age. On the other hand, the *Rites of Durham*, written *c*. 1593 but describing the monastic buildings and conditions of two generations earlier, mention boys attending their school at the age of seven, with the eldest monk acting as their tutor. One or two monasteries also founded grammar schools. Indirectly they made other contributions to education, and we read of endowments to help pay for masters at secular schools, for example Winchcombe or Sherborne, where the abbot paid for three or four boys to attend the local grammar school.[29]

The contribution of the mediaeval monasteries to the education of the masses might have been vastly overrated. "I do not think," wrote Coulton, "anyone who has studied the monastic records would reckon, at the Dissolution, more than thirty almonry and thirty choir schools in the country, with an average attendance of twelve and six respectively."[30] At the Dissolution, 1536–9, it has been estimated that there were only 8,000 monks, friars and nuns altogether in England.[31] With their disappearance the gravest blow to learning resulted from the destruction of their libraries and priceless manuscripts rather than from the loss of concrete teaching activities at the primary stage. The part played by the nunneries will be considered later (see page 53).

Let us now look briefly at the general qualifications and social background of the clerics who were directly responsible for encouraging the teaching of reading as a basic element.

Qualifications of the Teaching Clerics

Happily the leaders of the early Roman Church in England were men of distinct academic attainment. Theodore, consecrated Archbishop of Canterbury in 669, was "a man well educated in secular as well as religious literature, both in Greek and Latin."[32] With him came Abbot Hadrian, who was later principal of the monastery school and was described as "an African well versed in the Holy Scriptures, experienced in monastical and ecclesiastical discipline and most able in both Greek and Latin. . . . They attracted a crowd of pupils, and from them flowed rivers of knowledge ·to water the hearts of the hearers. Together with the books of Holy Scriptures, they also taught them the art of sacred poetry, astronomy and arithmetic. . . . The fact that some of their scholars are as well versed in Greek and Latin as in their own native languages is proof of this. Never have there been happier times since the English landed in Britain. . . . All who wanted to be instructed in sacred reading found masters available to teach them."[33]

Despite this promising start, one cannot assume that the rank and file of the clergy were wholly literate, In the Christianization of England, as in twentieth-century missionary expansion in Africa, crash courses were probably organized to prepare natives of good heart but limited attainment for evangelistic service. The partial success of their educational drive can be gauged from the fact that by the mid-seventh century English-born men such as Deusdedit and Damian had already been preferred to bishoprics. To improve matters, Bede in a letter to Archbishop Egbert of York in 734 had urged that "the uneducated [idiotas], who are familiar with their own tongue, should learn [the Creed and the Lord's Prayer] and recite them sedulously in English. This should be done both by lay people and by clerics or monks learning in Latin. . . . I myself have often allowed the uneducated [priests] to use English versions of the Creed and the Lord's Prayer." We hear too that Bede was engaged in translating St John's Gospel into English, as he lay dying.

Even so, the authorities frequently complained about the low educational standards of the clergy and urged them to do something about it. Writing about 894, King Alfred in his preface to his English version of Pope Gregory's *Pastoral Care* commented that learning had so fallen off "among the English that there are few on this side of the Humber who would know how to render their [Latin] services into English, and I do not think there would be many beyond the Humber. So few were they when I became king that I cannot bring to mind a single person south of the Humber."

Like Bede, King Alfred was also stimulated to prepare vernacular versions of specific books which he felt would be "very necessary for all people to know. . . . Among other things, I began to put into English the book which is called *Pastoralis* in Latin but the *Shepherd's Book* in English. . . . It is my will to send a copy to every bishop's see in my kingdom. . . . All youth of free men now in England [should commit themselves] to learning . . . until such time as they are able to read English well. Afterwards, he who wants to have further advancement and to reach higher office, could be allowed to learn the Latin language." But the valiant efforts of King Alfred and others like Aelfric, the Abbot of Eynsham, who died *c.* 1020 and who spent his life translating Latin books into English for the benefit of the people, often fell on stony ground. In his *Gesta Regum Anglorum*, which he finished in 1127, the historian William of Malmesbury dolefully recorded: "For some years before the Normans arrived, interest in literature and religion had decayed. The clergy were content with only a slight degree of learning and, as a result, could scarcely stammer out the words of the Sacraments. Anyone who understood grammar was looked upon with wonder and astonishment."

By the Middle Ages the state of illiteracy among the princes and chiefs of the Church was startling. About 1200 Robert, the Abbot of Malmesbury, was reported to the Pope by his own monks for his illiteracy and, when examined by the Pope's representative, managed to translate the Latin word *repente* (suddenly) as *"il si repentit"* (he repented).[34] Louis of Beaumont, Bishop of Durham (*c.* 1330), was so ignorant of Latin that he was given special coaching just before his consecration. At the consecration itself "when he had faltered his way, through the help of kind prompters, to the word *metropolitanus*, he gasped a great deal because he was unable to pronounce it. So he said, 'Let us take that word as read.' Another time when he was interviewing candidates for Holy Orders, he came to the phrase *in aenigmate* and whispered to those around him, 'By St Louis, he wasn't a very kind person who manufactured this word.' "[35] The Latin of a Bishop of Chichester also was so ludicrous that he raised laughter every time he tried to utter it.[36]

In view of this we must not be surprised at the low standards of the lesser members of the Church. The Lateran Council, convoked by Pope Innocent III in 1215 and regarded as the most important of all Lateran Councils, admitted that it was "almost impossible to find an educated man to serve a church where the owner allowed him but a meagre subsistence."[37] Giraldus Cambrensis reported that one priest, when reading his breviary, translated the Latin *in diebus illis* (in those days) as "in the days of Busillis," and another turned *piscis assus* (broiled fish) into "ass fish."[38] A Council of Oxford, 1222, referred to the general priesthood as "dumb dogs."[39] About 1260 Roger Bacon called them boys who gabbled "through the Psalter which they have learnt, and as clerks and country priests recite the Church services, of which they know little or nothing like brute beasts."[39] Archbishop Peckham of Canterbury in a statute in council in 1287 lamented that "the ignorance of priests is casting the people into a ditch of errors."[39]

The illiteracy among the clergy persisted for centuries. About 1510 William Melton, later Chancellor of York Minster, in a sermon addressed to ordinands and their examiners, complained of the poor learning displayed by entrants to the Church.[40] William Tyndale, the translator of the Bible (1494–1536), asserted, "I dare say that there be twenty thousand priests, curates, this day in England and not so few that cannot give you the right English unto this text in the Paternoster *'Fiat voluntas, sicut in coelo et in terra'* ['Thy will be done, in earth as it is in heaven'] and answer thereto."[39] Sir Thomas More, who was involved in controversy with Tyndale and others at the time, urged that "there should be more diligence used in the choice not only of their learning but *more especially* of their learning."[41] In 1530 Bishop Stokesley of London examined his curates "in letters and in their capacity and suitability . . . to the cure of souls" and found twenty-two of the fifty-six to be ignorant.[42] Bishop Hooper's visitation in 1552 revealed that of the 311 parish priests examined for the Gloucester see 168 could not repeat the Ten Commandments correctly, nine were unable to count them and ten could not say the Lord's Prayer.[43]

Depths were also plumbed in their mode of living. The amorous and intriguing cleric was a characteristic figure of the mediaeval tale, and forgers, counterfeiters and highwaymen strolled the ecclesiastical scene. The rector of East Barming and the vicar of Sarratt (1462) were both involved in the deaths of parishioners;[44] the rector of St Mary Axe about 1450 was said to enjoy prostitutes; and Margaret Harrison kept a brothel for the benefit of clergy in the parish of St John Zachary.[45] The monasteries had also descended into sloth and laxity of religion. "Flocks and fleeces, crops and barns, leeks and pot herbs," wrote Richard de Bury, the fourteenth-century book-collector, "cups and drinkings are today the readings and studies of monks."[46] When Archbishop William Warham visited one monastery in his Canterbury diocese in 1511, he noted the lack of "a skilled teacher of grammar . . . to teach the novices and other youths grammar. . . . In defence of such instruction it happens that most of the monks celebrating mass and performing other divine services are wholly ignorant of what they read, to the great scandal and disgrace of both religion in general and the monastery in particular."[47]

Much of the responsibility for this unsavoury state of affairs derived from the slipshod way in which candidates were accepted for the priesthood. Instead of sitting a written test, which might have somewhat extended the candidate's claim to literacy, he was rarely subjected to anything more rigorous than a *viva voce*, which was conducted by the bishop or his representative. Usually he was asked to recite a few Latin formulae or read the Latin service, either of which could have been learnt off by heart, and to sing. A few questions about moral background or marital status might have been thrown in because, if there was any suspicion that he might become a financial embarrassment to the Church, they immediately shied off him! In that case, he could always seek a better turn of fortune in other parts of the country.

Really, not much could have been expected of many priests. Most of the aspirants came from humble origins, and from time immemorial they had been looked upon as placed on earth to work for the lord of the estate. Probably thinking little about the elevation from the slough of illiteracy, they were more concerned about their being raised, however slightly, above poverty and so securing some freedom from social bondage.

There were many who sought this social escape. For example, though there were only 8,838 parish churches in the whole of England on the eve of the Reformation, 5,349 men were ordained in the diocese of Worcester alone between 1282 and 1302.[48] Once they were ordained, they found a variety of opportunities ahead of them, though large numbers became parish or chantry priests, gild or private chaplains. "There was," wrote Sir Thomas More, "such a rabble [of priests] that every man must have a priest to wait upon his wife. . . . There are more . . . priests now than of good men. Every rascal offers himself as qualified for the priesthood."[49] When Lord Mounteagle died in 1524, though he had made provision for only thirty priests to attend his funeral, eighty turned up.[50]

Some were lucky and rose to the highest positions. So it had been for centuries, if reliance can be placed on the chronicler's account for the year 879. "Dunberht, the Bishop of Winchester, died," he wrote, "and was succeeded by Denewulf. This man, if report can be trusted, was not only illiterate but also a swineherd in the early part of his life. When he was yielding to the fury of his enemies, King Alfred had taken refuge in a forest and chanced to light upon him as he was feeding his swine. Observing his intelligence, the King caused him to be taught learning and when he was sufficiently instructed, made him Bishop of Winchester, a thing that may be considered almost miraculous."[51] John Peckham (c. 1225–92), Archbishop of Canterbury, and William Wykeham, the founder of Winchester College in 1387 and also Chancellor of England, were both sons of peasants. "The child of cobbler or beggar has but to learn his book," summed up William Langland. "He will become bishop and sit down among the peers of the realm."

Others who failed to find livings sought employment elsewhere, such as keeping accounts for the monastery or manor or, from the fourteenth century when these posts were becoming more numerous and lucrative, as clerks or supervisors of commercial interests. Many were also becoming teachers, as we shall see presently.

How did these allegedly low standards of learning and morality affect the clerics in their teaching duties? The list of ecclesiastical lapses and illiteracies could be multiplied enormously. For example, there might be added the ludicrous instance of the thirteenth-century priest who thought that *te igitur* was the name of a saint![52] Nor are we reassured when we hear that things were much worse elsewhere in Europe. One must, however, wonder if the overall picture was really as gloomy as the accumulated instances might suggest. Though the ordinary parish priests, and especially others in Minor Orders, might have been no great scholars or persons of impeccable character, it is most improbable that all clerics were totally ignorant, undisciplined or lacking in moral fibre. Possibly many were far below the standard which we might consider appropriate for the men of the cloth today. Possibly too inability in Latin was considered a serious defect in the equipment of any mediaeval cleric. The fact remains that many were devoted to their preaching, social duties and teaching and that they were able, among other things, to help lay a firm base for the growth of English literacy. Most of them too had just that sufficiency of knowledge and expertise to be able to share their own rudiments of literacy with the unlettered masses.

The extent and standard of teaching must have varied from place to place and according to the responsibilities, ability and energy of the clerics engaged in the work. Some children were lucky in that they enjoyed the services of a man like Gilbert of Sempringham, c. 1083—1189, the later founder of the Gilbertine Order. When he was a parish priest, he was "a master of learning to the small petits, such as learn to read, spell and sing. He taught the children who were under his care not only their lessons on the book but also how to play in a seemly manner. He instructed them to be honest and joyful, without shouting or excessive noise, in their games."[53] Or like the Poor Parson of Chaucer's fourteenth-century *Canterbury Tales,* whose "parishioners devoutly would he teach."

The clerics must have done their work with some adequacy, for "it may be stated with some confidence that at least in the later Middle Ages the smallest towns and even the larger villages possessed schools where a boy might learn to read and acquire the first rudiments of ecclesiastical Latin and . . . except in very remote and thinly-populated regions, he would never have had to go very far from home to find a regular Grammar School. That the means of education in reading, writing and the elements of Latin were far more widely diffused in mediaeval times than has been sometimes supposed is coming to be generally recognized by students of mediaeval life."[54]

We must now look at the more clearly defined types of schools where reading instruction at the initial stage was being specifically offered.

3 Schools for the Teaching of Reading and the Rise of the Professional Teacher of Reading

Song Schools

For many centuries the *schola cantorum* or "song school" had been an important instrument in the organization of the Christian Church (see page 18). As its name indicates, its prime function was to teach song and music so that the finished product was a trained chorister who could help in the serving of the Mass and could join in the Responses, all of which had to be learnt by heart. In addition, all pupils were expected to learn to read, not in the vernacular but in Latin, the language of the Church service.

The earliest reference to such a school in mediaeval writings occurs in an English version of a thirteenth-century French romance, where the children are said to go to school to learn French and Latin and to write with a gold stylus on a wax tablet. The school must have accepted both boys and girls, for one pupil exclaimed amid his tears, "I cannot sing or read in any school without Blanchefleur."[1]

A more detailed account appears in Chaucer's "The Prioress's Tale": "At the far end of the street there had been established a small school where a number of Christian children received each year the kind of instruction that was normally prescribed for youngsters in that country, that is, learning to read and sing. . . . As this little child was learning his primer, he heard the others singing 'Alma Redemptoris Mater' just as children who have learnt their hymn-books are wont to do. As much as he dared, he drew closer and closer, listening intently all the time to the words and the tune till he knew the whole verse off by heart. As he was so young, he had no idea what the Latin meant, so one day he begged one of his friends to tell him the meaning of the song in simple language." His older companion then confessed, "Yes, I am learning to sing but I don't know much Latin."

In Henry VIII's reign there was also attached to Exeter Cathedral "a free song school, the schoolmaster to have yearly from the said pastor and preachers xx marks for wages and his house free, to teach xi children freely to read, write, sing and play upon the instruments of music, and to teach (them) their ABC in Greek and Hebrew."[2]

The Statutes of York (1307) nominated a precentor to be responsible for the appointment and control of the staff of the song school but the later history of St Paul's School put similar duties in the charge of an official called the chanter. He appointed the master of the song school, whose task it was to instruct those who could not sing and to teach them good manners as well. Judging from the words of a boy-bishop in Gloucester in 1558, when talking about the song school, some of the pupils needed training in good manners, or discipline as we should say nowadays. "It is not long since I was one of them myself . . . but I cannot let this pass untouched how boyishly they behave themselves in church [and] how rashly they come into the choir, without reverence. [They] never kneel down or lower their countenance to say any prayer or the Lord's Prayer but rudely squat down on their tails, and jostle with their fellows for a place . . . whose behaviour is in the temple as it was in their school, their master being absent, and not in the church, God being present."[3]

Sometimes the various teaching functions, such as song and grammar, were carried out by the same person but occasionally the song school existed in its own right, away from the grammar section. The records for 1426 for the Northallerton Grammar School, Yorkshire, which probably existed even before 1321, showed separate appointments for the teachers of the song and reading schools. Later, in 1443, the functions were again combined, with the song and grammar sections under the chaplain, whose duty it was to teach reading, song and grammar.[4] In 1483 Archbishop Thomas Rotherham of York, when founding Jesus College at Rotherham, arranged for a teacher of grammar, another "learned in song" and a third "learned and skilled in the art of writing and accounts."[5]

That the pupils learning the rudiments of letters were looked upon as distinct from and often inferior to the others is implied in the Ordinances of Ipswich (1477), which gave the grammar school master jurisdiction over all the scholars of the town, with the exception of "the petties called ABCs and Song." Disputes about the status of the various types of schools were rife. A famous one took place in Warwick in 1315 "between the Master and the Music Schoolmaster over the Donatists [i.e. grammarians] and the little ones learning their first letters and the psalter. . . . That undue encroachment of scholars on one side and the other may cease for the future," it was decreed "that the present Grammar Master and his successors shall have the Donatists, and thenceforward have, keep and teach scholars in grammar and the art of dialectic if he shall be expert in that art, while the Music Master shall keep and teach those learning their first letters, the psalter, music and song."[6]

On leaving school, many served in the church choir or migrated into minor orders but others moved into the outside world where frequent references can be found to their becoming farmers, fiddlers, jugglers or acrobats. Their training in letters and song also made them eminently suitable for acting roles in the miracle and morality plays that were so popular.

Reading and Writing Schools

Lines of definition are not always clear about educational affairs in the Middle Ages and, in addition to the song schools, the Chantry Certificates (1545—6) refer to reading schools. One existed at Bocking in Essex,[7] and another was found at Kingsley in Staffordshire where the chantry priest was directed "to keep school, and to teach poor men's children of the said parish, grammar and to read and sing."[8] There was another at Bromyard in Hereford, where lands and tenements producing three pounds nine shillings and eleven pence per annum were left "for the maintaining of God's service and bringing up the children born there in reading, writing and grammar."[9] Sir William Ilkes taught at Montgomery "young beginners only to write and sing, and to read as far as the accidence rules and no grammar."[10] In all of these the purpose of teaching song that was pre-eminent in the traditional song school seemed subsidiary to the purpose of teaching the basic literary arts.

The Chantry Certificates also have records of schools teaching the allied art of writing, for example at Normanton and Rotherham.

4   *A page from the Canterbury Psalter (c. 1150), showing the scribe,
Eadwine, at work*
Trinity College, Cambridge, MS. R.17.I.f.283 (by permission of the Master and
Fellows of Trinity College, Cambridge)

both in Yorkshire, with some of those mentioned in the previous paragraph as being both reading and writing schools. At Brough or Burgh-under-Staynsmore, Westmorland, "a free grammar school" was also intended to "teach scholars to write."[11]

By the Middle Ages writing was no longer confined to the scriptoria of monasteries for religious purposes. As we shall see in Chapter 8, professional copyists were already on the scene and, as the demand for literature grew, so scribes, illuminators for the painting of letters and illustrations of manuscripts, and binders were required in increasing numbers. Away from the monasteries, too, young men were being trained for the various specialized skills involving the essential detail of ink and parchment and the production of different types of script. So great had grown the demand for liturgies, biblical and devotional works, *Horae Beatae* and primers that importation of such books from abroad was necessary even before the invention of printing.

The occupational face of England was also changing. New industries such as shipbuilding, coalmining and the manufacture of armaments had already started, the cloth trade was being expanded and the peasants were migrating from the country to the town. To improve the standards of craft and manufacture and facilitate the machinery of trade and commerce, there was a widening demand for skilled men and clerks who knew letters and figures. There was an urgent need for the writing of correspondence, the composition of charters, the compilation of documents and the drawing-up of contracts, etc. When, for example, Richard II met the Wat Tyler rebels and agreed to grant them their freedom and absolve them conditionally from their dues, he had to employ a force of thirty clerks to draw up the charters.[12]

In the schoolroom too the method of learning was being modified. Whereas learning previously was wholly oral, teachers were now making their pupils commit the material to be learnt to writing as an aid to further reference and more effective recall. "Sententiae" and facts of history were now being preserved, and there was a demand for more instructional books. All these were in Latin and all copies had to be made in Latin. Hence one line was constantly used because it contained all the letters of the alphabet: "Adnexique globum Zephyrique Kauna secabant."

For such reasons as these attention had to be given more and more to the scriveners' art, and the skill of writing was being taught concomitantly with that of reading in the schools. For example, a private Act of Parliament (1483) concerning the College of Acaster,

Yorkshire, which had been founded by Robert Stillington, the Bishop of Bath and Wells, stated that of the three masters to be appointed, one was to teach grammar, another was to teach song but the third was to "teach to write and all such things as belonged to the Scrivener craft to all manner of persons."[13] By the sixteenth century this had become, with the casting of accounts, a popular subject in many schools, e.g. St Olave's, Southwark (1561), and Hartlebury (1565). The statutes for a school in Giggleswick, Yorkshire, in 1592, though it had been founded forty years earlier, prescribed that their scholars should "be exercised in writing under a scrivener."[14]

Gild and Chantry Foundations for the Encouragement of Literacy

The gilds were especially active in education. Basically a gild was formed by a group of men of like interests or ideas, who felt that association might best serve their mutual benefit or protection. Inspired at first possibly by religious motives, various other gilds, merchant, craft and social, gradually sprang up. By the twelfth century there were also gilds of trades, such as weavers, fullers and glovers, controlling the sale of their own articles and drawing up the regulations for the training of their apprentices. Where possible, they sought the consent of the king or the grant of a charter to strengthen their own position, and so they became formidable gatherings of important citizens.

They realized too that social recognition might follow from success and wealth in commerce and that education was a means of entrenching any newly acquired respect for their families. They set about establishing their own schools. Stratford-on-Avon had one before 1295. Another Free School at Farthinghoe, Northamptonshire (1443), was "to teach and instruct the little ones of the parish . . . freely and gratis without taking any pay or profit."[15] At Eccleshall, Staffordshire, the inhabitants "did erect two gilds . . . and one of the same priests has always kept a school and taught poor men's children of the same parish freely."[16]

The gilds appreciated the importance of the 3 Rs for the furtherance of their trade and the standards of their craft. In 1422 the Brewers Company of London had stated that "there are many of our craft of Brewers who have the knowledge of reading and writing in the said English idiom but in others, to wit, the Latin and French, before these times used, they do not in any wise understand."[17] The Goldsmiths Company levied fines early in the fifteenth century on any members who failed to have their apprentices taught to read and write and who refused at the same time to take on apprentices who could not do so.[18] The Skinners Company

5   *An English fourteenth-century school*
   B.M. M.S. Royal 6 E VI.f.541 (by permission of the Trustees of the
   British Museum)

had similar rules, for a record of 1496 informs us that two of their apprentices from the provinces were sent to school for that purpose.[19] Appreciating too the importance of spending their leisure profitably, they showed a keen interest in the development of drama and music, a contribution to the social awareness of literacy that cannot be dealt with here.

Gilds also helped through the establishment of chantries. These were foundations whereby a priest was provided to say Masses for the memory of a nominated person, who might have endowed for that purpose while he was still alive, and also for the souls of Christians in general. John Westley of Endford left 1,000 sheep for a priest to sing for ever: "The incumbent has always occupied himself in the teaching of children."[20] The sort of work they did can be pictured from the Chantries Acts, which mention 259 such schools, though there were probably over 2,000 of them in England as a whole.

Much of their educational work was similar to that of the song schools. Often they paid for a priest, who in addition to his chaplaincy duties acted as a schoolmaster for the children of members of the gild. As priests they conducted services and so required boys to act as servers and help in the liturgy. A chantry with the express aim of forwarding education was founded at Basingstoke as early as 1244.[21] Other records observe that "they teach freely all manner of children grammar" or that "John King, chantry priest, at the age of thirty-four years, having no other promotion, literate and [who] teaches children to write and read there and of good conversation, is now incumbent thereof."[22] At Newland, Gloucestershire (1445), the chantry priest provided "meat, drink, cloth[ing] and all other necessaries" for a scholar who in return helped to teach the little ones.[23] At Aldwinkle, Northamptonshire, a reading and spelling or syllable school was founded in 1489, where "the said chaplain . . . shall teach and instruct in spelling and reading six of the poorest of the town of Aldwinkle . . . freely, without demanding or taking remuneration from their parents or friends."[24]

Their real contribution can perhaps be gauged from the Injunction of Edward VI (1547) which exhorted "that all chantry priests shall exercise themselves in teaching youth to read, write and bring them up in good manners and other virtuous exercises."

Mediaeval hospitals also contributed to the teaching of literacy. St John's, Exeter, helped those "beginning with the alphabet and going on to the great psalter of David."[25] A licence was also granted to Lady Hungerford in 1482 so that she could found an almshouse with a master, whose duty it was "to teach and inform all such children and all other children that shall come to the place . . . from the beginning of learning until such season as they learn sufficient . . . grammar."[26]

Reading Instruction in the Grammar Schools

The cathedral or collegiate church schools of Anglo-Saxon times, such as those at Canterbury and York, had embraced song, grammar and theology in the one institution. Already in that period, however, a differentiation in teaching function between the various types of specialisms was being urged (see page 19).

The term *scola grammatica* was used in a document as early as the eleventh century but the English version, "gramer scole," seems to have first appeared in John of Trevisa's translation of Ralph Higden's *Polychronicon* in 1387. Schools which could be regarded as such, catering mainly for what would now be called the secondary tier of education, were being mentioned soon after the Norman Conquest. For example, York was refounded in 1075 and Warwick College was named in a deed of 1123. It was also stated of London in 1173 that "three principal churches have by privilege and ancient dignity, famous schools. Yet very often by support of some personage or of some teachers who are considered notable and famous in philosophy, there are also other schools by favour and permission."[27] Other such grammar schools were founded under the auspices of gilds or as adjuncts of colleges in Oxford and Cambridge, e.g. Merton (1270).

One of the principal differences between the cathedral school and the mediaeval grammar school was in the curriculum. The cathedral school had an encyclopaedic approach to education, ranging from the basics of the song school to the most sophisticated elements of the seven liberal arts. On the other hand, the mediaeval grammar school confined itself to the early branches of the seven liberal arts, the "trivium," that is, grammar, rhetoric and dialectic or logic, taught through the medium of Latin. The higher branches of the "quadrivium," that is, arithmetic, geometry, astronomy and music, were considered the rightful province of the university. As such, the grammar schools became the feeders of the universities and, jealous of their status, they thrust the teaching of the rudiments firmly on the song school and their like. So successful were the grammar schools in the provision of education and so keen had become the demand for entry to them that a profusion of foundations followed at places like Chichester, Manchester and Ipswich. Just before the Reformation there were already 400 in this country. With the increase of these schools with their qualified teachers and their reputation for success, pressure also grew for them to accept the "petties," as the youngsters who were entering upon the primary stage had come to be called. If accepted, more often than not they had to be taught to read.

Some grammar schools accepted the petties, and in 1522, for example, Christopher Walton provided for a person to keep a grammar school for all the poor children in Penwortham, Lancashire, so that he could teach them the "Absay, catechism, primer [and] accidence."[28] In consequence, the grammar schools began to face acute problems. Who was to teach the petties? Where were they to be housed? How were they to be taught?

How embarrassed the grammar schools were by the entry of non- or poor readers can be judged from the strict qualifications which were being prescribed for entry. Colet, when founding St Paul's in 1509, stipulated that the master must "first see they know the Catechism and also can read and write competently."[29] The authorities for Canterbury Grammar School (1541) stated that "no one shall be admitted into the school who cannot read readily."[30] In 1560 Westminster School prescribed "as a minimum that they have learnt by heart the eight parts of speech and can know to write at least moderately well."[31] Merchant Taylors' School in 1561 directed that they should "first see that they know the Catechism in English or Latin, and that every one of the said two hundred and fifty scholars can read perfectly and write competently, or else let them not be admitted in no wise."[32] The regulations of Alford School, Lincolnshire (1599), instructed that no one could "be admitted into this Grammar School before he can read perfectly and write legibly."[33]

One particular difficulty which keeps on cropping up in a study of the teaching of reading in this period is the exact identification of the reading act. In certain contexts the term used for "reading" does not necessarily signify the teaching or the learning of the rudiments of the skill. In his *Institutes* the Roman educationist, Quintilian, was quite specific in his meaning because he relied on phrases such as "those beginning letters," "the beginnings of letters" or "the elements of letters." Other classical authors generally employed such phrases as "learning the first elements" or "the names of letters" or "the alphabet." Whenever they wished to denote the act of continuous reading, they used the Latin word *lectio*. Many mediaeval records follow the same practice. When the statutes of Warwick School (1315) refer to the earliest stages of instruction, they employ the phrase "for the little ones learning their first letters" (*primas litteras*). The Convocation of Canterbury (1529) also made a clear distinction between "instructing boys in the alphabet" and *lectura,* where the latter term obviously implies a stage more advanced than the first rudiments.[34] One must therefore question if many of the grammar schools which have been credited with teaching the initial stages of reading were not actually teaching the skill at a higher level. The terms of the appointment at the Northallerton School, where the master would be required to teach the boys *lectura* and "grammar," would seem to support this.

The grammar school masters certainly disliked the entry of the petties to their institutions. John Brinsley in his *Ludus Literarius* (1612) considered it "an unreasonable thing that the grammar schools should be troubled with teaching ABC, seeing that it is so great a hindrance to those pains which we should take with our grammar scholars. . . . It does take up almost one half of our time. . . . It is an extreme vexation that we must be toiled amongst such petties and in teaching such matters whereof we can get no profit or take any delight in our labours." He felt that teaching "children to read . . . may seem unbefitting to our profession," and so he urged "all such schoolmasters who are encumbered with this inconvenience . . . to labour to have it reformed in their several schools."

Brinsley also suggested that everyone should "make it easier, if it lie on him," and so, in those grammar schools where the problem was acute, provision was often made for an usher, rather than the regular teacher, to teach the rudiments of the ABC, the Catechism and the primer. St Olave's School, Southwark, according to the deed of 1561, used an usher to help the schoolmaster teach the principles of the Christian religion, writing, reading and casting accounts, Oswestry School in 1571 had a schoolmaster and also an usher "for the teaching of the younger sort to read the ABC, the English primer," and Burford School, Oxford (1571), had both a master and an usher to teach grammar, reading and writing to "boys of the town."

Other schools made use of the older or more advanced pupils to help with the teaching of reading. In 1520 Robert Sherborne, the Bishop of Chichester, advised the master of Rolleston School, Staffordshire, to encourage his brighter pupils to "act as pupil teachers, to teach small boys who may be brought to him the alphabet and first rudiments."[35] The statutes of Rivington School (1566), though hoping that anyone who could not read would not be admitted, suggested that if those usually taught by the usher should be too many, then the schoolmaster should make use of some of the older pupils.[35] St Bees School (1583) also allowed that "the schoolmaster for the time being shall have authority to appoint some poor scholar that understands grammar and can read a reasonable hand to be his usher under him, who shall teach the children to read and write English."[36] Here it would seem that the schoolmaster was responsible for the Latin and the usher for the English.

Sometimes the petties were pushed out of the grammar school to be taught by any partially literate person in the town. We know, for instance, that help of a sort was available in Stratford in 1604, when the bailiff and burgesses petitioned the Chancellor of Worcester for a licence to be renewed to Thomas Parker who "has for a reasonable time . . . employed himself in the teaching of little children (chiefly such as his wife one time of the day does practise in needlework whereby our young youth is well furthered in reading, and the Free School greatly eased of that tedious trouble)."[37]

Educationists in this country had become aware by now of the existence of the petties and their problems. They were also recognizing that the petties should be kept apart from the grammar school. For instance, when Burford School was founded in 1571, Simon Wisdom provided for the petties "so that every man in the town and parish, minding to set his children to school, being mere children, having no infirmity or sickness, should be taught his ABC, his Catechism (and) primer, and to read and write, until he should be able to be preferred to the grammar school." A more clear-cut step was taken at Evershot near Sherborne in 1628 when the children on the threshold of learning were specifically allocated a separate building for their purpose. The sixteenth century also saw the first positive contribution being made to the most appropriate and effective methods of teaching the skills of reading and writing, and the most eminent in this respect, Mulcaster, Hart, Kempe, Coote and Brinsley were themselves grammar school masters.

The Rise of the Professional Teacher of Reading

From the beginning of this period the control of education in England had been vested wholly in the hands of the Church and, as external payment for teaching had been despised, the teaching clergy were dependent for their keep on the common fund. The Lateran Council (1179) had directed: "For a licence to teach no one shall exact money even if on any pretence of any custom he ask anything from those who teach." The English Council of Westminster (1200) had also emphasized that "the priests shall keep schools in their town and teach little boys gratis. . . . They ought not to expect anything from the relations of the boys for their instruction, except what they are willing to do of their own will."[38]

To ensure that these directives were carried out, supervisory powers were entrusted to a specially appointed officer of the Church, who was variously called the *scholasticus*, *archiscolus* or latterly the *cancellarius* or "chancellor." The duties of this official were set out by the Statutes of York in 1307. He alone could approve the appointment of staff to grammar schools or decide where schools could be established. He was responsible for the issue of a licence to anyone aspiring to teach in that diocese and, as Latin was required by entrants to Holy Orders, he excluded all who were incapable in that language. His powers of arbitration were particularly necessary therefore when several churches existed in the one district and all were desirous of organizing schools. The map of Lincoln (*c*. 1100), for example, shows thirty-nine churches on St Francis Hill alone. With the expanding educational programmes of other bodies like the gilds later, the problems of this official were further exacerbated.

From the late thirteenth century there was an increasing demand for education among the lower ranks of the population. Most of them were probably content, or had to be, to work for the lord in his fields and so those who wanted education had first to obtain his permission. The Articles of Clarendon (1164) had ruled that the sons of tenants in villeinage should not be ordained without the consent of the lord on whose lands they had been born, while many manors put restrictions on the education of their tenants. A register for 1325 for the manor of Burcester near Oxford forbade anyone's son to be "placed for letters" or for a daughter to be married without the lord's authority.[39]

Despite these restrictions, the manorial records of the fourteenth century abound with entries for fines inflicted for attendance at "clerical schools." For instance, Walter, the son of a carpenter, was "licensed to attend school" in 1295, provided a previous fine was paid. A villein of Coggeshill, Essex, was fined in 1344 for sending his son to school without a licence, and another villein was deprived of his horse in 1384 for the same reason.[40] There must have been a host of unrecorded instances.

The authorities in turn tried to stop the flow of men from the land. A Statute of 1388 had decreed that "he or she which used to labour at the plough or cart or other labour or service of husbandry till they be of the age of twelve years . . . from henceforth . . . shall abide at the same labour, without being put to any mystery of handicraft. And if any covenant or bond of apprentice be from henceforth made to the contrary, the same shall be holden for none."[41] In 1391 the Commons prayed Richard II that "no serf or villein henceforward put his children to school in order to procure their advancement by clergy" (see Chapter 7).[42]

It was like trying to stem the waves of the sea, and the failure to prevent the migration to the towns and into trades and for schooling was finally admitted by the Statute of Artificers in the reign of Henry IV (1406), which allowed, among other things, "every man or woman, whatever their estate, [to be] free to set their son or daughter to learn letters at any school which may please them in this realm."[43] The effect of this statute on education was tremendous.

In addition to the willing pupils, there was also a numerous supply of teachers who were eager to break the monopoly of the Church. "Are there not," the question was asked for the years 1119–35, "nearly as many skilled schoolmasters in France and Germany, in Normandy and England, not only in boroughs and cities, but even in country towns, as there are tax-collectors and magistrates?"[44] About 1260 Roger Bacon observed that there had never been "such a show of wisdom" or "such prosecution of study" as "in the last forty years. Doctors are found everywhere, particularly in theology, in every city, castle and burgh."[45]

Some areas welcomed this abundance of schoolmasters. In the history of the miracles of St John of Beverley we read that in 1100 when "a certain scholar came to Beverley . . . wishing, as the place was full of clerks, to keep school there," he was "received by the prelates of the church with unanimous approval. . . . Outside the church he taught a crowded school diligently: inside he governed the choir harmoniously."[46]

The authorized schoolmaster or priest frequently clamoured for the protection of the ecclesiastical watchdog against the unlicensed intruders. As early as 1138 Henry Blois, the Bishop of Winchester, issued a writ against unlicensed schools with the threat of excommunication if they continued without the consent of the licensed schoolmaster.[47] A document of 1289 reminded others in Kinoulton, Nottinghamshire, that "only the clerks of our parish . . . may, if they wish, attend the school which has been from times ancient customarily kept in that parish, all other clerks and strangers whatsoever being kept out and by no means admitted to the said school."[48] Later (1446–7) a Writ of Privy Seal concerning two

new grammar schools in London complained of the "great abuses
. . . within our city of London that many and divers persons, not
sufficiently instructed in grammar" presume "to hold common
grammar schools in great deceit as well to their scholars as unto
the friends that find them to school."[49]

Resort to proceedings against unlicensed offenders was common.
Two chaplains, Sir John Bernard and William Brynge, were sum-
moned in 1423 before the Abbot of Walden "to show why and on
what authority they practised the exercise of teaching small boys
of Walden and instructing them in the alphabet, graces and other
books . . . though they had previously been reproved for their pre-
sumption in doing this."[50] As they had repeated the offence, they
were interdicted from teaching at all, but after the parents had
appealed on their behalf they were permitted to teach the alphabet
and graces to one boy in each Walden family.

The licensed teachers themselves were not above cheating, and
there is an amusing story in 1321 about Robert de Henneye, the
Rector of St Martin's parish just outside Canterbury, and Ralph of
Waltham, the rector of Canterbury Grammar School. Robert had
been authorized to keep a reading and writing school for as many
pupils as he wished but he was not allowed to register more than
thirteen grammar pupils in addition. Ralph suspected that Robert
de Henneye was violating the conditions of his licence, so he complained to the authorities. He kept on sending his usher round to
count the pupils but the smart Robert always got wind of his projected visits and managed to hide the extra grammar pupils![51]

As such fierce disputes about school or teaching monopoly were
going on, one suspects that teaching was a profitable source of
income. Unfortunately, evidence about teachers' earnings in this
period is rather scarce, though the average income of a schoolmaster under the Chantries Acts was about six pounds nine shillings
and sixpence per annum, with the chantry priest earning about
five pounds per annum.[52] Part-time assistants were paid much less.
For example, John Balmok, the bellringer at Launceston, was paid
thirteen shillings and fourpence for his rudimentary work, while
John Pound at Penryn received two pounds per annum for ringing
the bell and teaching reading. The rates of pay also varied according
to the section of the school where one might be teaching. At Rotherham in 1483 the teacher of grammar was paid ten pounds per
annum "and not more," the teacher of song six pounds thirteen
shillings and fourpence "and not more," and the teacher of writing
five pounds six shillings and eightpence "and not more."[53] A

schoolmaster in Hackney in 1613 was paid fourpence for teaching grammar to a class but only twopence for teaching reading.[54] In Coxwold, Yorkshire, in 1603 a schoolmaster was appointed to teach the petties to "read English," for which he was paid two pounds thirteen shillings and fourpence per annum.[55] A more interesting instance is reported in 1552 of Christ's Hospital, where the authorities appointed, in addition to the grammar-school master and usher, two other schoolmasters "for the ABC," each being paid two pounds thirteen shillings and fourpence. A little later one of these was regraded as the school barber.[56]

The charges for tuition also varied. At the grammar school in Hull the scale of fees was "eightpence for teaching grammar and sixpence for teaching reading."[57] At Ipswich the tariff for pupils in 1476 was tenpence for "grammarians," eightpence for "psalterians" and sixpence for "primarians," that is, those learning the primer, but the petties learning the alphabet were excluded.[58] Moreover, this school was described as being "very well haunted" (attended). At a chantry school founded by Richard Gryndour at Newland, Gloucestershire, c. 1480, those learning grammar were charged eightpence a quarter and those learning to read fourpence a quarter.[59]

There were also endowments, both by organizations and individuals, for the education of those who were unable to pay for it. The foundation statutes of Merton College, Oxford (1270), when attaching a grammar school, stated that "if any young children of my kin need support in consequence of the death or poverty of their parents, while they are under early instruction in the rudiments of knowledge, in such case the Warden shall cause them, to the number of thirteen, to be educated in the house until they can make their way in the schools, if they turn out to be of ability."[60]

By the middle of the sixteenth century teaching was a somewhat populous profession, and some practitioners were issuing broadsheets advertising the advantages of attendance at their private academies. In 1570 Humphrey Baker, the author of *The Well Spring of Sciences*, drew attention to his pedagogic wares in these words: "Such as are desirous, either themselves to learn, or have their children or servants in any of these Arts and Faculties hereunder named: It may please them to repair to the house of Humphrey Baker, dwelling on the north side of the Royal Exchange, next . . . to the sign of the Ship. Where they shall find the professors of the said Arts, etc., ready to do their diligent endeavours for a reasonable consideration. Also if any be minded to have their children boarded at the said house, for the speedier expedition of their learning, they shall be well and reasonably used, to their contentation. . . . God save the Queen."

Generally teachers were not held in much respect. In his *Book of the Governor* (1530) Sir Thomas Eliot casually remarked that his peers seldom had "any regard to the teacher, whether he be well learned or ignorant. For if they hire a schoolmaster to teach in their house, they chiefly inquire with how small a salary he will be content, and never do in search how much good learning he has. . . . Undoubtedly there be in this realm many well learned . . . if the name of schoolmaster were not so much had in contempt."

An even more contemptuous attitude was being shown towards the teachers of the elements of reading. In fact, this had also been the case with the ancients. In his satire *Menippus* the Greek, Lucian, left his readers in no doubt about what he thought of them: "Our kings are all in straitened circumstances there and, on account of dire poverty, are either selling salt fish or are teaching the alphabet and are receiving foul abuse and being hit over the head by all and sundry." Quintilian too in his *Institutes* commented that previous writers on the subject of oratory had ignored or despised the primary stages of learning because they were none of their business or because there was very little money to be made in an educational patch which, however fundamental, did not capture the public eye.

It is not surprising therefore that Mulcaster in his *Elementary* (1581) declared that "good scholars will not abase themselves to it. It is left to the meanest and therefore the worst." Edmund Coote in *The English Schoolmaster* (1596) observed that it was "lamentable to see into what ignorant handling silly little children chance." Anyone other than a respectable schoolmaster could teach reading. In *The Petty School* (1576) Francis Clement suggested that the learners of the rudiments should be referred to the parish clerk, the tailor or any seamstress for instruction. Coote directed his counsel about reading methods to "the unskilful which desire to make use of it for their own private benefit, and to such men and women of trade as tailors, shopkeepers, seamsters and such others as have undertaken the charge of teaching others." John Brinsley in his *Ludus Literarius* (1612) shrugged them off: "There might be some other school in the town for these little ones. It might help some poor man or woman who knew not how to live otherwise and who might do that well if they were rightly directed." Richard

Hodges in *The English Primrose* (1644) concurred with these opinions: "so many are the difficulties in the common way of teaching to read English that few will undertake to be masters in that kind unless necessity and want cast them upon it. Nor will they long continue in the profession, if by any other employment they can subsist. And if masters find the work so tedious and grievous, it is impossible it should be pleasing to the scholars." He added a most ingenious suggestion to explain why the job was so hazardous. "It is most true that the poor boys be often chided, rebuked, knocked and whipped, when the fault is not in them that they apprehend not what is taught, but in the uncertain, perplexed and intricate expressing of our tongue by letters wrongly named and by their various sounds and forces attributed to them. This is not any singular opinion of mine. . . . [It] has been, and is, averred by divers learned and industrious men both in the former and this present age."

In the meantime, amid this throng of teachers the Church had not forgotten her rights in the licensing of schoolmasters. In the post-Reformation period the controlling power was in the hands of the monarch and the bishops rather than the Pope, and stringent supervision was necessary for reasons additional to those of the pre-1530 period. The Convocation of Canterbury (1571) directed "that the bishop shall approve no schoolmaster as worthy of the office of teacher, unless in his judgement he has sufficient knowledge and unless he is recommended as worthy in life and morals by the testimony of pious men."[61] In 1580 Elizabeth's Council wrote to Archbishop Edmund Grindal of Canterbury that "as a great deal of the corruption in religion, grown throughout the realm, proceeds of lewd schoolmasters, it is thought meet for redress thereof that you cause all such schoolmasters as have charge of children to be by the Bishop of the diocese, or such as he shall appoint, examined touching their religion. And, if they shall be found corrupt and unworthy, to be displaced . . . and fit and sound persons placed in their rooms."[62] On many occasions in the reign of Elizabeth (1581, 1583, 1585 and 1588), inquiries were made by the successive Archbishops, Grindal and Whitgift, whether anyone was teaching without the bishop's licence. In fact, teaching without the bishop's licence was not legalized in this country till the reign of Queen Victoria.

As women teachers were becoming more frequent, these too were included in the injunctions. An article of Bishop Edmund Bonner for the diocese of London (1554) concerned "schoolmasters and teachers of children, men and women. . . . Whether they that take upon themselves to teach children, whether it be in English or in Latin. . . . Whether any teacher or schoolmaster do teach or read to the scholars any evil or naughty corrupt book, ballad or writing."[63]

Instances of women teachers had been recorded from early in the fifteenth century, e.g. Matilda Maresfleet in Boston in 1404 and Ellen Schoolmaster at Taunton in 1494, but from the sixteenth century it was their increasing numbers that roused this sudden interest in them by the Church officials. The dissolution of the nunneries had forced the inmates to seek a livelihood outside the convent walls, hence the ready availability of seamstresses and others of similar trades offering instruction in reading. Later, the influx of refugees from abroad saw the emergence of small schools of calligraphy, music, languages and crafts, where the teaching of reading was probably supplied as an additional extra.

Teaching Girls to Read

The multiplicity of these women teachers reminds us of an aspect in the early history of education that has been rather perplexing — where and by whom girls were taught the elements of literacy. "The trend of mediaeval thought" according to one historian "was against learned women."[64] "A girl," so ran an Italian proverb, "must be taught to sew and not to read, unless she is to become a nun," and the same attitude was more explicitly stated by Francesco da Barberino (1264—1348). Reading, he observed was absolutely imperative for the daughters of kings and princes to help them with the later art of government. Possibly it was necessary for those of marquises and counts, and it might be tolerated for the daughters of judges and gentlemen. But there were no grounds at all for the art to be considered for the daughters of mechanics and craftsmen.

Despite these views, throughout this period we meet a succession of well-educated women but, reflecting da Barberino's scale, they almost wholly occur in the highest social échelons. For instance, Egitha, queen to Edward the Confessor, once challenged a scholar to a battle of wits in the fields of grammar, logic and verse, and Matilda, wife of Henry I, was well acquainted with the works of Cicero and loved poetry. The wife of Ralph Fitzgilbert (c. 1150) requested Geoffrey Gaimar to translate his work, *Estoire des Engles*, especially for her and even went to the trouble of procuring rare books, one in Welsh, to assist him in his task. Many Norman ladies were popularly represented as reading "sometimes in their hours of grief, from golden psalters, sometimes from books of romances."[65] The fact too that guides for letter-writing were available for them in French indicates an appreciable level of literacy among them. Curiously enough, the work *Advice to Ladies* (1371), whilst recommending reading, a knowledge of church music, embroidery, confectionery and surgery as useful accomplishments for ladies, preferred that they knew nothing about writing.

There is scant reference to the acquisition of reading skills by women of the lower classes till the Statute of Artificers (1406) (see page 45). From then on there is increasing evidence of literacy among women of the agricultural and artisan classes, and such instances are frequently quoted in the expanded 1563 edition of Foxe's *Book of Martyrs*. In 1429, for example, Margery Backster, the wife of a wright in the Norfolk village of Martham, invited her friends to come and hear her husband, "well learned in the Christian verity," read "the law of Christ . . . written in a book that her husband was wont to read to her by night."[66] The wife of a tailor could "read English very well and, yet servant, had a copy of the New Testament left her by Sir Hugh Pie."[66] Alice Harding in 1511 was said to "instruct better than many others," She could recite the Scriptures and other good books; and therefore when any conventicle of these men did meet at Burford, commonly she was sent for to recite unto them the declaration of the Ten Commandments and the Epistles of Peter and James."[67] The ownership of books by women, and the legacies of books to and by women, occur often from the early fifteenth century, and in 1395 a Lady Alice West left "all the books that I have of Latin, English and French . . . to my daughter-in-law."[68]

Again the Church played the all-important part. Women were required to attend services and so, to quote Mulcaster, they must have found "reading . . . very needful for religion." It has been suggested that to that end the earliest English primers were made specially for them, and that the smaller works printed by Caxton and others were aimed directly at women. Several pictures of the period also feature St Anne teaching Our Lady to read or Our Lady reading to the Child Jesus.

As we have seen, the song schools trained recruits for the choir and the clergy and, as girls were not eligible for either, boys enjoyed a monopoly of their places. Where then did girls receive the education to make them literate? In the early days, with "every house," in the

The grammar schools were also making their contribution to the education of girls. The school at Canterbury, it is true, categorically refused entry to girls, as "it seems very unfit girls should be taught in a school within the precincts of the Church, especially seeing they may have instruction by women in the town."[80] Others were more charitable in their attitude and accepted them. Bunbury Grammar School (1594) took in a few girls to learn to read English but only up to the age of nine.

By the sixteenth century the need for the education of girls was accepted unequivocally. "Our country," wrote Mulcaster in his *Positions* (1581), "does allow it, our duty does enforce it, their aptness calls for it, their excellence commands it." At the top there were some outstanding examples of female brilliance gracing the intellectual scene. Margaret Roper, the eldest daughter of Sir Thomas More, was called by Erasmus "the ornament of Britain and the flower of learned matrons of England." Lady Jane Grey was once found by Ascham "reading the *Phaedo* of Plato in Greek . . . with as much delight as some gentlemen would read a merry tale of Boccaccio."

At the other end of the social scale things may have been very different. The greatest Elizabethan of them all, William Shakespeare, had two daughters — Susanna, who could barely write, and Judith, who had to rely on her mark.

Aristocratic Disparagement of Letters

So far this chapter has been concerned with the facilities that were available in England for people who were eager to learn to read. Not all social groups, however, regarded the acquisition of letters as a laudable accomplishment and some, for example, were like the aristocratic Goths of the fifth century who exhibited a bitter hostility to them. Procopius tells us that when "Amalasuntha wished to make her son resemble the Roman prince in his way of life and was already compelling him to attend the school of a teacher of letters . . . the Goths were by no means pleased with this. All the notable men among them gathered together and . . . made the charge that their king was not being educated correctly from their point of view or to his own advantage. For letters, they said, are far removed from manliness."[81]

Despite the enthusiastic encouragement of letters by Charlemagne and Alfred the Great, a supercilious attitude persisted among the Norman nobles on the Continent. Hugh of Fleury, in a dedicatory letter to his *Historia Ecclesia*, referred to "those unlettered nobles [to whom] the art of letters is a thing of disdain," while Walter Map in his *De Nugis Curialium* (I.x) (*c.* 1190) said that the nobles were "too scornful or indifferent even to put their children to learn their letters." What their own leaders thought of learning is colourfully illustrated in the story of Lanfranc (*c.* 1005– 89), himself a member of a noble Lombard family and later Archbishop of Canterbury. When still on the Continent he had once received a visit from a Bishop Herfest, accompanied by some of Duke William's courtiers. So strongly did Lanfranc disapprove of their ignorance that he dared offer them a spelling-book. The insult was considered so gross that Lanfranc had to go into hiding for some time. The attitude of the early royal leaders themselves could not be painted more favourably. Not one of the first half-dozen dukes from Normandy was interested in letters.

When the Norman settlement of England was more stabilized, the attitude of the nobles underwent a remarkable change. Robert, the son of Henry I (1100–53), was a scholar of some renown, and King Stephen (1135–54) was brought up in the liberal arts. Henry II too had a more than useful competence in letters, ran a school at court, organized discussions on learned topics and gave much of his time to reading in public. Naturally this interest in the liberal arts spread to their fellows, and "it would seem that the sons of nobility in twelfth-century England received far more instruction in letters than is generally supposed."[82]

Moreover, if the upper social crust were so inclined, they had both the means and the opportunity to give their children a training in letters. Some, like the Earl of Salisbury, sent them to school in Bologna, while a school in Laon in France at the same time had five English boys. Others entered the Church where ready promotion awaited them. Ordericus Vitalis tells us that "at five (after my baptism) I was handed over by my father to Siward, a noble priest, to be trained in letters, to whose mastery I was subdued during five years learning the first rudiments."[83]

The majority, conforming to the customs of their class, sought a training for a life of adventure without the serious contemplation of letters, an education that would fulfil the requirements and privileges of the social class to which they belonged. For them an essential education embraced a competence in horsemanship, the use of weapons and the art of being a knight, a knowledge of the code of courtesy and manners, and a familarity with the procedure of religion.

To acquire this, they were often sent to the establishment of another peer or ecclesiast, where a sort of miniature school was organized. Thomas Bromele, the Abbot of a monastery near Winchester, received eight young gentlemen "for the purposes of literary instruction,"[84] and the Earl of Northumberland in 1511 took "young gentlemen at their friends' finding" into his household. As with the placement of girls, life was no picnic in any of these houses. In the *Paston Letters* we read of Anne Paston in 1457 actually begging her fifteen-year-old son's master to "truly belash him [if] he has not done well or will not amend." Often too the supervisory lords neglected their wards lest they should grow too proud to marry their daughters.

On first entering, the wards were put in the charge of the lady of the house who taught them the elements of language, including the skill of reading, the rules of courtesy and the elements of the Christian religion. At the age of fourteen they were promoted to the rank of squire when they were taught their duties and skills in war. A chaplain also gave them some book-learning. They were taught to write but with the direct object of being able to record the details of their own glorious exploits on the tablets which they later carried with them.

From such education little intellectualism was likely to result and within this narrow noble circle the contemptuous attitude towards letters displayed by the fifth-century Goths and the eleventh-century Normans died hard. As late as 1520 Alexander Barclay observed that "at this time the understanding of Latin was almost condemned of gentlemen"; yet it was the vital ingredient in the educational diet of all others. The fifteenth-century Pace relates a revealing incident in his *De Fructu*.

"When two years ago, more [or] less, I had returned to my native land . . . I was present at a certain feast, a stranger to many. . . . When enough had been drunk, one or other of the guests — no fool as one might infer from his words and countenance — began to talk of educating his children well. And, first of all, he thought he must search out a good teacher for them and that they should at any rate attend school. There happened to be present one of those whom we call gentlemen, and who would always carry some horn hanging at their backs, as though they would hunt during dinner. He, hearing the letters praised, roused with sudden anger, burst out furiously with these words. 'Why do you talk nonsense, friend?' he said. 'A curse on those stupid letters! All learned men are beggars. Even Erasmus, the most learned of all, is a beggar (so I hear). . . . I swear by God's body I'd rather that my son should hang than study letters. For it becomes the sons of gentlemen to blow the horn nicely, to hunt skilfully, and elegantly carry and train a hawk. But the study of letters should be left to the sons of rustics!' "[84]

Notwithstanding the derisory outburst of this coarse aristocrat, the fact remains that long before the sixteenth century the skill of reading was being successfully taught to "the sons of rustics" and others throughout the length and breadth of England. Let us now consider the general pedagogic principles which the teachers of reading observed when they were engaged in this elementary but fundamental stage of education.

Principles and Practice in the Teaching of Reading

4 Basic Methods of Teaching Reading

Instruction in reading had a long history among the Greeks. A law of *c.* 640 B.C., probably attributed wrongly to Solon, had required every boy to learn to read and swim. The Greek historian, Herodotus, referring in his *History* (vi) to the sea-fight of 494 B.C., has a tragic paragraph telling how "a house in the city collapsed on some boys as they were learning to read and only one boy out of one hundred and twenty escaped."

Over the centuries the Greeks had evolved their own methods of teaching the skill and, as the subsequent Roman methods were almost wholly based on theirs, one must regard the Greeks as the genuine formulators of what has been traditionally called "the alphabetic method" of teaching reading. But reading methodology today is a large subject with its own branches of specialisms, and it would be more appropriate to deal with each aspect separately throughout the period under review.

The Age of Reading Readiness

The Greeks had various opinions about this. Xenophon in his *Constitutions* felt that a start should be made with reading "as soon as there is a beginning of understanding," while Chrysippus the Stoic (*c.* 280–204 B.C.) (Quintilian's *Institutes,* i), proposed the age of three. Aristotle in his *Politics* (vii) put the age of five as the termination of that stage of the child's first development when he should not be required to study or work lest his growth might be impaired, and Plato in his *Laws* (vi) suggested the age of six. It would appear that as the skill of reading had to be mastered before the Athenian child could enter upon a study of grammar, the first element of the liberal sciences, an immediate start was made as soon as he entered school at seven. Yet even in those days there were theorists of advanced educational views, and the old Greek poet, Hesiod (*c.* eighth century B.C.), was supposed to favour a delay in introducing reading till the age of eighteen.

The views of Quintilian, the Roman educationist (*c.* 35—*c.* 95), about the teaching of reading merit serious attention. Not only was Quintilian the first officially recognized professional teacher in Rome but he offered more valuable advice about the acquisition of literacy, as the threshold to rhetoric, than any other classical writer. In the fourth century A.D. St Jerome was confidently recommending the use of his methods for Christian children, and later when *The Institutes of the Orator* were rediscovered by Poggio Bracciolini in the monastery of St Gall in 1416, his impact on educational methodology was greater still. Erasmus himself apologized in 1512 for daring to discuss the aims and methods of teaching because "Quintilian has said in effect the last word on the subject." This reverence for Quintilian principle prolonged English homage to the alphabetic method even in the Elizabethan age, which was so progressive in educational theory, so prolific in ideas about language reform and so profuse with books on pedagogy. For instance, one of the reformers, John Hart, in *A Method*, while pushing his own scheme of orthography, was happy to claim that his "manner of teaching is after the counsel of the excellent rhetorician, Quintilian. . . . Towards the latter end of the seventh Chapter of my treatise . . . I declared Quintilian's opinion in the teaching of letters, where I also professed that if I did set forth an ABC for teaching of the rude, I would follow closely his counsel, which I do hereafter very near."

While Quintilian prescribed no definite age for introducing the child to the formal act of reading, he had firm views about it. "If the child's age is considered suitable for moral training, why cannot it be deemed suitable for literary training as well? I fully understand that hardly as much progress can be made in the whole of this period as might be possible in one year afterwards. But still, those who disagree with my views seem in this instance to be doing so more out of sympathy with the teachers than with the children.

What is there better for the child to do as soon as he has learnt to speak? Surely it is necessary for him to be kept occupied? Anyhow, why should we despise any gain made, however slight, just because it was achieved before the age of seven?"

At the same time Quintilian appreciated the dangers inherent in forcing learning on the very young. The child might come to hate it and "start back in dread when he recalls the bitterness he once had for it, even though it was way back in his earliest years." This was a clear statement of principle which still gives concern to our contemporary psychologists whenever an earlier introduction to reading is being urged.

Particular care, he urged, should be exercised in the choice of nurse for the young child, for hers were the words the child would hear first and so try to imitate. If "mother" or "Infants teacher" were substituted for "nurse," this advice would remain wholly relevant today when research is demonstrating the incalculable influence of early language training on subsequent achievement.

After Quintilian, till the sixteenth century, apart from the infrequent reference to the age of school entry, usually by way of personal reminiscence, the problem never seems to have been seriously considered. Just as we often hear of children today learning to read merely from television captions or glancing daily at hoardings on the way to school, or learning to read both French and English from the label of an HP sauce bottle, so the skill was occasionally acquired in curious ways in Anglo-Saxon times. One infant prodigy of the fifth century, Bishop Samson, was supposed to have learned with the help of God all the letters of the alphabet in a single day and to recognize whole words in a week.[1]

Thoughts of the young Brontës at Haworth are also stirred by the story of a precocious lad, Leodegar (c. 616—79), the later Bishop of Autun. As soon as he could walk and talk, he showed no enthusiasm of any sort for boyish games out of doors. Instead he used to immerse himself in books and, while his friends were romping around noisily, he used to strip the bark off trees and make little books for himself, using any handy fluid for ink.[2]

Another tale concerned a little boy, Anskar or Anscharius (801—65), who later became the Bishop of Bremen and earned the title of "The Apostle of the North." Though he had been sent by his parents to a monastery at the age of five, he preferred to spend his time in play rather than study. One night, as he was strolling along a path that led to a wood, he was suddenly confronted by Our Lady, dressed in white and accompanied by a group of saints.

"My lad," she said, "if you intend getting away from these fool-ish things and leading a decent life, you had better get on with your study."

The young lad was so impressed by the encounter that he changed his life on the spot and from that time gave his whole life to reading and meditation.[3]

Among the conflicting stories told of King Alfred, there is one about his early genius. One day his mother "showed him and his brothers a book of Saxon poetry, which she had in her hand and said, 'I will give this book to the one among you who shall the most quickly learn it.' Then, moved at these words or rather by the inspiration of God, and being carried away by the beauty of the initial letter in that book, anticipating his brothers who surpassed him in years but not in grace . . . he said, 'Will you of a truth give that one book to one of us? To him who shall soonest understand it and repeat it to you?' And at this she smiled and was pleased and affirmed it, saying, 'I will give it to him.' Then forthwith he took the book from her hand and went back to his master and read it and, when he had read it, he brought it back to his mother and repeated it to her."[4]

Such stories die hard, and some eight hundred years later an almost similar story of early genius was told by Boswell about Dr Johnson in his *Life of Samuel Johnson* (1791). Apparently "Mrs Johnson one morning put the common prayer-book into his hands, pointed to the collect for the day, and said, 'Sam, you must get this by heart.' She then went upstairs, leaving him to study it: but by the time she had reached the second floor, she heard him following her. 'What's the matter?' said she. 'I can say it,' he re-plied; and repeated it distinctly, though he could not have read it over more than once." Dr Johnson was then three years old.

The age of going to school, and therefore of beginning to learn to read, varied in this early period. Ordericus Vitalis (1075—1143) went to a school in Shrewsbury to learn reading, grammar and singing at the age of five (see page 55), and the little cleric of Chaucer's "Prioress's Tale" and Floriz and Blanchefleur were already in school at the age of seven (see page 32). The most tender age seems to have been that of "The Wise Child of Three Years Old," who figures in a sixteenth-century tract of that title and who was questioned on the most abstruse religious matters by the Emperor Hadrian. Another, George Medley, quoted as an expense for 12 July, 1550, the provision of "a pound of sugar plate and great 'confets' to make him learn his book, xx d: for two ABCs i d"[5] for his four-year-old nephew, Francis Willoughby. Mary Tudor, the daughter of Henry VIII, started her education at the same age. Francis Clement in *The Petty School* considered that "although he be but four years of age, yet at the least let him learn to discern the vowels from the consonants" but he hastened to add that the teacher should exercise discretion about introducing him to all or some of the rules of spelling until "he is of years and capacity." Lord Herbert of Cherbury, born 1583, recalled in his *Autobiography* that his "schoolmaster in the house of my lady grandmother began at the age of seven years to teach me the alphabet and afterwards grammar."

Most English children were not in the social position to enjoy the advantages of individual tuition by special tutors employed in most of these instances, and the vast majority had to seize their opportunity at any age. From the *Ludus Literarius* of John Brinsley we gain a firm impression of what was happening about 1612. In the country, he wrote, children were first sent to school "commonly about seven or eight years old. Six is very soon. . . . If any begin so early, they are rather sent to the school to keep them from troubling the house at home, and from danger and shrewd turns, than from any great hope and desire their friends have that they should learn anything in effect."

By the sixteenth century the topic of reading readiness seems to have assumed the proportions of a popular controversy, and many varied opinions were being vehemently aired.

Roger Ascham in *The Schoolmaster* (1570) put the argument in favour of an early introduction to schooling rather prettily. "For we remember nothing so well when we be old, as those things we learned when we were young. And this is not strange, but common, in all nature's works. Every man sees . . . new wax is best for printing, new clay fittest for working, new shorn wool aptest for soon and surest drying, new fresh flesh for good and durable salting. This similitude is not rude or borrowed of the larder house but out of the schoolhouse, of which the wisest of England need not be ashamed to learn. Young grafts grow not only soonest but also fairest and always bring forth the best and sweetest fruit."

Ten years later Richard Mulcaster in his *Elementary* wrote of the dilemma. "One of the first questions is at what age children should be sent to school, for they should neither be delayed too long, so that time is lost, nor hastened on too soon, at the risk of their health." Writing in the key of the modern psychologist, he stresses the importance of individual variation. "The rule therefore must be given according to the strength of their bodies and the quickness of their wits jointly. If the parents be not wanting in means and there is a convenient place near . . . and a teacher with sufficient knowledge and with discretion to train him up well by correction . . . and if the child has a good understanding and a body able to bear the strain of learning, methinks it were then best that he begin to be doing something as soon as he can use his intelligence, without overtaxing his powers either of mind or body, as the wise handling of his teacher will direct. What the age should be I cannot say, for ripeness in children does not always come at the same time, any more than corn is all ripe for one reaping, though it is pretty nearly at the same time. Some are quick, some are slow. Some are willing when their parents are, and others only when they are inclined themselves." This is advice which could be taken to heart by every Infants teacher today.

His advice is so full of sound common sense that one cannot omit the frightening picture he paints of the child who has been pushed into learning both prematurely and unwillingly. "Those who fix upon a definite age for beginning have an eye to that knowledge which they think may be easily gained in these early years and which it would be a pity to lose. I agree with them that it would be a greater pity for so small a gain to risk a more important one, to win an hour in the morning and lose the whole day afterwards. For experience has taught me that a young child with a quick mind pushed on for people to wonder at the sharpness of its edge has thus most commonly been hastened to its grave . . . and even if such a child lives, he will never go deep but will always float on the surface without much ballast, though continuing for a long time to excite wonder. Sooner or later, however, his intelligence will fail, the wonder will cease, while his body will prove feeble and perish." Mulcaster knew all about keeping up with the educated Joneses! Do the child no harm, he advises, "by hurrying him on so fast and measuring his forwardness not by his own knowledge but by the notions of his friend."

Brinsley was equally candid in his plea for a start at the age of five "at the uttermost or sooner" but reiterating the arguments which Mulcaster had previously tried to refute.

"1. Because . . . then children will begin to conceive of instruction and to understand. [They will] be able not only to know their letters, to spell and to read but also to take a delight therein and to strive to go before their fellows. . . .

"2. If they be apt much before five years of age to learn

shrewdness and those things which are not hurtful, which they must be taught to unlearn again, why are they not as well fit to learn those things which are good and profitable for them?. . .

"4. This first age is that wherein they are most pliant and may be bent and fashioned most easily to any good course. . . .

"5. Above these, this is the principal benefit that by this means two or three years may well be gained to fit your scholar so much sooner for the university or any honest trade or calling."

Brinsley suggests that, to help the act of learning with such of tender years, "the school be made unto them a place of play and the children drawn on by that pleasant delight which [it] ought to be." As a counter to the old arguments that (i) "it will cause them to hate school," (ii) "they can but little learning then" and (iii) there is a smaller loss of a year or two" at that time, he emphasized that "the loss will be found at the end, though it indeed be in the beginning." By starting earlier, he was certain, such a loss could be prevented.

In his book *A New Discovery of the Old Art of Teaching School* (1660) Charles Hoole returned to the same problem, giving more information about the age of children going to school for the first time. "It is usual in cities and greater towns to put children to school about four or five years of age, and in country villages, because of farther distance, not till about six or seven. I conceive [that] the sooner the child is put to school, the better it is, both to prevent ill habits which are got by play and idleness, and to enure him betimes to affect learning and well doing." He suggests yet another reason for an early start. "I observe that betwixt three and four years of age a child has a great propensity to peep into a book, and then is the most seasonable time . . . for him to begin to learn. Though perhaps then he cannot speak so distinctly, yet the often pronunciation of his letters will be a means to help his speech, especially if one takes notice in what organ or instrument he is most defective, and exercises him chiefly in those letters which belong to it." He adds an interesting item about a "Mr Roe and Mr Robinson, the latter of whom I have known to have taught little children not much above four years old to read distinctly in the Bible in six weeks' time or under. Their books are to be had in print, but everyone has not the same art to use them." It is unfortunate that these works have not survived for our inspection.

In short, as it might be noticed, all the views and arguments offered are still being put forward today and we are still without a solution, though the latest proposal for an earlier start to reading is based on the fact that children are maturing earlier.

The Alphabetic Method

The actual method of teaching reading was a formal affair. The learner began by learning to recognize the shapes and then to remember the names of the letters. When learning to read, wrote Plato in his *Republic*, one must "know the various letters in all their recurring sizes and combinations. One cannot dismiss them as unimportant according to their large or small format but one must identify them wherever they occur. Nor can one consider oneself competent in the art until one can recognize them on every possible occasion." Aristotle added in his *Politics* that "one must always learn the same name for the same letter wherever it appears. In any class where boys are gathered to learn their letters, they are invariably asked about the letters that make up any word."

Automatic recognition of the letters was the basic principle of the Greek method, and so they had to be learnt from all directions. They were first learnt from alpha to omega, the first and the last letters; then as alpha and omega, the first and the last, beta and psi, the second and the twenty-third, etc.; or in sequence with a prescribed number of letters omitted, e.g. first, twelfth, second, thirteenth, etc.

Some interesting information about the teaching of reading and writing among the Greeks was revealed when some ostraka were purchased in Karnak in Egypt early this century.[6] Dating from the second century A.D. and written on pottery, the ostraka were found to be exercises for the young child. One was a catalogue of trades in alphabetical order for the child to learn, and another list required the insertion of letters to complete words. Yet another, a list of familiar names, was set out alphabetically and in columns to be learnt by heart, a practice still recommended today as a distinct aid to memory learning.

To us this sheer concentration on the conning of letters might be distasteful but it must be remembered that letters were of vital importance to the Greeks. Being the key to man's thoughts, they were looked upon as items of magic and, as they were also used as figures in trade and commerce, they had practical significance. All writing was in the form of printed capitals, set out in solid chunks, compact without any spacing, so as to conserve the material being written on, as in the sentence at the top of the next page.

" HISPERSISTENTENEMYNEHEMIAH
THEATHEISTHISSEDATTHEHIRSTS."

This sentence is not easily decipherable even by the expert reader of contemporary English and, with such an arrangement, an emphasis on letters was obligatory. Greek and Latin were also inflected languages, and so a close scrutiny of the ends of words was also required. This remained the arrangement of writing for many centuries, and it was not till there was a need for quicker and easier reading that a space between the word blocks was introduced.

6   *A passage from Virgil (fourth or fifth century A.D.)*
     (From Sir E. M. Thompson's An Introduction to Greek and Latin Palaeography, *Oxford, 1912)*

Standardized punctuation, as we understand it, came about only some 250 years ago.

Such rote learning was also laborious and difficult for the Greeks, and we hear of various games and gimmicks being used to ease the pain. In his play, *Amphiaraus* (*c.* A.D. 200), Athenaeus introduced a person who danced the form of the letters, while he also mentioned the popular practice of composing speeches in which the letters of certain words were concealed. One such example was supposed to have been written by Euripides (*c.* 480– 406 B.C.): "In that play there is an illiterate herdsman who plainly described the name of Theseus as it is inscribed, thus: 'Though I am not skilled in letters, yet will I tell the witness of their shapes. There is a circle as it were measured off by compasses: this having in its centre a plain mark. The second letter has two strokes, and these are kept asunder by another in their middle. The third is like a curl turned hither and thither, while the fourth again has one rising stroke, and three cross-lines are propped against it. The fifth

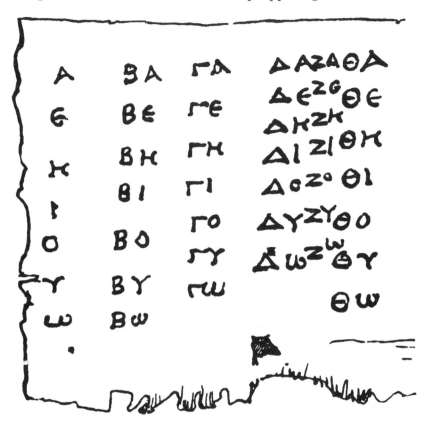

7   *Facsimile of a Greek abecedarium (third century A.D.)*
    (From A. W. Tuer's A History of the Horn-book, *London, 1897)*

is not easy to describe; for there are two lines standing apart, and these run together into one support. The last letter is like the third."[7]

From the letter the Greek learner moved on to the syllable, beginning with the combination of a vowel and a consonant, e.g.

alpha + beta   A + B   epsilon + beta   E + B
alpha + gamma, etc.   A + Γ   epsilon + gamma, etc.   E + Γ

Or reversed, with the consonant and the vowel, e.g.

| beta   + alpha | B + A | beta + epsilon, etc. B + E |
| gamma + alpha, etc. Γ + A | | |

Then to syllables of three letters, e.g.

| beta + alpha   + nu | B + A + N |
| beta + epsilon + delta, etc. B + E + Δ | |

Or to more complicated formations, e.g.

| beta + rho + alpha   + sigma | B + P + A + Σ |
| beta + rho + epsilon + sigma, etc. B + P + E + Σ | |

Plato tells us that the learner, though recognizing the short syllables in isolation, might experience difficulty with them when
they form part of longer and more difficult words. In that case, the
teacher must return to first principles and compare the structure
of the difficult word alongside words of simple syllables that they
have learnt already. For example, the English word "sprat" could
be split into: at, rat, sap, pat, spat, sprat, etc.

From syllables they progressed to the whole word, using the
names of mythical or national heroes, gods, rivers, mountains and
foreign places but the harder the word the better. Quintilian used
the same form of exercise later, making the child rattle off names
and sentences "made up of syllables that go ill together, harsh in
manner and clumsy in sound. The Greeks call them 'bridles'." This,
he believed, was the most effective way to eradicate defects in
pronunciation that would otherwise become incurable habits. The
modern teacher of reading might perhaps be aghast at this, when
he considers the importance shown nowadays to the use of familiar words and controlled vocabularies in our early primers.

The practice of writing was also thought to have a direct bearing
on the teaching of reading, and each was used to reinforce the
other. The writing was done on a tablet coated with wax. Letters
were inscribed at the top, and the learner was required to prick his
own copy with a stylus in the space below. If he was not skilled in
it, Plato, for instance, suggested in the *Protagoras* that he should
be given a tablet on which further guide-lines had already been
provided. These guide-lines were probably similar to the horizontal
lines in our modern exercise-books but they might also have been

incomplete dotted outlines of letters which he was expected to fill in, the guide-lines becoming fewer as he progressed. As the Greek word, υπογραψαντες, suggests an incomplete outline, this would support the latter interpretation. Further evidence for this is found in the *Epistles* (xciv) of the Roman, Seneca (*c.* 4 B.C.–A.D. 65), who observed that "when children are taught to write letters, their fingers are held and their hands grasped and guided to help them copy other letters. They are then told to imitate the models provided and to correct their own versions from them." St Jerome also advised that the learner should be taught to write either with another hand guiding her small fingers or following the tracks of letters already marked out on the tablet."

Quintilian was not at all satisfied that young children should be made to learn the names and sequence of letters before they learnt their shapes. He believed that the Greek method of attending to the names and order actually slowed down the process of recognizing the letters, "as the children don't pay attention to their shapes but rely purely on what they have previously learnt by heart. For this reason, when they think they have sufficiently inculcated in the pupils the letters in the accepted order in which they have been used to write them from the start, they reverse the order and then mix them in every possible permutation till they recognize the letters just by their look and not from the order in which they appear. In the same way as they identify men, so the children should be taught to identify the letters by their shape and name."

In this respect Quintilian was forestalling by some two thousand years the proposals of some modern linguistic scholars who believe that the shape of the letter is of the greatest importance for the young learner. Automatic recognition of the letters from their shapes rather than their sounds or names forms the initial stage of their reading approach. Charles Fries, for example, arranges the letters of the alphabet in three groups of structural characteristics: those made up of strokes, e.g. I, F, X: those consisting of circles or parts of circles, e.g. C, Q: and those which are a mixture of both, e.g. D, P.[8]

Endorsing the Greek step to the syllable, Quintilian suggested that this necessary base of immediate recognition by their shape should be reinforced by letting the children play with ivory letters. "If anything at all should bring joy to that particular age, it would be found that the handling, the sight and the naming [sounding] of the letters would bring pleasure."

This system was the forerunner of the modern Montessori

method or the kinaesthetic or moving finger technique which has been more fully and scientifically developed by the Americans, Fernald and Keller, since World War I. But to Quintilian rather than the Greeks must be accorded the honour of pioneering the approach, because the Greek method seemed to be purely concerned with the teaching of writing, not reading, and nowhere in the Greek is it mentioned that the sound of the letter must be uttered at the same time as its shape was being written.

"When therefore," Quintilian continued, "he has been sufficiently instructed to follow the patterns of the various letters, it would be profitable for their shapes to be cut as accurately as possible into a board, so that the stylus can be made to follow the tracks made." As its hard edges prevented mistakes being made through the straying of the writing instrument, board was preferred to wax and, to help the learner gain steadiness, the teacher was also advised to increase the speed and number of the exercises as they went on. Above all, there was to be no haste. If the child was forced to attempt more than he was capable of, he would begin to hesitate, repeat and finally stop.

Surely no apologies need be offered for the lengthy treatment of the views of this educationist from classical antiquity. Apart from his support of the alphabetic method, which barely accords with the phonetic circumstances of our current English and his firm proposal to introduce formal reading earlier than usual, most of his recommendations are in keeping with the soundest contemporary practice. His insistence on attention to the shapes of letters and the integration of reading and writing as co-operative skills are just two other features which have been important characteristics of various modern systems which have been popular both in the United States and in this country since World War II.

From the mastery of the word, the learner progressed to complete sentences. Quintilian agreed with the Greeks that they should illustrate some moral lesson, because then they would be remembered more easily in age and would contribute to the moulding of a better character. Of the sentences which have survived for our consideration, some contain what might have been sound practical advice for the youngster. e.g. "You must work hard, if you want to avoid a whipping." Others would be considered out of taste even in the laxity of today, e.g. "The asp is buying poison from the viper," referring to a woman seeking advice of another.

In Anglo-Saxon times the pattern of early reading instruction hardly deviated from the classical grind. "For those first lessons, reading, writing and arithmetic," wrote St Augustine in his *Confessions*, "I thought as great a burden as any Greek."

About teaching methods themselves, little can be found in this early period apart from some snatches of practical advice offered by St Jerome in his letter to Pacatula. Before she could read, he advised, Pacatula would have to learn her alphabet, spelling and grammar and, to help her with the alphabet, he said in another letter to Laeta (*c.* 403), she should be given a set of ivory or box-wood letters. Occasionally these should be mixed up so that she could learn to pick out the last from the middle ones or the middle from the first. From Quintilian's precepts it showed a difference only in minor detail. He suggested that the correct order of the letters could be best learnt through play, while their names would be best retained through the use of a simple song. No such song directly concerned with alphabetic sounds has come down to us from this early period but the first hymn to be composed in Irish, the "Secundinus Hymn," which was supposed to have been written in praise of St Patrick himself, illustrates the probable arrangement. With each line or stanza beginning with a different letter of the alphabet in sequence, the Latin version began:

> *Audite omnes amantes Deum sancta merita viri in Christo,*
> *beati, Patricii episcopi. . . .*
> *Beata Christi. . . .*
> *Constans in Dei amore, . . .* etc.

This individual hymn, however, was hardly intended for pedagogic purposes (see pages 124—5).

Quintilian, demonstrating an enlightened attitude to punishment, had already suggested that the child's studies should be based on amusement and that the child should be stimulated by competition and praise. This was also St Jerome's opinion, for he believed that the young learner needed companions to share the activity, because "praise is the best incentive for the mind" when one is doing well but one must also be reprimanded when one falls behind.

Similarly, St Jerome proposed that "little gifts" (*munusculis*) should be distributed as prizes for successful spelling, and in the letter to Pacatula he varied the reward by giving a honey-cake (*crustula mulsi*) or something like a flower, a toy or a pretty doll (see page 82). This too he borrowed from the ancients, as the Latin poet in his *Satires* (i. 25—6) had recommended that "smooth-coaxing teachers" should occasionally give their pupils small pieces of pastry (*crustula*) to make them better disposed to the task. St Jerome stated pointedly that the lessons should be interesting and attractive, for any dislike incurred at that fundamental stage would long persist.

Whereas Quintilian had urged the teacher of reading not to waste time by giving children words of everyday usage, St Jerome seems to have been the first to suggest the use of carefully chosen and graded vocabulary. Further, while he approved another practice common among the ancients, that is, learning off by heart long lists of complicated names, he substituted Biblical names for the mythological. He proposed the use of names of prophets, apostles and patriarchs from Adam downwards, as mentioned in "St Matthew" and "St Luke," because the young learner would then be studying the Bible as well as learning to read. This Biblical innovation was also sanctioned by the Rule of St Basil, and so began a Christian practice which remained an important feature of reading instruction throughout the whole of this period. A thousand years later one such list compiled by Henry Hawkins (*c.* 1450), a *History of the Old Testament*, started with Adam and went on to Ptolemy Philopater. Sometimes the monarchs of England were also included in such lists, and one anonymous series compiled before 1500 covered the succession of kings from Adam down to Edward IV.

Otherwise the same ancient alphabetic, syllabic or spelling method, as it was variously called, was used in all the countries of Western Europe, including France, Germany and Switzerland. The thirteenth-century romance of Blanchefleur and Floriz tells us that when children begin school, they have

> On the book letters to know
> As men do, both high and low.

Vives, the Spanish educationist (1492–1540), lent his authority to it. Grammatical science, he advocated, must be taught by people who know their own language better than those who are learning it. As one's elders surely know best, so he felt that he could safely advise that the single sounds of vowels must be learnt first, then the consonants, syllables and words. "The boy," he says in his *De Tradendis Disciplinis* ("On the Subject of Study") (1531), "must get used to naming letters speedily and sweetly and then to combining them." The names of letters, he stressed, are more important than their sounds.

The Church regulations for the town of Wurtemburg in Germany (1539) directed the children to learn the alphabet first slowly and thoroughly, repeating letters several times before proceeding to new words. The children should then be tested in their knowledge of letters out of their conventional order before they moved on to syllabification. In his curriculum for the teaching of French, John Calvin, the austere reformer of Geneva (1509–64), advised pupils also "to learn the letters of the alphabet and to write them to form syllables."

Hallowed then by the ancients and practised widely in all continental countries through approval by the Church, the method was similarly employed and revered in England. Mulcaster never questioned its efficacy, as he wrote: "When by gradual practice in combining letters and in spelling out words under direction, the child has acquired the faculty of reading easily, what a cluster of benefits thus comes within his reach. . . . It should be thoroughly learned, when it is first begun, as facility will save trouble both to master and scholar at a later stage."

Despite the fresh ideas about the teaching of reading that were current by the late sixteenth century, the alphabetic method was a long time dying, if it has ever fully died in this country. In fact, in a survey of reading in sixty Kent schools in 1959 it was found that "four schools . . . used the alphabetic method in teaching reading. In them the infants were taught by experienced teachers who, having obtained satisfactory results with a previous generation, continued using what they considered was a valuable method . . . used . . . in conjunction with others."[9]

The Oral Approach

How a language or Latin reading lesson might have been conducted in an Anglo-Saxon monastery school is illustrated in the *Colloquy* of Aelfric, who died *c.* 1020.

The dialogue form in which it appears had long been a favourite structure for philosophical debate and was also the popular means of instruction. In it the teacher so framed his question that the pupil had to give the direct answer required, and the lesson moved along at the pedagogue's prompting. As it developed, the teacher introduced the topics that he wished to be studied, reminded the scholars of their moral duties, offered the material in such a way as to permit repetition and also selected the vocabulary to be practised. As such, it was the "direct approach" which is so favoured in language lessons today.

In the *Colloquy* the master is a monk, while the pupils are attending the monastic school.

Pupil: We boys beg you, sir, to teach us to speak Latin properly because we are ignorant and do it badly.
Master: What would you like to talk about?
Pupil: We don't mind what we talk about provided our speech is correct and useful, not silly and vulgar.

To stimulate further oral work, the master asks each boy in turn who he is and what he does, with each assuming the role of a member of the monastic community.

Pupil: I am getting ready to be a monk, and every day I sing seven times with my brethren and I am kept very busy both with singing and reading. Meanwhile I want to learn to speak Latin.

Ploughboys, shepherds, oxherds, tailors and bakers, all take their turns and the repetition of vocabulary, with the words grouped according to occupations and sentence structure, provides the necessary practice. One pupil dares to suggest to the master that he should avoid using words and ideas that are beyond their grasp. "So far your talk has been concerned with things that are too hard for us to follow. Please speak to us in our own manner and not too abstrusely." Later the master is asked to "remember how young we are when you talk to us, so that we can understand what you are talking about."

This was the catechetical approach which became so deeply ingrained in education that it remained the method of instruction in reading primers long after the invention of the printing press. As late as 1761 Isaac Watt still started his manual, *The Art of Reading and Writing*, like this:

Question: What is reading?
Answer: To read is to express written words by their proper sound.
Question: What are words made of? etc.

Oral methods of instruction were a pre-eminent feature of early education (see page 36). This was due not merely to the fact that books were scarce and costly but because it had been long believed that the uttering of something aloud strengthened its retention in the memory. "Open your mouth," the Jewish Talmud advised, "in order that you may retain the subject of the study and that it may remain alive within you." We read of a Jewish woman severely chastising her student for learning his lessons quietly, as that was not the proper way to learn. Rabbi Elieser complained how he once had a pupil who studied the words of his lesson without articulating them and as a result he forgot everything within three years.[10] Many centuries later Vives in his *De Tradendis Disciplinis* was equally insistent on the virtues of the practice. "Anything we want to remember must be inscribed on our memory while other things are silent. We need not remain silent ourselves, for the things we read aloud are usually better retained. Similarly we remember best what we have heard from others rather than what we read ourselves." Mulcaster put it even more succinctly: "Memory I will force."

Teachers of reading in England also relied on these methods. We read in the chronicle of Reginald of Durham that in 1170 a school attached to the church of St Mary's, Durham, taught the children the first elements of letters by "hearing, reading and chanting them." Woodcuts of the later mediaeval period often show the interior of some sort of school where the pupils appear to be repeating what the teacher is reading from the book. The *Parvus* of Caxton (1481) has a similar scene with the tutor holding the book and five pupils kneeling before him. Consequently the children had to listen carefully to what the teacher said and then they had to chant it several times. If they succeeded in learning to read, that was a real bonus but, even if they did not master the skill, something might stick in their memory for later reproduction in the church service. An account of such a service in 1066 illustrates this, when we read that the boys in the choir "walked, stood, read and chanted like brethren in religion and whatever had to be sung at the steps of the choir or in the choir itself they sang and chanted by heart, one or two or more together, without the help of a book."[11]

By the sixteenth century there were undertones of disquiet about learning to read by this practice, and this supercilious exchange about it occurs in Shakespeare's *Romeo and Juliet* (I.ii. 59–64):

Servant. God gi' god-den, I pray, sir, can you read?
Romeo. Ay, mine own fortune in my misery.
Servant. Perhaps you have learned it without book; but, I pray, can you read anything you see?
Romeo. Ay, if I know the letters and the language.

The myth about the value of rote learning in reading was not effectively exploded till the "Little Red Hen" issue three hundred years later.

The Practice of Reading Aloud

An interesting point of comparison that might be made between reading as taught and practised by the ancients and that of our

Hic finis parui catonis

8   *Pupils reading with the schoolmaster. Woodcut from Caxton's* Parvus (c. 1481)

own age concerns technique. Today the technical aim of most reading instruction is to develop ultimately the art of silent reading. The technique of reading aloud is reserved mainly for the building of confidence in the early stages, assessing the pupil's progress and diagnosing defects in his performance. With the ancients the position was different.

To the early reader any written material was a precise record of what a speaker had originally said. If the real intent of the speaker was to be recaptured and the spirit behind the words to be "read into" them, then the writing had to be spoken aloud by the reader. One writer has shown that the Greek word ακουεω and its Latin. equivalent *audire* on many occasions have the meaning "to read" rather than "to hear,"[12] and he quotes several instances to illustrate his point. For example, King Croesus made up his mind on one occasion to test the authenticity of the oracles by asking each to say what he had been doing at a particular moment. All the replies, which were written down, were brought back to Croesus who "when he heard [i.e. read aloud] the answers of the one at Delphi . . . knew it was the genuine one."[12]

While it is not advanced that silent reading was not practised among the Greeks and Romans, it seems to have been such an unusual procedure that when indulged in, it denoted some special reaction on the part of the reader. When, for example, the legacy-hunter Nasica in the familiar Satire of Horace (65—8 B.C.) gets hold of a will and *tacitus leget* (reads it silently), he betrays his discomfiture at slighted personal hopes. Or the fact that Cydippe in the *Heroides* of Ovid (43 B.C.—A.D. 18) said that *legi sine murmure* ("I read it without a sound") was to indicate her fear. Otherwise she would have read it naturally, that is, aloud. In "The Ignorant Book-Collector" Lucian even implied that it was an inferior way of reading. "What good, you strange person, will it do you to own them when you do not understand their beauty? . . . To be sure you look at your books with your eyes wide open . . . and you read some of them aloud with great fluency, keeping your eyes in advance of your lips; but I do not consider that enough, unless you know the merits and defects of each passage in their contents, unless you understand what every sentence means, how to construe the words."[13]

Another indication that reading was meant to be done aloud rather than silently can be deduced from the passage in Quintilian's *Institutes* where he advises that "reading should in the first place be sure, then smooth-flowing, but regulated to a controlled pace for some time till an efficient speed will result from the practice. The act of looking ahead to the right, as is universally encouraged, and the habit of thinking ahead come from practice rather than precept. . . . While keeping one's eye on what is coming next, the points that have gone earlier must be kept in mind and, what is very difficult, the attention of the mind must be divided so that while the voice is concentrating on one course of action, the eyes have something else to do."

Evidence is fairly conclusive too that in the early Christian period it was still the accepted practice. The Book of Acts (viii. 26) describes how "a man of Ethiopia, an eunuch of great authority under Candace . . . was returning and sitting in his chariot reading Esaias the prophet. . . . And Philip ran thither to him and *heard him* read the prophet and said, 'Understandest thou what thou readest?'"

St Augustine also describes how interested he became in the silent reading of his colleague, St Ambrose. "When he was reading, his eye glided over the pages, and his heart searched out the sense, but his voice and tongue were at rest. Oft-times when he had come (for no man was forbidden to enter, nor was it his wont that any one who came should be announced to him) and we saw him thus reading to himself and never otherwise; and having sat silent (for who dare intrude on one so intent?), we were fain to depart, conjecturing that in the same interval, which he obtained, free from the din of others' business, for the recruiting of his mind, he was loath to be taken off; and perhaps he dreaded lest, if the author he read should deliver anything obscurely, some attentive or perplexed hearer should desire him to expound it or to discuss some of the harder questions. . . . But with what intent soever he did it, certainly in such a man it was good."[14] That he described the process in such detail must point to the fact that silent reading was not generally practised.

Later, when St Benedict (480–543) formulated his Rule for his monks, he also included an instruction about the noise made by the inmates while they were supposed to be reading to themselves: "On rising from table after the sixth hour, let them rest on their beds in strict silence but, if anyone shall read, let him do so in such a way as not to disturb anyone else."[15]

The monks must have been perturbed about the noise they made while reading, because some devised a series of signals to indicate the type of book they wanted to borrow, without having to utter a word. "The general sign for a book . . . was 'to extend the hand and make a movement as if turning over the leaves of a book.' For a missal the monk was to make a similar movement with the sign of the cross; for the gospels the sign of the cross on the forehead; for the antiphon or book of responses he was to strike the thumb or the little finger of the other hand together; for a book of offices or gradale to make the sign of the cross and kiss the fingers; for a tract lay the hand on the abdomen and apply the other hand to the mouth; for a capitulary make the general sign and extend the clasped hands to heaven; for a psalter place the hands upon the head in the form of a crown, such as the king is wont to wear."[16]

Reading aloud was also used as a source of private and public entertainment and was much favoured in the homes of the wealthy. According to his letter to Arrianus, the Roman, Pliny the Younger, born A.D. 62, once read his own works to his guests "for two days in succession," and King Alfred arranged for his secretaries to read to him when he was at leisure. The same occurred in monastic establishments. St Benedict also included instructions about it: "There ought always be reading whilst the brethren eat at table. Yet no one shall presume to read there from any book taken up at hazard. . . . The greatest silence shall be kept so that no whispering, nor noise, save the voice of the reader alone, be heard there. . . . Let no one ask any question there about what is being read or about anything else, lest occasion be given to the evil one; unless perhaps the prior shall wish to say something briefly for the purpose of edification. The brother who is a reader for the week may take a mess of potage before."[16]

In some reading sessions the reader was merely a puppet, giving a mechanical performance without any understanding of what he was reading. For instance, when the Anglo-Saxon missionary from Devon, Winfred, later called St Boniface (680–754), visited a monastery at Treves, he and the other inmates were entertained by a public reading of the Latin Scriptures by a fifteen-year-old boy. "You have done well, my boy," remarked Winfred, "that is, if you were able to follow what you read." Despite the lad's protestations that he did, further questioning betrayed his total ignorance.[17]

Particular care had to be exercised in the art, and in the eighth century Leodegar was returned forthwith to England for further training because he had made a mistake in one public reading. The Rule of St Benedict also referred to such lapses: "If anyone, whilst reciting a psalm, responsory, antiphon or lesson, make any mistake and do not at once make humble satisfaction for it before all, let him be subjected to greater punishment, as being one who is unwilling to correct by humility what he has done amiss through negligence. For such a fault let children be whipped."

Lapses in reading performance were looked on askance and by the Middle Ages an extra devil, Titivillus by name, had been invented to deal with the offenders. It was his job to note all the words that had been glossed over, mumbled, slurred or omitted by clerics in their religious readings and then book up their offences for later qualification for Hell!

To us today such an extravagantly meticulous attitude to trifling errors might seem astounding but we might fail to realize how the whole atmosphere of life in those days was charged with the service of God. The services, the prayers, the chanting and the readings were all a vital part of the people's daily life. It was not such an unusual request on the part of Charlemagne for his peasants to sing the Church canticles as they drove their ploughs homeward. Only a few centuries earlier an Irish monk, Aengus, according to his biographer, made three hundred genuflections daily in his lonely retreat. He also recited the entire psaltery in an extraordinary fashion. He arranged his self-imposed task in three parts. After saying fifty psalms in his cell, he recited fifty more in the open air and then repeated the last fifty with his neck chained to a post, and his body plunged in a huge tub of cold water. The Elizabethan *Rites of Durham* (see page 25) tell us that when a monk died, the pupils of the almonry school had "to sit on their knees" all night by the corpse and read the Psalter till 8 a.m.

When therefore we remember the severe demands made by the Church of the individual Christian, we might be less critical of the rigorous standards expected of the reader and more tolerant of the unremitting, grinding drill of learning to read.

Above all, we might also remember that change was outrageous to the Christian way of life. For centuries people were being born into this scheme of things, and any attempted alteration could bring unpleasant, even dangerous, consequences. One chronicler has this entry for 1083: "There was a dreadful quarrel between the monks of the dignity. Among his acts of folly, he attempted to force the monks to relinquish the Gregorian chant, which he despised. . . . They were very upset about this, as they had long grown accustomed to its use. . . . So one day when they were not expecting it, he suddenly broke into the chapter-house at the head of a band of armed men and pursued the terrified monks . . . to the altar. . . . Two of the monks were killed and fourteen wounded, and some of the soldiers also received wounds."[18]

No wonder the teacher of reading also had an unshakeable belief in the efficacy of the rod, and that its use or misuse was accepted as the natural part of learning.

Corporal Punishment as an Aid to Teaching Reading

"The young fellow has a back," the Egyptians used to observe complacently. "He hears it when you beat it." In early Hebrew too the word *mûsar* could be translated as either "education" or "chastisement," and the same parallel idea became inherent in the educational approach of the Greeks. They believed implicitly that there could be "no progress without painful effort." The teacher decided what the children had to learn, he repeated it to them and the children chanted it aloud. If there was a breakdown in the learning process, then they were beaten. It was the same with the teaching of the elements of reading, with the result that "the characteristic figure that stayed in the memory of the men who had been educated at those little schools (i.e. the primary schools of the Greeks) was . . . the terrible schoolmaster, stick in hand, inspiring terror."[19] The Romans also accepted the Greek approach, and the Latin *manum ferulae subducere* (to put out one's hand for the cane) was an equivalent phrase for "to study."

There was also the sacred precedent of the Bible. The Book of Proverbs (xii) advised "He that spareth the rod hateth his son, but he that boweth him, chasteneth him betimes" and (xxii) "Foolishness is bound up in the heart of the child but the rod of correction shall drive it far from him." St Augustine in his *Confessions* acknowledges that he had been thrashed when he was slow to learn, because his forefathers had considered such punishment praiseworthy. Elsewhere in his *De Civitate Dei* (XXI. xiv.) he reveals the harshness of the reality of punishment when he asked, "Who is there who would not start back in terror and choose death, if he was invited to choose between dying and going back to childhood?" Pope Gregory the Great was not averse to using the stick on his song-school pupils to effect an improvement (see page 18).

Corporal punishment may not have been viewed therefore with the same sense of abhorrence as it is today, and the literature of this early period in England has a number of references to its use to accelerate the learning act. In Aelfric's *Colloquy*, for example, when the master asks the pupils if they are willing to be flogged when they are learning, one boy speaks up stoically for them all: "We'd rather be flogged so that we can learn than remain ignorant. Of course we know that you are a kind person and you'll not beat us unless you really have to."

The birch was also the symbol of the schoolmaster in England. One poem, "The Birched Schoolboy" (*c.* 1500), speaks in frank terms of the brutal punishment he himself had received:

I would fain be a clerk
   but yet it is a strange work.
The birching twigs be so sharp
   it makes me have a faint heart.
What avails me though I say nay?

My master looks as he were mad:
  "Where have you been, you sorry lad?"
  "Milking ducks, my mother bade."
It were no marvel though I were sad.
  What avails me though I say nay?

My master peppered my arse with well good speed:
  it was worse than finkle seed.
  He would not leave till it did bleed. . . .

Thomas Tusser in *Points of Good Husbandry* offers similar testimony to the harsh treatment:

From Paul's I went, to Eton sent,
To learn straightways the Latin phrase.
Where fifty-three stripes given to me
  At once I had
For fault but small or none at all.

In fact, by the first century A.D. the Romans themselves had been advocating less severity in their educational methods, and Quintilian was already pleading for a softer approach both in respect of corporal punishment and the teaching means employed (see pages 71–2). Such inroads had these progressive influences been making that one Roman writer, Petronius, complained that "nunc pueri in scholis ludunt" (nowadays children play as they learn).

Though St Jerome had also proposed more lenient methods in the teaching of reading, nothing concrete seems to have been done about it till the late Middle Ages. Erasmus, the great Dutch scholar, philosopher and educationist (1466–1536), commented in his work, *Of the First Liberal Education of Children*, that drill in reading and writing was tiresome and he urged that the teacher should palliate the process by a more attractive method. "The ancients," he reminded his readers, "made dainty tasties in the form of letters and thus caused their children to swallow, as it were, the alphabet." Ascham, the English educationist, pulled no punches in *The Schoolmaster*: "Some will say that children of nature love pastime and dislike learning, because . . . the one is easy and pleasant [and] the other hard and wearisome. The matter lies not so much in the disposition of them that be young, as in the order and manner of them that be old. . . . For beat a child if he dance not well, and cherish him though he learn not well, [and] you shall have him unwilling to go to dance and glad to go to his book. Knock him always when he draws his shaft ill, and favour him again when he fault at his book, you shall have him very loth to be in the field, and very willing to be in the school."

Such educational suggestions as these certainly bore fruit in the teaching of reading, as we shall see in Chapter 6, but much time was to pass before lenity became an integral part of the teaching pattern. Not till 1669 was a tentative document laid before Parliament as "The Children's Petition: or a Modest Remonstrance of that intolerable grievance of our youth . . . the accustomed severities of the school-discipline of this nation."

The Reading Failure

Despite the almost professional approach of the Greeks to the teaching of reading, they too had their failures or reluctant readers. The poet, Herodas, in his mime, "The Schoolmaster," has a vivid picture of a truant schoolboy who was fast developing into a young delinquent.

Kottalos had been behaving so badly that his mother had been forced to drag him before his schoolmaster to be given a sound thrashing. A thoroughly bad lot, so it seemed, Kottalos had almost stripped the roof off his mother's house with his gambling and he had wasted all his time with spivs and runaway slaves, instead of attending the writing school as his mother believed. Every month his mother had his tablet re-coated with wax but it remained untouched by the side of his bed. "He can't even remember the letter 'A,'" she moaned, "unless you yell it at him half a dozen times."

Then, citing what might be the first case recorded of a mirror reversal in history, she complained that "Only a few days ago, when his dad showed him how to arrange the letters for the word ΜΑΡΩΝΑ, the ass wrote ΣΙΜΩΝΑ instead. I feel really stupid for not letting him learn to feed donkeys instead of learning letters." When he was asked to recite a few lines from a tragedy, all he could do was to stammer it out like a sieve, so haltingly that his grannie or slave could have done better. Worst still, if he was ever reprimanded, then he just refused to come home and hid at his grandmother's, eating her out of house and home. Sometimes he sat on the top of the roof, legs astride it, leering like an ape at everyone. Of course, when the holidays were near, he knew more about them than any astrologer whose job it was to fix them! An interesting case of possible dyslexia for any educational psychologist . . . and the date was 270 B.C.

The Greeks had various ways of dealing with pupil intransigence, stupidity and backwardness. In the case of Kottalos, he was dragged before his master, Lampriskos, and thrashed with the "tough leather strap, the bullock's tail" which Lampriskos used "to beat rebellious boys," but when the Greek orator, Herod Atticus (A.D. 101—77), found that his son was too dull to learn to read he decided to do something else about it. He employed twenty-four slaves to be brought up with his son and each was given the name of a letter of the alphabet, which he also had to carry around with him each day. This device reminds us of the famous "Sounds in Colour" method of Miss Nellie Dale of Wimbledon, which was so popular at the beginning of this century in England. Apart from other features, each child carried a large letter above the head and, as the children were uttering the letters in sequence, so they moved inwards to illustrate the blending of letters/sounds to form the unity of the word.[20]

The Greeks also tried to remove or alleviate some of the circumstances of learning disability by allowing the teacher to object to being given too many pupils in the class.[21] Quintilian supported this idea of cutting down class numbers and he was extremely frank about the varying capabilities of children. Comparing them to vessels, he said that those with very narrow mouths could not hold all the liquid if one tried to pour too much into them. Likewise, consideration should be given to the amount of learning a child's mind was able to receive. Children differed from one another. Some were slack, others were uncontrollable but many required constant supervision. In Quintilian's view there were few who could not learn. On the contrary, most lads were quick in this respect and the number of ineducables was so small that they could be regarded as prodigious births or monstrosities. If boys were unable to learn, the fault would be found not in their inborn talent but in the insufficiency of attention paid to them by others.

In the Anglo-Saxon period in England one meets little evidence of backwardness or reading failure, as we now understand it, because there was only minimal literacy among the masses as a whole. For example, King Alfred, when he found any ealdorman or reeve unable to read either through advancing age or slowness of wit, ordered him to seek help from a member of his own family, a friend or even a serf. "And they deemed the youth of this age happy, since they were able to be happily learned in liberal arts, but they considered themselves wretched, since they had not in their youth learned letters, nor were able to do so in old age, though they ardently desired to do so."[22] This refers to a national adult illiteracy problem rather than individual disability.

King Alfred himself has been involved in mystery about his early reading capabilities. Asser reported of him that "the culpable negligence of his relations, and some of those who had care of him, allowed him to remain ignorant of his letters until his twelfth year, or even to a later age. Albeit, day and night he listened attentively to the Saxon poems, which he often heard others repeating, and his retentive mind enabled him to remember them."[23] Later Asser added, "because there were no men really skilled in reading in the whole realm of the West Saxons," it was not till his thirty-seventh year that "the oft-mentioned Alfred . . . by the inspiration of God began first to read and interpret at the same time on one and the same day."[24] Various attempts have been made to explain this. For example, the suggestion has been made that the Latin word *recitare* could mean "read aloud" or "recite" or "repeat after another," and so it might refer to a polished skill in reading aloud. It has also been suggested that till he was twelve he could read no English, and no Latin till he was thirty-seven. That he could not read at all was hardly likely when his father, Ethelwulf, maintained frequent correspondence with others on the Continent or that a man with such a taste for native literature as Alfred could have come to the skill so late.

Another curious item concerns Charlemagne (see pages 20–1). It has been widely believed that, despite his drive for education, he himself could not write. His secretary, Eginhard, revealed that though Charlemagne carried little tablets around with him to practise the formation of letters, he never succeeded in mastering the skill. No special interpretation need be placed on this, as Eginhard might have been referring to some intricate ornamental script rather than straightforward writing.

The first available account of a boy's indifference to, and possible slowness in, learning to read in English is found in a *Testament* (c.1389) by John Lydgate. The boy concerned probably attended a Benedictine monastery school. The speaker, in this paraphrase, recalls his early life. "I remember the green seasons of my life, those years beginning at childhood and extending to my fifteenth year. . . . I was quite unreasonable and given over to wilfulness. I just did not want to learn or do anything other than fool around and enjoy myself. I was an utter stranger to spelling and reading. . . . I was forever being thrashed and, hating school, I wasted my time like a young colt that runs wild, bridleless. I also made my friends squander their time in idleness. . . . I had fallen into the habit of being late for school, never punctual for lessons and always picking arguments with my mates, gossiping and playing tricks on them. . . . When I was chastised for it, I got used to telling lies and even inventing them ready as an excuse for the next occasion. . . . I hated getting up and I loathed going to bed in the evening still more. Usually I went to food with my hands unwashed, not caring twopence about the Lord's Prayer or the Creed."

As one might expect, by the sixteenth century with its amazing spread of literacy, we hear more frequently about the difficulties involved in the process of learning to read. The *Jests of Scogin*, a very popular work of the time of Henry VIII, has one section which tells "How a Husbandman put his son to school with Scogin." Despite his father's ambition to put him into Holy Orders, the lad was hopelessly backward, lazy or just stupid. "The slovenly boy would begin his ABC and he was nine days in learning them. When he had learned the nine Christ-cross row letters, the scholar exclaimed, 'Am ich past the worst now?'" A similar experience occurs in John Cooke's *Pleasant Conceited Comedy* (III) (1602), when a man-servant declares: "I had rather play the truant at home than go seek my master at school. Let me see what age I am. Some four and twenty, and how have I profited? I was five years learning to criss-cross from great A and five years longer coming to F. I stuck there for three years before I could come to Q and so in process of time I came to pere and compere."

Teachers too were candid about the misery they themselves experienced in dealing with slow or reluctant learners and the appallingly low standards of some of their pupils. In *The Petty School* Francis Clement laments "how few there be under the age of seven or eight years that are towardly abled and praisably furnished for reading. And . . . there be many above those years that can neither readily spell nor rightly write even the common words of our English. The cause . . . to me surely appears to be either untowardness in the scholar or ignorance in the teacher or negligence in both." He directs the blame unequivocally. "Children . . . almost everywhere are at first taught either in private by men or women altogether rude and utterly ignorant of the due composing and just spelling of words or else in common schools most commonly by boys, very seldom or never by any of sufficient skill."

Nor does John Brinsley pull his punches about the standards of English reading in the grammar schools of 1612. "I have had some who have been with me two or three years before they could read well. . . . I have sometimes been so abashed and ashamed that I have not known what to say, when some are being a little discontented or taking occasion to quarrel about paying my stipend. [They] have cast this in my teeth that their children have been under me six or seven years and yet have not learned to read English well. I myself have also known that their complaints have been true in part, though I could have taken all the pains with them that ever I could devise."

Things were no different half a century later. Charles Hoole in *A New Discovery of the Old Art of Teaching School* admitted that "some have been certain years daily exercised in saying lessons therein, who after much endeavour spent have been accounted more blockheads and rejected altogether as incapable to learn anything. . . . Some teachers have essayed a more familiar way and have professed that they have not met with any such thing as a dunce amid a great multitude of little scholars. . . . Others of a slower apprehension. . . could scarce tell six of their letters at twelve months."

Though he lies just outside the period under study, one must mention the attitude of George Robertson to reading backwardness, as it may have been quite different from that of the so-called reading experts of that period. In his work, *Learning's Foundation Firmly Laid* (1651), he acknowledges[66] no such thing as a dull person either young or old. But though there are degrees in that as in all other things, all are capable. . . . These that are called blockheads are much injured, because the reasons do not proceed from themselves but either from the carelessness of parents who do not keep their children close to school or their too much indulgence that will not commit them wholly to the tutor. Or [it might arise] from the rigour of a rigid cruel teacher or from an endless method of teaching, of many years practice but in the end no perfection. [The method might be] impossible to be comprehended of a tender-brained child and therefore [he] must be beaten with rods and scourges. What he gets must be dearly bought with blood and sweat, whereby he is discouraged and his affections quite crushed and withdrawn from all learning and from school, which turns to a grinding and tormenting house to him, and not a delight."

As is so often claimed by most reading schemes today, there is an unfailing cure for their reading difficulties — Robertson's own. "If they have an easy ingression by a pleasant method, and a smiling tutor, who in the first place labours to get into their affections, to find out their dispositions and follow them according

87

thereto, then will they run the way of learning with alacrity, rejoicing in their loving master and triumphing in their victories by their easy method of reading. Every degree of progress [will] encourage them to a further advance, so that nothing shall be more pleasant than the school, nothing more delightful than their master's company." One wonders if the sales of his method were greatly increased by this blatant self-advertisement.

It was not a period that cared much for the failure. In *The Schoolmaster* Roger Ascham considered that "a child that is still, silent, constant and somewhat hard of wit is either never chosen by the father to be made a scholar or else, when he comes to school, he is small regarded, little looked into. He lacks teaching, he lacks encouragement, he lacks all things [but] he never lacks beating or any word that may move him to hate learning or any deed that may drive him from learning to any other kind of living."

"No one," wrote Sir Walter Raleigh, "who understands the real thing cares twopence about the dull student, except as a man and brother. Drink with him; pray with him; don't read with him."[25]

The attitude of the schoolmaster is amply demonstrated too in a document of Rolleston School, Shropshire (1520), which sets out that "the clever boys [are] to teach small boys, who may be brought to him, the alphabet and first rudiments. He is to take particular care of the clever boys, while the stupid, the lazy and those in human judgement incapable of learning he is to sharpen as far as he can by reading, writing and casting accounts, lest they should seem to have come to the school for nothing."[26] Some fifty years later Bishop Richard Barnes of Durham in his *Injunctions*, while providing schools for the "apt," added that the parents of those who were "inapt and of no pregnant wit or good capacity [should put them to] learn husbandry or other good crafts so that they may yet learn to be good members of the country and commonweal"[27] (see page 23).

Let us now turn to the various devices, primers and other essential books that were being used to introduce the learner to the skill of reading and to improve his necessary technique.

5 Devices and Basic Books for Initial Reading Instruction

Glossaries and Vocabularies

Before the Norman Conquest, books concerned even indirectly with the teaching of the rudiments of reading were few and far between. The first language manual or dictionary produced by a native-born Englishman was *On Orthography*, compiled by Bede (672–735), but this was aimed more at the teacher than the pupil in the Anglo-Saxon classroom. Written in Latin, it begins with the alphabet, with each capital form of the letters in sequence and followed by a succinct definition with explanatory matter, e.g.

> *A*, a letter: it is also the mark of a forename: when alone it stands for Augustus.
> *B*, related to the letter *p*, for which it is often substituted, e.g. *supponit, opponit*.
> *C*, the mark of a forename, standing for Caesar: likewise of a number, when it signifies a hundred, etc.

After the alphabet comes a long list of words arranged alphabetically and illustrating meanings and correct usage, e.g. *acer, acerrimus*, not *acrissimus*. The book was probably an invaluable reference work for the learning of letters and Latin phrases or the checking of difficult words.

Various other pedagogic works on grammar, music and rhetoric have been attributed to Bede, and he is also credited with the compilation of one on arithmetic. These two problems were supposed to have been invented by him or Alcuin:

(a) A swallow once invited a snail to dinner. He lived one league from the place, and the snail travelled at the rate of one inch a day. How long would it be before he dined?

(b) An old man met a child. "Hello," he said. "I hope that you will live as long as you have lived already, and the same period again, and then three times as much as those two periods together. Then, if God lets you live one year more, you will be a hundred years old." How old was he?

Alcuin (735–804) also produced a language manual called *Orthography*. This also served the function of a dictionary, with the

9 Title-page of John Stanbridge's Parvulorum Institutio *(edition of 1530).*
One of the earliest grammar books in English
(*By permission of the Provost, King's College, Cambridge*)

words arranged alphabetically and accompanied by comments on their spelling, pronunciation and meaning. One of his quaint definitions gave the Latin *coelebs* (bachelor) as "one who is on his way to heaven" (*coelum*).

Generally speaking, the lines of instruction hardly varied from those advocated by the Greeks and Romans. The child was made to learn his letters, syllables, words and sentences of moral injunction and then moved on to grammar. Books were available for that vital subject of the *trivium* (see page 40). The English used the universally-popular grammatical primer of the fourth-century Roman professor, Aelius Donatus, the *Institutes of the Grammatical Art* of the sixth-century Priscian and the *Doctrinale* of Alexander de Villa Dei, born *c.* 1200, whose work went into 260 editions between 1460 and 1520 alone. From the fifteenth century the English themselves began to produce their own Latin grammars. The charmingly-entitled *Lac Puerorum* ("Milk for Children") of John Holt of Magdalen College (1497) was the first to be printed and published in England, and this was followed by many others. The most famous was the *Latin Grammar* of William Lily (1513).

But what elementary books were available for the important stage between the initial mastery of the mechanics of reading and the ultimate entry to grammatical principles? In the absence of other evidence, one must assume that the books used for this further practice and the building up of essential confidence in Latin reading were similar to those that had been traditionally employed, that is, nominalia, vocabularies and glossaries.

One such glossary was that of Aelfric, which consisted of lists of Latin nouns and adjectives with their English/Old English equivalents. The first section began:

About Tools for Farmers

Uomer uel uomis	scear (a ploughshare)
Aratrum	sulh (a plough)
Aratio	eriung (the act of ploughing)
Buris	sulhbeam (the plough-beam)
Stercoratio	dingiung (casting fertilizer)

Then came groups of words for the limbs of the body, fish, wild beasts, trees, etc. "This lesson book," wrote the author, "is intended for little boys who know nothing, not for their elders," though he knew that many would blame him for turning the art of grammar into English.

Where any doubt might arise about the meaning of a particular word, the native equivalent was inserted as an interlinear gloss. Aelfric's *Colloquy* (see page 73) had a sort of running translation above the Latin version, e.g.

we   cildra biddath the eala   lareow that thu
nos pueri rogamus te   magister   ut

taece   us   sprecan (rihte)
doceas nos loqui   latialiter recte, etc.

This approach was still more popular after the Norman Conquest. One work *De Utensilibus* ("About Materials") by Alexander Neckham (1157–1217), which was an easy Latin reader intended for use by children, had interlinear glosses in Old French, e.g.

> quisine   table   cholet   mincé
> *In Coquine sit mensula, super quam olus apte minceatur,* etc.

A wide-ranging book, it covered a number of aspects that the child might meet in his daily life and so provided the necessary vocabulary for him, e.g. the parts of the house, tools, cooking terms, the garden, the building of a castle and affairs of navigation.

Another popular book was the *Dictionarius* of Johannes de Garlandia (*c.* 1220), a sort of phrase-book which dealt with aspects of life in France and especially Paris, with its trades, gardens, houses, furniture and items of practical advice for the child, e.g.

> pye-makers   pasteys
> *Pastillarii quam plurimum lucrantur, vendendo clericis pastillos de*
>   chykens   hely
> *carnibus porcinis et pullinis et de anguillis.*

i.e. Pie-makers make as much as they can by selling pork, chickens and eel-pies to the clerics! Yet another was the *Phraseologia* or *Anglo-Gallic Dictionary* of Walter de Bibbesworth (*c.* 1270). Arranged in rhyming couplets, this too was a very simple lesson book in both English and French. Using interlinear glosses, it started at birth and went through a variety of activities, including the toilet.

Only one other book in this particular vein deserves mention. This was published three hundred years later in 1562 by Alexander Lacy as a small quarto specially compiled by Thomas Newbery to teach children to read: *A Book in English metre of the great merchant man called Dives Pragmaticus, very pretty for children to read, whereby they may the better and readier read and write wares and implements in this world contained.* On its title-page appeared the caution, "When thou sellest ought unto thy neighbour or buyest anything of him, deceive not nor oppress him," Deut. xxiii.

This book of verse has as its chief actor a merchant who shouts aloud a range of goods which he invites people to come and buy, so that the children can learn to read and write the occupations, tools and commodities that are being advertised. As a preface it has this verse:

> God, the great giver of virtue and grace
> Has planted a man here but for a space
> To live and to learn by his vocation
> To serve God and man, by their ordination.

He goes on to mention all sorts of implements and goods, e.g.

> I have to sell carpets, chests, coffee and locks,
> Presses and keys, wheels, spindles and rocks,
> Pig, goose and capons, hens, chickens and cocks.
> What wares do you lack? Come hither to me. . . .
>
> I have here to sell fine needles and thimbles,
> Nail piercers, small pod chisels and wimbles,
> Blades, and for weavers fine shuttles and brimbles.
> What do you lack, friend? Come hither to me. . . .

Nor was there lack of moral advice for the young learner.

> Honest mirth in measure is a pleasant thing:
> To write and read well be gifts of learning.
> Remember this well, for all you that be young,
> Exercise virtue, and rule well your tongue.

Naturally the need for interlinear glosses had disappeared by the sixteenth century. But meanwhile other learning devices more directly concerned with the teaching of reading were already in use, and these must be considered in turn.

The ABC

The first reference to the alphabet in English as "abece" occurs in 1297 but from that date this particular word assumes a number of different forms, such as abc, a b c, apece, apecy, apsie, absey, abeesee, abice, a-pece, apesy, etc.

When, however, Piers Plowman remarked that Abstinence the Abbess had taught him the "Abc," the term had undergone a further extension in that he could have been referring to either the letters of the alphabet or the skill of continuous reading itself. When, in 1389, Philippa and the seven-year-old Blanche, the two daughters of Henry IV, were given two books "of ABC" for two-pence, the term had also come to signify the actual book itself.

The ABC was the most basic element in learning to read, and all sorts of devices were used to make the alphabet more easily available and its learning more palatable. For instance, a child's porringer, not later than 1400, had on it a decoration formed from the letters of the alphabet.[1]

The most common arrangement for the ABC was to have the letters in the shape of a Cross, with A at the top and Z at the bottom. Thus it came to be called the Christ-cross or Criss-cross row or Chriss-crosse or Christ's cross. The arrangement took different forms, the simplest being the first nine letters of the alphabet put in the form of a cross with the rest of the letters strung in bead-fashion on a frame. Others were more elaborate and had the capitals along one arm of the Cross, the small letters along the other, and the numerals down the centre-piece. Both were used as rosaries as well.

At a later stage of development, instead of the cruciform shape, the rows of letters were set out in ordinary lineal fashion with a small cross placed separately at the beginning "to show," in Dr Johnson's words, "that the end of learning was piety." The cross acted as a reminder to the learner to cross himself before he started to read. The function is described in the sixteenth-century printed version of "De Proprietatibus Rerum" of Bartholemew Glanville (1360):

> Cross was made all of red
> In the beginning of my book,
> That is called "God me speed,"
> In the first lesson that I took.
> Then I learned a and b,
> And other letters by their names
> But always God speed me.

The end of the criss-cross row was usually indicated by three pricks, once again a religious reminder that while three pricks meant one stop, there were also three persons but only one God. Thus the instruction was also given a moral and religious bent.

It was used too for divination. Divination by books, often called bibliomancy, had been a popular practice from the earliest times, and the ancients used to open the works of famous classical authors, Homer and Virgil, at any chance page to try and forecast the future from any lines on which the eye might have rested. The early Christians also tried their luck but using the Scriptures, especially the Psalms. St Augustine himself indulged in it. Once when he was troubled in spirit, he heard a voice advising him, "Take up and read, take up and read." Realizing it was the voice of God, he took up the book of the New Testament and read, where his eyes first alighted, "Not in rioting and drunkenness, not in chambering and wantonness, not in strife and envying; but put ye on the Lord Jesus Christ; and make not provision for the flesh, to fulfil the lusts thereof" (Romans xiii. 13). As a result St Augustine no longer sought a wife or any worldly hopes. (*Confessions.*) In France certain books of the Bible were actually placed on altars or shrines for the direct purpose of divination till the practice was forbidden by Louis the Debonair, who died in 840. As the criss-cross row was so easily accessible and simple to interpret, it was a handy substitute, however rough and ready, for the members of an ordinary family.

So fundamental was the ABC in reading instruction that in time the horn-book or any elementary reader or primer was given the same name.

The Horn-book

Although the criss-cross row was convenient to handle, it had only limited space, and room had to be found for the provision of other important language elements, such as the syllabic combinations, and other religious matter. Again, parchment or vellum was costly and scarce, and some other means had to be devised that could stand up to the rough treatment that was being meted out by the dirty, clumsy hands of the youngsters. To meet the need, there arose the horn-book, described again by Dr Johnson as "the first book of children, covered with horn to keep it unsoiled."

Basically the horn-book was just a tablet, usually of oak or other firm wood, on which the letters of the alphabet or other syllabic formations were either embossed or incised. Later, instead of the incision or embossment, a sheet of parchment or paper with the learning material written on it was fastened to the board, over which was placed a thin sheet of horn, sufficiently thin to allow the writing to be read but sufficiently strong to prevent the paper being torn or soiled. Both the paper and covering were secured to the board, according to a fourteenth-century poet, by five nails in token of Christ's death:

> When a child to school shall be set,
>   A book to him is brought,
> Nailed on a breed of tree,
> That men calleth an abece,
>   Practically i-wrought.
> Wrought is on the book without
>   V paraffys [nails] great and stout,
>   Rolled in rose-red;
> That is set without doubt
>   In token of Christ's death.[2]

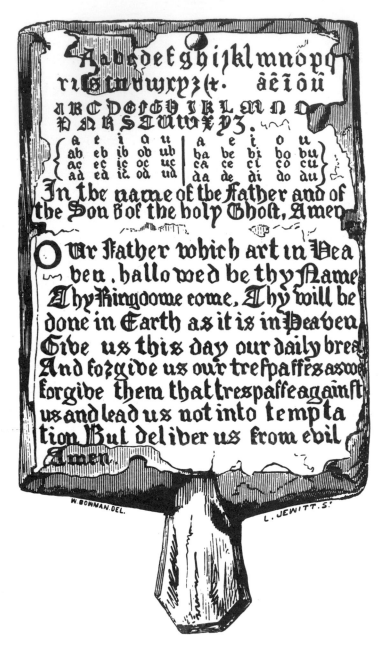

10　*Early seventeenth-century horn-book*
(*From A. W. Tuer's* A History of the Horn-book, *London, 1897*)

Some horn-books had handles for them to be easily held up, while others had a hole at the end to allow their being slung from the pupil's waist. The early versions were probably bulky, sometimes made of lead.

We do not know when the horn-book was introduced but we can discount the claim of Edmund Coote in *The English Schoolmaster* (1596) that he was responsible for it. "But methought," he wrote, "I heard you say that my reasons have persuaded you to be willing to teach this [i.e. his method] but you cannot move all their parents to be willing to bestow so much money in a book at first. Tell them from me that they need buy no more, and then they shall save much by the bargain. But they will reply that this little child will have torn it before it be half learned. Then answer that an answer is provided for that also, which is this: First, the printer upon sight thereof framed the horn-book according to the order of this book, making the first part of my second page the matter thereof, which in my opinion he did with good reason. For a child may by this treatise almost learn in as little time as well learn the horn-book. But this latter being first learned, being the ground-work of spelling, all the rest of this work will be gotten with small labour. Secondly, I have so disposed the placing of my first book that, if a child should tear out every leaf so fast as he learns, yet it shall not be greatly hurtful: for every new following Chapter repeats and teaches again all that went before."

The device was well-known before Coote's day. For example, a Latin record (1421) states that Thomas Hornar de Petergate was paid two shillings and sixpence for "horning and nailing the above-mentioned books," and there is also a reference to a "Horn ABC" being licensed to James Wolfe in 1587. What seems fairly certain is that it was an English invention, though the Dutch used what they called an "a b boordjie," which was simply an abecedarium.

From the end of the sixteenth century all sorts of horn-books were being made. Some were cruciform in shape, others were mounted in silver or made of filigree silver with protective covering of talc rather than horn, and then laced with red silk. Others were slabs of ivory, with their sunken letters filled with a black pigment. Another, now known as the Bateman horn-book, has an equestrian portrait of Charles I with a crown on his head and a church above it. Other later representations were of St George and the dragon.

The instructional side began with the sign of the Cross on the top left-hand corner. This was followed by the alphabet in both capital and small letters, syllabic combinations and the Roman and/or Arabic numerals. Others, more ornate, had as many as three alphabets, Roman, Black and Italic, together with the signs for etcetera and the ampersand, with the various marks for the stops, interrogation mark, hyphens and brackets. Most had the preface "In the name of the Father and of the Son and of the Holy Ghost," followed by the Lord's Prayer.

One interesting reference to it is found in Shakespeare's *Love's Labour's Lost* (V. i. 45):

> *Armado* (*to Holofernes*): Monsieur, are you not lettered?
> *Moth.* Yes, yes; he teaches boys the horn-book. What is a, b, spelt backward, with the horn on his head?
> *Hol.* Ba, *pueritia*, with a horn added.
> *Moth.* Ba! most silly sheep with a horn. You hear his learning.

It has been suggested that the pun on "horn" here might be an attempt to make it known to Holofernes that he is just an abecedarium, a teacher of the ABC, with little or no status. Others have commented that a horn on the head was a mnemonic device for the benefit of beginners. The connection of "ba" with sheep, however, may also have been a traditional joke. In the *Dialogues* of Vives (1538), there is a scene in which the master is trying to teach Lusius the difference between the vowels and the consonants. "Every one of these signs," said the Preceptor, "is called a letter. Of these, five are vowels A, E, I, O, U. They are present in the Spanish word *oueia*, which means sheep. Keep that word in mind, for any one of these, together with any letter you like, or even more than one, can form a syllable. Unless you have a vowel, you can't make a syllable, though sometimes the vowel is a syllable on its own. And so all the other letters are called consonants, because they can only form sounds if a vowel is joined to them. . . . Out of syllables we get words, and from words comes continuous speech, which all animals lack. And if you can't talk properly, you will be no better than an animal."

To direct the reading, the teacher or child used a sort of pointer, stick or pin, which was called a fescue. "The fescue," commented Halliwell in his Folio Shakespeare, "was an important instrument in the process of instructing from the horn-book." Or, as Nicholas Breton wrote in his *Melancholic Humours in Verse* (1600):

> I never lov'd a book of horn,
> Nor leaves that have their letters worn;
> Nor with a fescue to direct me,
> Where every puny shall correct me.

The horn-book was in popular use right down to the nineteenth century, various names being applied to it. John Florio in his *World of Words* (1598) referred to "Horn-book, Abecedario and Abee-cee book" as being synonymous. Other names often employed were just plain "horn" or "criss-cross row" or later, owing to its shape, "a battledore," which has remained enshrined in our saying, "not to know one's B from a battledore."

Its place in the reading process was fundamental. Nicholas Breton remarked in his *Cornucopiae* (1612):

> Even so, the Hornbook is the seed and grain
> Of skill, by which we learning first obtained;
> And though it be accounted small of many,
> And haply bought of twopence or a penny,
> Yet well the teaching somewhat costly be
> Ere they attain unto the first degree
> Of scholarship and art.

To Charles Hoole also its use was the first step along the path of learning to read: "The usual way to begin with a child . . . is to teach him to know his letters in the horn-book, where he is made to run over all the letters in the alphabet or Christ-cross-row both forwards and backwards, until he can tell any of them, which is pointed at, and that in the English character."

After the letters of the alphabet had been mastered, there was little doubt where the child should proceed next — to the reading of religious matter.

The Psalter, the Primer and the Catechism

Ordericus Vitalis reminisces that after learning "the letters of Carmen Nicostrata," he went on to the psalms, hymns and other religious material (*Historia Ecclesiastica,* XIII), and John of Salisbury, the famous English scholar (died 1180) related how as a boy he was placed in the care of a priest, together with other boys, to learn the Psalms (*Polycraticus,* II. 28). This might have been a very pleasant assignment, for this same priest's hobby was magic and he was in the habit of using the boys as his assistants. But the Latin phrases, *psalterium discere* (to learn the psalter) and *psalterium docere* (to teach the psalter), demonstrate the basic importance of the psalms because these two phrases were frequently used to indicate an elementary pupil and elementary teacher respectively.

Directives about reading responsibility were more precise later. The Clerk's School at Skipton, for instance, founded in 1555, directed the clerk "to teach the children to spell, and read the ABC, called the ABsc, the Primer and Psalter in Latin and not in English."[3] The foundation deed for a song or elementary school at Childrey in Berkshire also set out the full curriculum to be followed by the priest who had been appointed to teach at the school. First, he was to teach the alphabet, in Latin, the Lord's Prayer, the Hail Mary, the Creed, all things necessary for the serving of Mass, De Profundis, the Collects for the departed, graces, for dinner and supper; and then, in English, the Fourteen Articles of Faith, the Ten Commandments, the Seven Deadly Sins, the Seven Sacraments, the Seven Gifts of the Holy Spirit, the Seven Works of Mercy, the Manner of Confession, and various points about manners and good conduct.[4] A hefty assignment for the fittest of men!

Still, this was the sort of reading syllabus that was being prescribed by the experts. William Bullokar (1580) directed the child to learn first with a spelling pamphlet and then progress to the Psalter and the Primer, "because these be the first books that are handled of learners. . . . I have altered no sentence or word in the Primer from the former and commonest impression thereof at this day."

William Kempe in *The Education of Children in Learning* (1580) advised that "after the four and twenty letters, and the tables of the syllables . . . he shall proceed to practise the same in spelling and reading other men's works, as the Catechism and Primer." Mulcaster in his *Elementary* was even more explicit: "Wherefore to lay the first ground of learning, which is to learn to read, in religion towards God, and in religion itself to observe the law and ordinances of my country, I will after the Abc, set down the ordinary Catechism set forth by my prince, the state of my country, with all such appendants for graces, and other prayers, as shall seem most pertinent to the elementary training of the Christian child. Thereunto I will join some other pretty short treatise concerning the same religious argument being of good importance for those years to understand [i.e. the Catechism] ; and as warily appointed as God shall appoint me." From this it would appear that the learning of the Catechism was required by law.

Brinsley too advised the children to "go through their Abcie and Primer," the "Abcie" here referring probably to the Catechism. Charles Hoole also directed them next to "the ABC or Primer, and therein to make them name the letters, and spell the words, till by often use they can pronounce [at least] the shortest words at the first sight. This method takes with those of prompter wits, but many of more slow capacity . . . go on remissly from lesson to lesson, and are not much more able to read, when they have ended their lesson, than when they began it. Besides, the ABC now being . . . generally thrown aside, and the ordinary Primer not printed, and the very fundamentals of Christian religion [which were wont to be contained in those books, and were commonly taught children at home by heart before they went to school] with sundry people . . . slighted, the matter which is taught in most books now in use, is not so familiar to them, and therefore not so easy for children to learn. But to hold still to the sure foundation, I have caused the Lord's Prayer, the Creed, and the Ten Commandments to be printed in the Roman character," etc.

As early as 1520 *The Day-Book of John Dorne*, a bookseller's account book, showed that he held in stock such books as an ABC "for to learn [to] read" and a boy's "primer"; and a hundred years later, in 1620, the names of books on the stock-list of the Stationers Company leave little doubt about their longevity: *The ABC with Catechism, The Horn ABC, Spelling ABC*, Primers, Psalters and Psalms, all as separate volumes.

Let us now turn to the development of the primer.

In order to help people take part in the church service, the devotional obligations had been collected into a single volume, which was called the *Horae Beatae Mariae Virginis* or the "Book of the Hours," and this became the prayer book or the private devotional of any ordinary layman who could afford to buy one. As one might expect, in due course the book had come to be called *primarium* in Latin or the "prymer," "primmer" or "primer" in English, obviously deriving the name from its position of prime importance in religion. The name must have been adopted early, for there is a reference to Mathew of the Exchequer leaving his *primarium* in his will in 1294.[4] One of the earliest versions, *The Primer or Lay Folks' Prayer Book* (*c.* 1425), contained the Hours of the Blessed Virgin Mary, with prayers, hymns and psalms; Matins and Lauds; the Seven Penitential Psalms; the Fifteen Gradual Psalms; The Litany of the Saints; and the Offices for the Dead; and Commendations. While this issue had no ABC as a preface, another *Horae Beatae Mariae Virginis ad Usum Sarum* (i.e. after the custom of Salisbury), published in Paris, 1514, contained an ABC, a syllabarium, the Lord's Prayer and Creed.

This was the *Primus Liber,* which was used in church, home and school and which came to be regarded as the basic elementary reader which every child was required to read before he could enter the grammar school. No attempt was made to grade the reading material, and the book was very expensive to buy. In 1447, for instance, the Pastons had to pay two shillings for their copy, a prohibitive price for most. Later John Dorne listed them for sale from threepence to sixpence.

At this stage the Germans were beginning to exercise their influence on educational matters in this country, particularly the primer. Up to the Lutheran challenge to Papal authority in 1517 the Germans had been using primers which were Catholic in content and Latin in language. It was no surprise that when the people began to demand the Bible and their hymns in German, they should also look for primers that would similarly satisfy the religious and linguistic needs of their German children. In 1524 Philip Melanchthon issued a somewhat different sort of primer or *fibel,* as it was called, though still in Latin. "Philip Melanchthon," it began, "desires the salvation of all children." Then followed the alphabet, both small and capital letters, the Lord's Prayer, the Ave Maria, the Creed and other traditional religious material, but the last fourteen pages, for the first time in such a Christian compilation, were devoted to secular material, including famous Greek sayings. In 1525 Martin Luther issued his own version in German.

With students proceeding to England from Germany, especially Wittenberg, in large numbers, the ecclesiastical authorities in this country were acutely aware of the danger inherent in this situation. The threat of heresy from the Wycliffe Bible had been bad enough. Now they feared that an English primer, the basic reader for children, might spread infection even wider and deeper. The authorities sensibly decided that the safest way to counteract the danger would be to issue one in English, approved by themselves.

A primer that contained the Lord's Prayer in English had been issued by Wynkyn de Worde in 1523 but the first primer, wholly in English and so approved, was that of John Byddell for William Marshall about 1534. Consisting of 289 pages, it had the title *A Primer in English, with certain prayers and godly meditations, very necessary for all people that understand not the Latin tongue. Cum privilegio regali.* It had an Almanack, a General Confession, the Ten Commandments, the Creed and the Lord's Prayer, with explanatory notes, etc., but, interestingly, it had no prefatory alphabetic instruction.

With the official primer in the field, Henry VIII issued his Injunctions (1536), which instructed "the persons, vicars and other curates" to warn parents, masters and "governors of youth" that they had to teach, or have taught, their children and servants, from their days of infancy, the Lord's Prayer, the Articles of the Faith and the Ten Commandments in English. As the children were to be made "to repeat and understand" these pieces, the clergy were required to recite each of them in their sermons, one clause or article each day, till "the whole be taught and learned by little and little." They also had to "deliver the same in writing" or to inform "them that can read or will desire the same" where books containing them were sold.

Another Injunction (1538) directed that all had to be able to say the Lord's Prayer, the Ave Maria, the Creed and the Ten Commandments in English before they could receive the Sacrament, and "the petty teachers within the Church itself" were "ordered to teach these fundamental materials in the vernacular." From now on, with the urgent need for children to learn to read the authorized material in English, few primers or Catechisms were published without an ABC by way of preface.

One primer still preserved from about 1538 had the title *The BAC [sic] both in Latin and in English. . . . Printed at London in Paul's Churchyard at the sign of the Maiden's Head by Thomas Petyt.* Another famous primer, called *King Henry's Primer* (1545), was issued to bring about one uniform manner or form of prayer in English "throughout all our dominions." Others, with Cranmer's Catechism attached "for the singular commodity and profit of child and young people," had both the alphabet and syllable tables in the preface.

One primer rapidly superseded the next. In 1545–7 was issued *The ABC set forth by the King's majesty and his Clergy and commanded to be taught throughout all his Realm*, and this added some easy spelling exercises to the alphabet in the preface. In the eyes of Edward VI sloth, idleness, beggary, theft, murder, calamity and misery had been brought about by the failure of parents and friends to bring up their children "in good learning, some occupation or craft," and further primers were published in 1551 and 1553. Still another, *A Primer and a Catechism, and also the notable fairs in the Calendar . . . to be taught unto children,* was issued about 1560, while *The Primer and Catechism set forth with many godly prayers* (1566) was in use until 1651 when it was finally abolished.

The A.B.C

set forthe by the Kynges maiestie and his Clergye, and commaunded to be taught through out all his Realme. All other btterly set a part, as the teachers thereof tender his graces fauour.

 A.a.b.c.d.e.f.g.h.i.k.l.m. n.o.p.q.r.z.s.s.t.u.b.w.x. y.z.ɛ.ꝝ: Est. Amen.

A.B.C.D.E.F.C.H.J.K.L. M.N.O.P.Q.R.S.T.U.W. X.Y.

A.B.C.D.E.F.G.H.I.K. L.M.N.O.P.Q.R.S.T. U.W.X.

In the name of the Father, and of the Sonne, and of the holye Ghoste. So be it.

11   *First page of an early ABC, printed in London (William Powell,*
      c. 1545—7)

The pleasure derived by ordinary people from such a book as
the primer is seen in this contemporary description, headed "Brawl-
ing or Misconduct in the Church of Walsingham. The personal
answer of Arthur Chapman of Walsingham, blacksmith, aged thirty
years, 3 Feb. 1576."

"He said that upon St Matthew day last he . . . was in the church
of Walsingham the time of the morning prayer; at which time this
deponent was reading . . . an English book or primer while . . . the
priest was saying . . . his service, not minding what the priest read
but tending his own book and prayer. Marry, he read not aloud to
the hindrance of the priest to his knowledge, but the priest after
the first lesson willed him to read more softly, to whom this exami-
nate answered that he would make amends for that fault. . . . The
said Arthur said that he had a primer in English, which he had a
twelvemonth and more; which primer [he] has used to pray on,
and at such times as he is now blamed for."[5]

One curious book further indicates the importance paid to such
religious works. In 1575 Peter Bales wrote the Lord's Prayer, the
Ten Commandments, the Creed and some Latin prayers, together
with his name and motto, on a silver penny covered with crystal
and, after mounting it in a ring of gold, he presented it to Queen
Elizabeth. To complete the gift he added a pair of lenses "cun-
ningly devised."

Together with the Primer went the Catechism. Whereas the
Primer was basically a book of devotions for use by Christians of
any age, the Catechism was a plain summary of Christian principles which had to be learned by Christians from an early age. It
was arranged in the traditional form of disputation and the master
"opposed" the scholar with questions to test his Christian belief
before he could be brought to confirmation by the bishop. Such
catechisms had been in use from the early centuries (see page 16)
but by the sixteenth century their popularity was quite remarkable.
In 1527 Colet had inserted a "Catechyzon" in his *Accidence*, and
in 1533 Erasmus had composed his version in Latin. *The First
Book of Common Prayer* (1549) also had a section with the title,
"Confirmation wherein is contained a Catechism for Children,"
and from 1570 the famous Catechisms of Dean Nowell were being
regularly issued.

The use of the Nowell versions was widespread in Elizabethan
schools. For example, it was prescribed in the injunctions of Bishop
Horne for Winchester Cathedral for 2 October 1571: "The said
choristers shall not only learn to sing but also shall learn without

book the Catechism in English written by Mr Nowel, Dean of
Paul's, and every fortnight shall be examined how they profit
therein." The *Catalogue of Books,* compiled by Andrew Maunsell
(1595), listed no fewer than sixty different catechisms, while Hugh
Peter's in 1660 referred to "near a hundred" of them in *A Dying
Father's Last Legacy to an Only Child.*

The catechisms boasted a variety of names, e.g. "A brief and
necessary catechism very needful to be known of all householders"
(1575); one "to be learned of the ignorant folk," composed by
Bird; "the short questions between father and son"; "a short sum
of the whole catechism" (1618); and "so short a catechism that
whosoever will not learn are not to be admitted to the Lord's
Supper" (1626).

From the speech of Philip Faulconbridge in *King John* (I.i.
192ff) it seems more than probable that Shakespeare himself learnt
from an ABC with Catechism:

> Why then I suck my teeth, and catechize
> My picked man of countries: *"My dear sir,"*
> Thus, leaning on mine elbow, I begin,
> *"I shall beseech you"* — that is question now;
> And then comes answer like an Absey book:
> *"O sir,"* says answer, *"at your best command;*
> *At your employment; at your service, sir."*
> *"No, sir,"* says question, *"I, sweet sir,* at yours";
> And so, ere answer knows what question would. . . .

From the middle of the sixteenth century one meets an increasing number of books which sport the term ABC more prominently
in their titles, e.g. *An ABC with the Pater Noster, Ave Maria, the
Creed and Ten Commandments with certain instructions that
Schoolmasters ought to bring up children in* (1553–8); *An ABC
for children. Here is an ABC devised with syllables. . . . And by
this Book a man, that has such good capacity and can no letter on
the book, may learn to read in the space of six weeks, both Latin
and English, if he give thereto good diligence, as it has been divers
times proved. Also you may learn thereby to write English truly,
and to know the true Orthography of the English tongue.* (c.
1553); *A Ballad entitled an ABC with a Prayer* (1558); *An a.b.c. in
Latin* (1559); *The Olive Leaf: or Universal Abc . . . wherein is set
forth the Creation, Descent and Authority of Letters: together
with the Estimation, Profit, Affinity or Declination of them: for*

the familiar use of all Students, Teachers and Learners: of what Chirography soever, most necessary (1561); and *The Battle of the ABC* (1586).

Firms too were using the ABC as a designation of their publishing business, e.g. Richard Faques in 1523 had a printing shop near St Paul's "at the sign of the A.B.C." The term was also being used to denote the elementary, but basic, nature of books on other subjects, e.g. "The Aged Man's A.B.C.," "The Virgin's A.B.C." and "The Young Man's A.B.C."

Yet, though the Elizabethan age was teeming with ABCs and Catechisms, only a few leaves of an original copy have come down to us, and these were found as part of the binding of another book. The imperfect title-page of a book, generally dated as 1582, reads, *The ABC with the Catechism, that is to say the instruction of the Christian faith, to be learned by every child before he be brought to be confirmed of the bishop. . . . Forbidding all others to print this Catechism.*

The phrase, "Forbidding all others to print this Catechism," reminds us that these primers, Catechisms and ABCs were printed under licence. Interference with or encouragement of printing in this country had started as far back as 1484 when an Act had allowed any artificer or foreign merchant or any scrivener, illuminator, binder or printer to exercise his trade here, so that the growing demand for books could be met. So many entered the trade over the next forty years that by 1523 another Act, forbidding printing firms to employ more than two foreign journeymen apiece or to have any apprentices other than English, was passed. These foreign printers and bookmen were also ideal carriers of the virus of Protestantism, and in 1524 booksellers were forbidden to deal in Lutheran works. The ban was not entirely successful and books were still entering the country in large numbers. In 1531 Richard Bayfield was burnt for importing prohibited books.

The 1484 Act was repealed in 1534 on the grounds that there were already in the country "a great number cunning and expert in the said craft of printing, as able to exercise the said craft in all points, as any stranger in any other realm or country." Apart from these severe restrictions on foreign printers and stationers, it directed that no person should "buy to sell again any pirated books brought from any parts of the King's 'obeisaunce' ready bound in boards, leather or parchment." A close surveillance at the ports failed in its object, and in 1541, for example, Grafton was sent to prison for printing "a seditious epistle in the English tongue written by Melanchthon," and in 1543 eight persons were severely punished for printing books of a prohibited nature.

To make control more effective, the proclamation of 1538 declared that all printed works had first to be examined by the Privy Council or its agents, and, to demonstrate that approval for publication had been secured, the words *cum privilegio regali/Ad imprimendum solum* (i.e. with the royal consent/for sole publication) had to be inserted on the title-page.

In addition to repeating this proclamation in 1549 and 1551, Edward VI extended another practice which Henry VIII had started, the granting to certain individuals of the sole right to print books of a specific type. For example, Grafton and Whitechurch alone could print service-books. In 1552 Richard Tottell was awarded the right of printing law-books for seven years, Jugge was allowed to print Bibles and Testaments, and in 1553 William Seres was given the privilege of printing "all manner of Primers, English or Latin" and John Day the right of printing the ABC and Catechism in English. John Day's licence was renewed several times by Queen Elizabeth so that, in all, he held the monopoly for nearly thirty years.

One need hardly dwell on the financial advantage that accrued from these publishing monopolies, because primers, catechisms and ABCs approved by the authorities enjoyed a substantial circulation. As others tried to avail themselves of the privileges, disputes were inevitable and several of the unprivileged carried on illegal printing and clandestine publishing. Such a case was that of John Tysdale who was tried "for printing without licences the A.B.C. and other such like. For both he is fined iiij s. viiij d."[6]

Another, John Wolfe, openly declared his opposition to the nefarious traffic and, when John Day's right to print this class of book was reawarded to him in 1577, it was found that the manual, though not printed by Day, was already being sold on the open market. After an appeal by Day to the Star Chamber in 1582, proceedings were begun against Roger Ward who confessed to having printed the equivalent of about 10,000 copies of the ABC. Unfortunately for Day, though he won his case, his publishing empire was somewhat truncated, for John Wolfe, the real cause of the trouble, had to be taken into this particular monopoly. A few years later, when Day's son, Richard, took similar action against eighteen other defendants, Wolfe was cited as a plaintiff! Some were reputed to have sold as many as 10,000 ABCs in two months, eleven others had sold 2,000 Psalms and 10,000 ABCs, and three others had printed "great numbers of the ABC with the Little Catechism," and had put up for sale "the number of fifteen thousand of the said book."[7]

In 1588 R. Jones was licensed to print the *ABC for children, newly devised with Syllables* but in 1603, with the granting of the privilege to publish the *ABC with the Little Catechism* and others, the somewhat devious story of the child's first reader comes to an end.

If, however, one asks what the next immediate step for the learner was, the answer is best put in the words of John Brinsley: "Thus they go through their Abcie and Primer. And if they read these over that they may be perfect in them, it will be the better for them. For the second reading of any book does much encourage children, because it seems to be so easy then and also it does imprint the more. Besides that, they will run it over so fast at the second time, as it will be no loss of time at all unto them." Such second reading had also been sanctioned by no less an authority than Quintilian, who had prescribed that "when a book is finished, it is to be gone through again from the beginning."

After the primer and catechism, the next material stage was also marked out, and most Elizabethan books of pedagogy were agreed that reading practice should now reach out to an awareness of the child's duty to his country and his fellow man.

Mulcaster, for instance, wrote in his *Elementary:* "The matter itself is spread unto two branches . . . either for religion towards God, and right opinion in faith or for civility towards men, and right judgement in behaviour. I will therefore cast the matter of reading so, as it shall answer at full both to religion, in faith, and to civility in friendship." Brinsley also advised that, after "the Psalms in metre" and the Testament, the "'School of Virtue' is one of the principal and easiest for the first enterers, being full of precepts of civility, and such as children will soon learn and take a delight in . . . and after it 'The School of Good Manners' called 'The New School of Virtue.'" Charles Hoole itemized the stages thus: "Having all things which concern reading English made familiar to him, he may attain to a perfect habit of it. 1. By reading the single Psalter. 2. The Psalms in metre. 3. The School of Good Manners or such like easy books, which may both profit and delight him."

Books of Courtesy or Manners

Injunctions in good manners, the bases of "gentil behaviour," had long been regarded as an obligatory part of the study of the young nobleman both on the Continent and in England, and a number of instructional books in the art were available in the original Latin or French and in translation. One of the most popular works on the subject was the *Distichs* of Cato, which had been conveniently used to teach both Latin and manners together, while another, a fourteenth-century translation of Christine de Pisé's *Moral Proverbs*, a collection of wise sayings in French, was considered eminently suitable for young people.

From the early fifteenth century the study of manners had also come to be regarded as an essential part of the education of other social classes. Consequently, the native need for more books of this type was so great that originals in English verse were now being written. One of the earliest pieces extant, Symon's "Lesson of Wisdom for Children," illustrates the sort of advice that was being laid before the young reader:

> All manner [of] children, you listen and learn
> A lesson of wisdom that is writ here.
> My child, I rede [advise] you to be wise and take heed of this rhyme:
>
>> The child that has his will always
>> Shall thrive late, I will say [to] you;
>> And therefore every good man's child
>> That is too wanton and too wild,
>> Well learn this lesson for certain,
>> That you may be the better man.
>> Child, I warn you in all wise
>> That you tell truth and make no lies.
>> Child, be not forward, be not proud,
>> But hold up your head and speak aloud.
>> And when any man speaks to thee
>> Do off your hood and bow your knee.
>> And wash your hands and your face. . . .

The poet then advises the child to take good care of his book, cap and gloves and, after cautioning him not to pull faces at any man, he reminds the child that one must cultivate good manners to get on in life.

>> And namely to clerks to be meek and mild
>> And, child, rise be-time and go to school,
>> And fare not as wanton fool. . . .
>> A good child needs learning, and so
>> "He hateth the child that spareth the rod."

Another advisory poem, *How the Wise Man Taught his Son* (*c.* 1430), counselled the child to pray to God every morning, refrain from talking too much, not to marry a woman for her money, keep out of taverns and always keep himself busy. *How the Good Wife Taught her Daughter* (*c.* 1430) directed the girl to love God, not to chatter or gad about town, not to spoil her husband with extravagance, not to drink ale to excess and, when her children are cheeky, to give them a sound thrashing.

Another, *The Book of Courtesy* or *Stans Puer Mensam* of some 848 lines, also written *c.* 1430 and sometimes ascribed to John Lydgate, aimed more at the upper classes. The "young enfaunt," after being told how to behave before his lord, was reminded among other things not to stuff food into his mouth or harp on old grievances. Among the most popular of all such works and reprinted later by Caxton, it also stressed the elements of religion and the code of behaviour in church. Another, *Urbanitatis* (*c.* 1460) was more downright, including such directions as taking one's hat off in the presence of one's lord and keeping it off till told to put it back on, holding the chin upright and refraining from spitting!

Yet another, *The Book of Nurture*, was composed *c.* 1470 by John Russell, once servant to Duke Humphrey of Gloucester. As an usher who loved teaching, he tells how during a walk in a forest he chanced upon a young man stalking some deer. In conversation the young man admitted that at various times of his life he had wanted to be a butler, a chamberlain and a carver, but no one would employ him because he had received no training in any of these skills. Of course, this was grasped by the versifier as a glorious opportunity to launch upon an exposition of the various duties of these occupations, describing how to name the sundry wines, how to lay a table, wrap bread, carve meat and fish, and how to make sauce.

The Babees Book or *A Little Report of how Young People Should Behave*, translated from Latin *c.* 1470, also dealt with behaviour at meals and before one's lord. One should not, for example, scratch one's self or talk filth, one should not drink "with full mouth" or talk when eating, and one should always cut one's bread, never break it. Another famous book, *The Book of Nurture*, compiled by Hugh Rhodes (*c.* 1530), went straight to the point, beginning: "There are few things to be understood more necessary than to teach and govern children in learning and good manners, for it is a high service to God, it gets favour in the sight of men, it multiplies goods and increases your good name, it also provokes to prayer by which God's grace is obtained, if thus they be brought up in virtue, good manners and Godly learning." This is the advice he gives the young master about his servants: "Take them often with you to hear God's word preached, and then inquire of them what they heard, and use them to read in the Bible and other Godly Books but especially keep them from reading of feigned fables, vain fantasies, wanton stories and songs of love, which bring mischief to youth. For, if they learn pure and clean doctrine in youth, they pour out plenty of good works in age."

Caxton also produced books in this field and among others he published a translation of *The Knight of the Tower* from the French, to teach all young gentlewomen how to behave virtuously.

The best known of all was *The School of Virtue and Book of Good Nurture for Children and Youth to Learn their Duty by. Newly perused, corrected and augmented by the first Author, that is F. Seager (c. 1534)*, the book that was strongly recommended for use as a reader by Brinsley. An interesting feature of this work was the way in which it was aimed directly at the ordinary person rather than the member of the noble class. After beginning with instructions about morning and evening prayers, it directed the child how to behave himself on getting up and dressing:

> This done, your satchel and your books take,
> And to the school haste see you make
> But ere you go with yourself, forethink
> That you take with you pen, paper and ink. . . .

Then, when on the way to school:

> Your cap put off,
> Salute those you meet;
> In giving the way
> To such as pass by.
> It is a point
> Of civility. . . .
> When to the school
> You shall resort,
> This rule note well
> I do thee exhort:
> Your master there being,
> Salute with all reverence. . . .
> Unto your place
> Appointed for to sit
> Straight go you to

And your satchel unknit,
Your books take out
Your lessons then learn. . . .
Learning to get
Your book well apply:
All things seem hard
When we do begin,
But labour and diligence
Yet both them to win. . . .

On the way home from school, children should not run in gangs or whoop and shout as if they were out hunting foxes:

Gape not nor gaze not at every new fangle,
But soberly go you with countenance grave;
Humble yourselves towards all men behave;
Be free of cap and full of courtesy.

Various other items of advice are given about how to sit and serve at table, accepting the food which one is given, not looking for birds' nests and getting home from school before dark.

Many famous writers tried their hand at these books. Erasmus, for example, wrote *De Civilitate Morum Puerilium* for "a child of noble blood and singular hope," which was translated into English by Robert Whittinton in 1532, and a version of which was published by Wynkyn de Worde as *A Little Book of Good Manners for Children.*

Most writers did not pay much attention to the particular linguistic or conceptual limitations of the children who were expected to read them. One book, for instance, was advertised as *The Secret of Secrets of Aristotle, with the governale of princes and every manner of estate, and rules of health for body and soul, very profitable for every man, very good to teach children, newly translated out of French and printed.* In it the philosopher, instructing Alexander of Macedon, talks about the duties of kings, and their vices, giving details of their toilet, dress and sleep without any attempt to reduce the language difficulty to the probable level of the child learner.

Books of Pedagogy for the Teacher of Reading

The first manual of instruction on how to teach reading seems to have been John Hart's *An Orthography* (1569), and this was followed by his second book, *A Method*, a year later. Then came

THE
FIRST PART
OF THE ELEMENTA-
RIE VVHICH ENTREA-
TETH CHEFELIE OF THE
right writing of our Engliſh tung,
ſet furth by RICHARD
MVLCASTER.

Imprinted at London by Thomas Vau-
troullier dwelling in the blak-friers
by Lud-gate
1582.

12   *Title-page of Richard Mulcaster's* The First Part of the Elementary
(London, 1582)

Roger Ascham's *The Schoolmaster* (1570); Francis Clement's *The Petty School with an English Orthography* (1576); *Bullokar's Book at Large* (1580); Richard Mulcaster's *Positions* and *First Part of the Elementary* (1582); William Kempe's *The Education of Children in Learning* (1588); Edmund Coote's *The English Schoolmaster* (1596); and John Brinsley's *Ludus Literarius or the Grammar School* (1612).

One point that immediately catches the eye of the modern reader of Elizabethan books is the author's apparent lack of modesty about his own work. For example, *The Mirror of our Lady* (1530) was said to be very necessary for all religious persons, while *A Muster of Seismatic Bishops of Rome* of the same year was "to be read [by] all the King's true subjects." Another, *The Governance of Good Health* (1530), unashamedly warned the reader that he would "repent that this came not sooner" into his hands, while a Latin grammar (1569) was advertised as "a delicious syrup newly clarified for young scholars that thirst for the sweet liquor of Latin speech."

The professional teachers of reading had similarly exaggerated ideas about their books. John Hart averred that his learners could be brought "to read English in a very short time with pleasure," while Francis Clement claimed that he could teach "a child to read perfectly in one month." Bullokar intended his book both for the English nation and "all strangers [and pedagogues who] could thenceforth devote their time to being unhappy about something else"! He also boasted that his readers would think it "a plain lie if I should write that one who never knew a letter before has, within ten hours' teaching of ten days, been able to read the last six pages of this book." Mulcaster, writing of his *Elementary*, declared that he did not know of any other book of the same kind that was "so thoroughly fitted for such a purpose," as he intended to prove. He also promised that he would bring out a Latin version of his work to help "any foreign nation" solve any problems it might have with its native orthography. Coote considered that his work, *The English Schoolmaster*, was "the most easy, short and perfect order of distinct reading and writing [of] our English tongue that has ever been known or published by any." By its use "any unskilful person may easily . . . understand any hard English words [which he might meet] in Scripture, sermons or elsewhere." The person who used his book "need buy no other to make him fit from his letters unto the Grammar School, for an apprentice or for any other private reading in English. [He had written it] not only for children, though the first book be more childish for them, but also for all others, especially [those] ignorant of the Latin tongue."

Coote's approach was somewhat modest when compared with the arrogance and ill-tempered menaces written by George Robertson, whose book, *Learning's Foundation Firmly Laid* (1651) we have already met. "My genius," he boasted. "leads me so much to other studies . . . that I could hardly afford myself any spare time to look after this, if my conscience did not tell me that that candle, which the Lord has lighted to me in this way [must be put] on a candle-stick . . . to make it shine to all the world." When Robertson recalls the amount of work he has put into his teaching and particularly his method, and when he sees the affluence his professional imitators have gained for themselves, he is convinced there is no other way "whereby I can benefit the Commonwealth more than by this." Not only has he successfully educated persons who "for stature and years . . . were ready to be prentices, but void of all other qualifications" but he has "never met with any, young or old, desirous to learn, but I have brought them up to reading, unless it were the fault of the parents." Often they removed the pupil from his tuition just when the pupils were on the verge of learning to read! Fortunately, he adds, there were "very few of those." Poor Robertson certainly had his troubles, for he says that some of his rivals had tried to damage his professional reputation either by open attacks or by spreading malicious gossip about him among his neighbours and clients, while others had wickedly lured his pupils away from him. "In regard to them, the righteous Lord judged righteously and brought forth my righteousness as the sun and disappointed them of all their wicked and unjust plots." If anyone doubted his teaching ability, Robertson concluded, he could come and see "the vast difference between those that have been removed from me a time, and those who have been constant with me."

Continental writers on education made equally flamboyant claims. The German, Valentin Ickelsamer (1501–42), in his book *Ein Teutsche Grammatica* claimed that his work was set out with such "clarity, simplicity and entertainment" that "everyone through his own efforts, without the aid of a schoolmaster, can learn to read books, whether he is a woodchopper, a shepherd in the field or an apprentice in the workshop. Moreover, fathers can teach their children to read at home." Another Augsberg primer (1597) claimed that it could teach people of all ages to read within twenty-three hours.[8] Another Danzig headmaster, John Buno, advertised his reading primer in 1650 in these terms: "Newly set out ABC and reading book through which, by means of the instruction contained therein, not only the young but also adults can be brought to fluent reading of both German and Latin, small and capital letters, within six days, through the use of amusing tales and games."[8] Buno recommended that his pupils should read four long passages every morning and four every afternoon so that after forty of these lessons he would be able to cope with "Herr Saubertis's Reading-Book," the Bible itself and "some other good German history-book." Of such magnitude were the lessons and so prolonged the effort required that the undertaking would have daunted the bravest of young learners.

The titles of books were also long and cumbersome. Outside the field of instructional reading these books, for example, were published: *The truth of the most wicked and secret murdering of John Brewen, goldsmith of London, committed by his own wife, through the provocation of one John Parker whom she loved: for which she was burned and he hanged in Smithfield.*" Still more impressive was the title of another book, *True and Dreadful new tidings of blood and brimstone which God has caused to rain from heaven within and without the city Strale Sonet, with a wonderful apparition seen by a citizen of the same city named Hans Germer, who met him in the field as he was travelling on the way!*

After these we must not be too severe on similar tendencies among the writers of books on the teaching of reading. The full title of Francis Clement's book was *THE PETTY SCHOOL. WITH AN ENGLISH ORTHOGRAPHY wherein by rules lately prescribed is taught a method to enable both a child to read perfectly within one month and also the unperfect to write English aright. Hereto are newly added 1. Very necessary precepts and patterns of writing the Secretary and Roman hands. 2. To number by letters and figures. 3. To cast accounts.* Another was *Bullokar's Book at Large, for the amendment of Orthography for English Speech: wherein a most perfect supply is made for the wants and double sound of letters in the Old Orthography.*

Stock phrases or Biblical quotations were often placed under the title. *The Petty School* has "Proverbs xxii: 'Teach a child in the trade of his way and when he is old he shall not depart from it.'" *The Education of Children* quotes the same proverb and adds three more: "Father, provoke not your children to wrath but bring them up in learning and information of the Lord, Eph. vi. 4." "The rod and correction give wisdom but a child set at liberty maketh his mother ashamed, Prov. xxix. 15.".: and "Foolishness is tied in the heart of a child but the rod of discipline shall drive it away, Prov. xxii. 15." The most apt perhaps in the sphere of teaching reading is found on the frontispiece of *The English Primrose* (1644), by Richard Hodges, advocating the reform of spelling along the lines of one letter/one sound: "If the trumpet give an uncertain sound, who shall prepare himself to the battle? Cor. 14.8." John Hart's *A Method* has:

$$\left.\begin{matrix} \text{Reason} \\ \text{Order} \\ \text{Experience} \end{matrix}\right\} \text{ the } \left\{\begin{matrix} \text{Mother} \\ \text{Nurse} \\ \text{Teacher} \end{matrix}\right. \text{ of all human perfections}$$

It would be pointless to examine all the methods recommended by the various writers on the teaching of reading, for in the main their principles are very similar. Here and there the author might lay special stress on some minor point (e.g. Clement stresses the importance of the soft *c* or the danger of omitting *g* in "speaking") in the hope that it might distinguish his individual approach from that of another, though one suspects that it was really common practice. To avoid a mass of conflicting detail, it would be best to outline the methods proposed by the best-known Elizabethan reading-teacher, Edmund Coote, a master in the Free School of Bury St Edmunds, Suffolk. His work, *The English Schoolmaster* (1596), designed as a manual to be used by both teachers and pupils alike, was the first reading instructional textbook to receive wide and lasting acclaim. Twenty-six editions of the work were published by 1656, with another eleven by 1673 and the last recorded edition in 1704.

Very confident about what his book has to offer, he assures the users that "if peradventure for two or three days at the first it may seem somewhat hard or strange . . . yet be not discouraged . . . for, if they take but diligent pains in it but four days, you will learn many profitable things that you never knew. Yea, you shall learn more of the English tongue than any man of your calling, other than a grammarian, in England." They would become far superior teachers and, once familiar with the pattern of the book, they could get on with their work in the shop, at the loom or with the needle and still check on the reading of their pupils.

Page 2 of the manual sets out three different types of letters, both lower and large cases, with various consonantal combinations such as *ff*, *fl*, *ffl*, etc. He so arranges the layout of the page that the instructions are placed next to the reading material to be learnt, though he warns that the titles of the chapters are intended only to direct the teacher and not to be learnt by the scholar. The teacher begins with the vowels and, "after two or three days, when he is skilful in them," the pupil is taught "to call all the other letters, consonants." So he goes on "with the other words of art, as they stand in the margin [but] never troubling his memory with a new word before he be perfect in the old," e.g.

a	e	i	o	u		a	e	i	o	u
Ba	be	bi	bo	bu		Ab	eb	ib	ob	ub
Da	de	di	do	du		Ad	ed	id	od	ud
Fa	fe	etc.				Af	ef	etc.		

The pupil is now given exercises which he is required to read distinctly three times before he may go on to the next.

If we do ill: fie on us all   Up go on: lo I see a pie
Ah is it so: is he my foe?   So it is, if I do lie
Woe be to me, if I do so   Woe is me, oh I die
                            Ye see in me, no lie to be.

This is an historical exercise, because it is the first graded vocabulary exercise known in English, though in modern times word control has become an essential feature of most reading schemes both in England and the United States.

Syllables of three letters and diphthongs are introduced next: "and here you see that this, and every new Chapter, does so repeat all that went before [so] that your scholar can forget nothing."

"Ba bab ba bad ba bag bar bat bay," with a series of exercises, such as

Me   meg   men.   Mi   mil   mis.
Mor   mop   mos.   Mu   mul   mum   mur.
Na   nag   nam   nan. Ne   nel   net   ne   new. . . .

. . . Qua quaf quat. Qui quil quip quit"; and another "made only of the words taught before, where you are not to regard the sense, being frivolous, but only to teach distinct reading."

Boy go thy way up to the top of the
hill: and get me home the bay nag,
fill him well, and see he be fat, and I
will rid me of him: for he be but
dull, as his dame, yet if a man bid
well for him, I will tell him of it, etc.

In fact, most of these sentences could have been taken out of a certain modern Linguistic Reading Method book, in which meaning is considered to be an impediment to the acquisition of mechanical accuracy.

Next come the syllables of three letters but beginning with two consonants. e.g. *bla*, *ble*, *bli*, etc.; *squa*, *sque*, *squi*, etc.; with practice in the joining of words made of syllables beginning with two consonants and the single final consonant. e.g. *Bla + b*; then on to syllables of four letters but beginning with three consonants, e.g. *scra*, *scre*, *scri*, etc.; and then on to syllables ending with two consonants, the learner being required to spell them out. Again, this is followed by a reading exercise, bristling with a realism that must have had vigorous meaning for any Elizabethan lad with escapade coursing through his veins: "As I went through the castle yard, I did chance to stumble in a queach of brambles, so I did scratch my heels and feet and my gay girdle of gold and purple. Then I sought how I might wrestle out, but I dashed my hands in a bundle of thistles," etc.

Book 2 deals with "plain and simple rules" for syllabification. "I divide your syllables for you, until you have the rules of division, and then I leave you to your rule," e.g. "Do you think yourself so suf—fic—ci—ent—ly in—struc—ted to spell and read di—stinct—ly?" At this point too the traditional pattern of question and answer is introduced.

> Scholar. Sir, I do not un—der—stand what you mean by a syllable?
>
> Master. A syl—la—ble is a per—fect sound, made of so ma—ny let—ters, as we spell to—ge—ther: as in di—vi—si—on you see few—er syl—la—bles.
>
> Scholar. How ma—ny let—ters may be in a syl—la—ble?

From here Coote proceeds to the rules of pronunciation and how "to divide truly the longest and hardest English word that you shall find." He concedes that others teach these rules otherwise but he advises the teacher and pupil to "follow 'the Coote rules' without fear or doubt. And thus may you . . . spell truly, certainly and with judgement any English word that can be laid before you."

When the scholar questions the wisdom of using these rules for "little children," the master replies: "A child of ordinary capacity will, and has, conceived easily these rules, being orderly taught. But discretion must be used not to trouble them with any new rules before they be perfect in the old. . . . "If your child," he goes on, "be very young and dull, trouble him with understanding no more of them than he is fit to conceive and use. Yet, let him learn to read them all, if it is granted that he could understand none of them." The mere fact of his reading them will benefit him as much as if he were reading something else! What, he asks, does "he understand when he reads a chapter of the Bible, yet no man will deny the profit he gets from it?"

Next comes the disputation in which the scholars oppose some of their fellows in a sort of spelling-bee. "This opposition," said one pupil Robert, "does very much sharpen our wits, keeps our memory" and helps in many other ways.

Once the pupil has achieved some reading efficiency, he proceeds to a catechism, which Coote himself devised along the lines of Nowell's *Middle Catechism*, e.g.

> What religion do you profess?
> Christian religion.
> What is Christian religion?
> It is the true profession, believing and following of those things which are commanded and taught us by God in the Holy Scriptures.

Other reading material for further practice includes the Ten Commandments, the Creed, the Sacraments of the Baptism with the Last Supper, various observations about Sunday observance, a prayer and thanksgiving before and after meals. A few injunctions in verse complete the course.

> My child and scholar, take good heed,
>   unto the words which here are set:
> And see you do accordingly
>   or else be sure you shall be beat.

After directing the pupil to serve God and be dutiful to his parents, Coote offers hints about clothes, shoes, punctuality, loitering in the street, and earning the love of one's parents and the praise of teachers. After some numeration or arithmetic, he also provides the traditional Biblical names, a chronological series from Sheth to the "Goths conquered Italy: then increased barbarism and papistry," and a list of difficult words with their meanings.

His injunctions about the care of books leave one in little doubt about his own long experience as a teacher! "If, notwithstanding my former reasons, you doubted that this little child will have spoiled this book before it be learned, you may divide it at the end of the second book or you may reserve fair the written copies, till he can read." His abounding confidence in the system shines through to the last: "If you think me . . . unfit for children, plentiful experience in very young ones (believe one who has tried) does daily confute you. Therefore, to dislike before you have tried or diligently read, were either to be rash or unkind."

Despite Coote's conviction of the efficacy of his personal methods and the fact that *The English Schoolmaster* was the most prominent English manual on the teaching of reading in the period under review, one firm impression must still remain. Since the days of the Greeks, except for the Christian atmosphere in which it was now enveloped and the emergence of certain technical details, the basic approach to the teaching of the skill had hardly changed. There were, however, some fresh ideas about it already in the air, and we must now consider how they were being developed.

6 Some Progressive Ideas about the Teaching of Reading

Some educationists were already beginning to realize that the young child learning to read might be experiencing real difficulty in accommodating to the artificial academic processes to which he was being rigorously exposed. The rod was not a panacea for all learning ills. Even before the end of the fifteenth century some new and exciting ideas about the teaching of reading were being mooted, particularly in Germany, and these were beginning to affect pedagogic methods in England. Not a great deal perhaps had been done so far but some moves were being made in interesting directions. For example, it was felt not only that the boredom of the alphabetic grind might be somewhat intolerable for the young learner but also the material content and the language of the textbooks might be unnecessarily difficult.

Grading of Reading Material

As early as the fifth century St Jerome had advocated the use of carefully chosen and graded vocabulary in instructional readers (see page 72) but his proposal does not seem to have been generally adopted. By early in the sixteenth century simpler and more relevant material was being used in some Latin grammar books and one compiler, William Horman, in the 1519 edition of his *Vulgaria* included such sentences as these:

The Thames is frozen over with ice.
Old and doting churls cannot suffer young children to be merry.
I have laid many gins, pots and other . . . to take fish.
See that I lack not by my bedside a chair of easement, with vessels
    under and an urinal [near] by.
Paul's steeple is a mighty great thing and so high that a man may [just]
    discern the weather-cock

Such examples in other fields were also affecting the teaching of reading, and Mulcaster was also advocating an improvement in the material content and language of the readers for children. "I would be careful," he wrote in the *Elementary*, "that the matter, which he shall read, may be so fit for his years and so plain to his intelligence that, when he is in school," he would eagerly forge ahead with studies of his own accord. To that end, the matter of the initial readers should be "so easy to understand" and their language "so simple to follow" that both would encourage him still more."

"The easier and the more familiar the matter," Brinsley summed up, "the faster they learn" and, as we have seen (pages 119–20), this enlightened approach of graded vocabulary and realistic subject-matter was a welcome feature of Coote's manual.

The Use of Pictorial Material

From the fifteenth century attempts were also being made to enliven the monotonous procedure through the use of pictorial illustrations. As early as 1477 Christopher Hueber, a teacher in Bavaria, had issued an ABC book with small pictures above the letters.[1] In 1485 the Florentine humanist, Jacob Publicius, had prepared the *Ars Memoriae*, which also contained ABC pictures, and another picture primer (1496) had delicate miniatures which have been attributed to the hand of Leonardo da Vinci. In 1532 the German, Marcum Schulte, published his picture alphabet. This was significant in that he used the illustration to demonstrate the sound of the initial letter and, to make learning still easier, he placed a rhymed couplet of a moral nature alongside the picture.[2]

These books became very popular in Germany, and one of the best known was the *Poetic Calendar*, published in Strasburg, with a picture of the twelve-year-old Jesus on the title-page and the pictures of saints to illustrate the different letters. Another *Name-book* of Simon Kofferls (1570) dealt with "the whole ABC in order for young and old, and for those who have no time to go to an ordinary school. Teaching by rhymes." Alongside the names of

Adam, Abel and Abraham, for example, appeared this aphoristic couplet:

> You should first and foremost fear God,
> And you will become a wise man.

Next to the names beginning with *J*, such as John, Justin, etc., were these lines:

> If you turn to God, then he
> Will turn to you and bless you.

In time the accompanying rhymes tended to degenerate from their religious and moral nature. By the late seventeenth century such unworthy examples as these were being used in books of this type:

> The monkey is so ridiculous,
> Especially when he is eating an apple;

and

> The nun in the convent wants to do penance, so
> One will have to use a gimlet.

The English also used such an alphabetic arrangement but without accompanying pictures in the Middle Ages. The earliest extant version that might have been used for instructional reading was *The A.B.C. of Aristotle* by a Master Bennet, a rector of Essex *c.* 1430. This was designed to teach both the letters of the alphabet and to give counsel about personal behaviour. After beginning thus,

> Whoso wishes to be wise and worship desires,
> Learn he one letter, and look on another
> Of the A.B.C. of Aristotle.

It then went on right through the alphabet:

> A too amorous, too adventurous and argue not too much;
> B too bold, not too busy and board not too large;
> C too courteous, too cruel, etc.

By the sixteenth century various English primers were copying the German picture pattern, and one little tract entitled *Alphabeticum Primum Becardi* (1552) carried rhymes with each letter, and in 1575 another ABC was advertised with "All the letters whereof there is a good document set forth and taught in rhyme. Translated out of Bas Almaine into English." There was a similar deterioration from the standard of the moral rhymes that were originally used in England, and soon the most popular lines were such as these:

> A was an archer that shot at a frog.
> B was a baker that had a big dog.

Origin of the Whole Word/Look-and-Say Method

The importance of using illustrations was strongly emphasized by a German professor, Lubinus, at Rostock in his 1614 book, *The True and Ready Way to Learn the Latin Tongue*, translated and published by Hartlib in England in 1654. "Four-footed creatures," he wrote, "creeping things, fishes and birds which can neither be obtained nor live easily in these parts ought to be painted." Models should be made and likenesses should be "drawn with the pencil, yet of such a size that they can be easily seen by boys some distance away." There should be produced a book in which everything that can be seen should be fully and accurately described, with the correct linguistic term put alongside it, both in Latin and in Dutch. "Visible things," he stressed, "must be known by the eyes," and the best way for a child to learn anything is to let him say its name at the same time as he sees it. This, of course, was the essence of the Whole Word or Look-and-Say method some forty-three years before the "Orbis Pictus" of Comenius, who has been generously credited with its introduction to the world of reading. Lubinus further suggested that whole sentences, such as

> This bread was put on the table
> The cat devours the mouse

should be placed under the illustrative pictures. This was the germ of our modern Sentence method.

The practice of using pictorial illustrations had also been used in England before the introduction of printing, and one might point to the habit of the vocabularist of placing a miniature alongside a word to clarify or amplify its meaning. One pictorial vocabulary of the late fifteenth century[3] is a word list with English/Latin equivalents for the parts of the body and clothing, with illustrative sketches at the side of the list.

The Introduction of Phonics

Some German educationists were also drawing attention to the advantages of using the sound or phonic powers of letters rather than their names.

The first outstanding figure of the phonics school was Valentin Ickelsamer (1501—42), a schoolmaster of Augsberg and later Erfurt, who publicized his views about the teaching of reading in

Hic sal, saltis, A^{cc} salt.
Hoc coclear, A^{cc} a spone.
Hoc candelebrum, A^{cc} a cand-
    ylsteyke.
Hoc gausape, }   5
Hoc toral,. } a burdclothe.
Hec mappa, /
Hoc sissorium, A^{cc} a trench-
    ore.
Hoc manitergium, a hand- 10
    clothe.
Hec culingna, A^{cc} a line-
    shark.[1]

NOMINA VESTIMEN- 15
TORUM.

Hec vestis }
Hoc vestimentum, }*A^{cc}* clothe.
Hoc indumentum, /   20
Hoc superum, An^{cc} a pryn.[2]
Hoc pelicium, A^{cc} a pylchen-[3]
Hoc scapilorium, A^{cc} a scap-
    lorey.
Hec capa, A^{cc} a cope.   25
Hec sarabarda, A^{cc} a sclav-
    ene.
Hoc mantile, } a mantelle.
Hoc mantellum, }
Hec seclas, -cis, idem est.   30
Hoc capellum, A^{ce} a hat.
Hic capellus, idem est.
Hic pilius, A^{cc} a cape.
Hec tena, A^{ce} a hewd.[4]
Hoc capucium, A^{cc} a hode. 35
Hec armilansa, a cloke.
Hoc colobium, a tabare.
Hec toga, } a gowyn.
Hoc epitogium, }
Hec supertunica, a syrcote. 40
Hec roba, A^{ce} a robe.

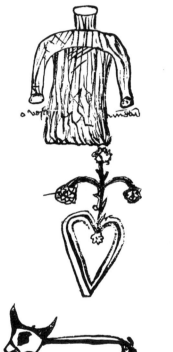

---

[1] *Lineshark. Culigna,* in good
Latin, signified a drinking bowl.
[2] *Pryn,* a woman's smock.
[3] A furred outer-coat.
[4] *Hewd,* the extremity of the
riband hanging from the bishop's
mitre.

13   *A late fifteenth-century pictorial vocabulary*

(*From T. Wright's* Anglo-Saxon and Old English Vocabularies, *edited
R. P. Wülcker, London, 1884*)

two works: *Ein Teutsche Grammatica*[4] and a small book, *Concerning the Quickest Way to Read*, the second edition of which appeared in 1534. His publications were so important in the history of teaching reading, particularly for their influence on English methodology, that they merit fairly substantial treatment.

Something of a fanatic where reading methodology was concerned, Ickelsamer advocated that the secret of quick acquisition of the process lay in the fact that the pupils had to learn to name the letters properly, that is, phonically, rather than depend on mere names which were actually an impediment to easy learning. Then, to emphasize the difference between the name of the letter and the genuine sound required for the same symbol, he investigates the physiological production of the sound. "With those letters which have a strong sound," he says, one "is obliged to open one's mouth as if for a hunting-call." For example, the vowel *a* sound is produced "with the breath just coming through the throat and the mouth wide open," whereas the *o* sound is formed "through the rounded mouth" rather like the sound which brings horses to a stop, and so it might be called "the waggoner's letter." Going on to the sounds of the consonants, he says that the sound of *g* resembles "the sound made by a goose chasing someone so as to bite him," and the letter *r* has a sound like the noise of a dog baring his teeth and growling.

Ickelsamer now demonstrates how one can teach oneself to read by means of this "oral analysis of sounds," the breaking-up of words into their constituent sounds rather than identification of letters, for this must have been the way in which man first learnt to read. Take, for example, the word "Hans." In this word one hears first "a strong breath like someone breathing into his hands, the *h* sound which one breathes onto the *a* sound. After the *a* sound, there comes a nasal sound and finally the sound of a young dove or snake, an *s*. Anyone who can break the word up into its parts [sounds] can say that he has learnt to read by himself, that is, without a book." He urges all schoolmasters to adopt his method and encourages parents at home to use games based on its procedure, with "someone saying a word and asking how many letters it has and with which parts of the mouth these letters are formed."

Not until the pupils can split the words up into their sounds mentally should they be introduced to "the visible symbols, the letters." To help with the recognition he recommends the use of pictures. "One should represent the actual sound of the letters by means of outlines and pictures of animals or other things which might best stand for the voice of the letters." These aids too should be made by the teacher himself. If, for example, the children are to read the word "März," they must first break it up into its sounds: "first the mooing cow *m*, then the goose sound *ä*, thirdly the dog's letter *r*, and finally the sound of the sparrow 'ʒ'."

The teacher should now show the letters to the pupil, together with the illustrations of a cow, a goose, a dog and a sparrow, and the child must find out to which of these drawings the various letters belong. "Eventually he will find the cow with its mooing (*m*), the goose with its cackling (*ä*), the dog with its growling (*r*) and the sparrow with its twittering (ʒ), and so the whole word 'März'. . . Obviously it is necessary that the pictures on such a picture-chart . . . should represent the sounds correctly." He also feels that it is best to confine the use of the picture to the first letter of a word, e.g. *m* with the picture of a monk, *r* with that of a ring, etc. Moreover, "one must exercise care in the choice of pictures. If one uses a stallion (*ross*) for *r*, it could be taken by the child as a horse (*pferd*) or a cart-horse (*gaul*) and he would say *pf* or *g* rather than *r*. Nor must the sounds be uttered disjointedly but always in an even flow from one to the next, "not breaking off in the middle of the word but reading it right through to its end." For this reason it is best to use only short, easy words with the beginner so that he docs not have to keep on turning back.

The controversy about the use of sounds, the how and why of phonics, started by Ickelsamer, is still raging four and a half centuries later, and the devices and arguments used by him are still being bandied around by our contemporary reading experts when they are advocating the virtues of their own phonic schemes or setting out the difficulties of blending. One set of phonic-based primers which have been so popular in our schools since the late fifties must have found generous inspiration in his pioneering work, and another programmed reading kit of the sixties also had Ickelsamer echoes.

Ickelsamer's work was soon imitated. In 1553 it was followed by a book entitled "*Leyenschul.* How one can quickly and skilfully learn to read and write. Together with this instruction how the uneducated person of low intelligence should be taught all that is necessary in the way of reading and writing, without letters but by means of figures and characters. Printed in Mainz."[4]

Petrus Jordan, the printer and probable author, acknowledged explicitly the help he had from Ickelsamer's books. He insisted that "the children should not be taught the names of the letters in their order," as had been the case with "reluctant and lazy school-masters," but that "a beginning should be made with the vowels. In addition, so that those of low intelligence can learn the nature of the letters more easily and quickly and therefore name and pronounce them properly and correctly, I have added to each letter a figure or character to give a sound or description of the letters which will act as a sort of introduction to the naming of the letters. If however anyone is so stupid that he doesn't know or can't name the letters, then by my method he can make his own Abc with the shapes and characters which are easiest for him."

Each of the five vowels is accompanied by a small picture, e.g. the *a* by an *arm-brust* (cross-bow), the *e* by an *ege* (harrow), the *i* by an *igel* (hedgehog), the *o* by an *ochs* (ox) and the *u* by an *uhr* (clock). The consonants are similarly illustrated, e.g. *b* by a *becher* (mug), *c* by a *circkel* (circle), etc. All pictures have been chosen in accordance with Ickelsamer's ideas but Jordan stresses that the teacher would be better employed in "showing his pupils which parts of the mouth are used to form the eighteen consonants." Thus, "to sound a *b*, together with the virtually identical *p*, he suggests that "one should close one's mouth and hold one's breath, so that the cheeks are puffed out. Then one must open the mouth. The *p*, however, is harder than the *b*." To make the *k*, he suggests that its sound is "rather like when one is choking and wants to vomit but cannot do so." Jordan's ideas have also been popularly imitated in contemporary phonic schemes, e.g. "Patterns of Sounds."

Let us now turn to the use of phonics in England, where it will be noted that our forefathers, while naming letters in the alphabetic process, were not unaware of the values of the sounds themselves. For example, despite his subsequent triumphant claim that his pupil was now "able to name the xxv letters." John Hart in *A Method* (see pages 148 ff.), relied on both the pictorial method and the phonic approach to assist him. "The first breath or sound, or both together, of the name figured under each letter is the breath or sound, or both together, of the letter above it, with examples thereafter in divers words. . . . The ease . . . is such that as soon as one is able to name the xxv letters perfectly and readily, wheresoever they may present themselves to his eye, so soon shall he be able to read. This may be in so short a time or shorter than he shall be able to learn to know xxv men, women and children, though he never met them before, and to name them readily and perfectly wheresoever he might meet them."

A Methode.

ſ	*b*	*p*	*d*	*t*
Sheares.	A Ball.	A Peare.	A Drum.	A Trumpet.
g	*ʒ*	*v*	*d*	*2*
A Graſhopper.	A Ierkin.	A Vane.	The Sunne.	Zacheus.
k	*ᴒ*	*f*	*th*	*s*
A Key.	A Chaire.	A Filbert.	A Thimble.	A Squirrell.

¶ Here is to be noted, for that there is not in my remembrance the names of any thing which beginne with the soundes of *d* or *ʒ*. I haue vſurped the article *de*, with the Sunne, for the beſt I could as yet thinke on: and the littlo man Zache, that climed in the wilde figge tree. Luk .xix.

¶ Now you may teach your Scholler, to remember the letters by the names of the portraitures, firſt the fiue vowels, forth and backe, which when he thinketh to know, you may doe the like with the reſt, and when he hath ſo gone o-uer all foorth and backe, then you may ſhew them vnto him downewardes, and vpwardes, and when he thinketh to know the letter alone, you maye doe
B.ij.   well

14   An Elizabethan phonics aid. (*From John Hart's* A Method or
Comfortable Beginning for all Unlearned, *London, 1570*)

Bullokar too brought phonics to bear on his teaching of spelling/reading. He has warned his pupils, he says, "of this turning and that turning, of this block and of that slough. . . . I mean by giving to double and trebled sounded letters, their double and treble names, agreeing to their sounds in words: also what letters were superfluous in some words and where some were misplaced . . . and such like means which did greatly comfort and further them in learning, with more speed and pleasure than any learner could do by any ordinary teaching or as I myself was taught."

There are many references not merely to the pronunciation of words but also to the sounds of letters and the length of sounds in Edmund Coote's *The English Schoolmaster*. For example, the pupil Robert remarks that when he used to be taught by the clerk, Goodman Taylor, he was made "to sound these vowels otherwise than (methinks) you do. . . . I remember he taught me these syllables thus: for 'bad,' 'bed,' 'bid,' 'bod,' 'bud,' I learned to say 'bad' ['bade'?] , 'bid,' 'bide,' 'bode,' 'bude' . . . for these vowels *e, i, u* are very corruptly and ignorantly taught by many unskilful teachers."

John Brinsley too was well aware of the importance of sounds. "First the child is to be taught how to call every letter, pronouncing each of them plainly, fully and distinctly. . . . More especially, be careful for the right pronouncing of the five vowels, in the first place as *a, e, i, o, u*. Because these are first and most natural and do make a perfect sound, so . . . they may be fully pronounced of themselves. They being rightly uttered, all the rest are more plain. After these vowels . . . teach them to pronounce every other letter. . . . But they are at least to be taught to pronounce their letters thus, as they do learn them — to prevent the grief and wearisomeness of teaching them to forget evil customs in pronouncing, which they took up in their first ill teaching."

In view of such statements as these, one must assume that, apart from the niceties of correct speech, phonics were also regarded, however unwittingly or perhaps naïvely to our ears, more frequently than most might now concede.

An interesting sidelight may be mentioned here.

From the evidence of Thomas Morley's *A Plain and Easy Introduction to Practical Music* (1608), the horn-book was at times set to music, e.g.

> Cantus.
> Christ's cross be my speed, in all virtues to proceed,
> A, b, c, d, e, f, g, h, j, k, l, m, n, o, p, q, r, s, etc.
> When you have done, begin again, begin again.

Cantus.

15 *A horn-book set to music. (From Thomas Morley's* A Plain and
Easy Introduction to Practical Music, *London, 1608*)

A similar idea is implied in Brinsley's suggestion: "You must teach
them . . . to call their five vowels and to pronounce them right. . . .
Cause them to repeat them oft over after you, distinctly together
thus: a, e, i, o, u, after the manner of five bells, or as we say: one,
two, three, four, five." This, he believed, was "the easiest, pleasan-
test and shortest way of all, where one would begin in a private
house with little ones playing."

The Quasi-Linguistic Method

Another system described by John Buno in his book, *Newly set-
out ABC and reading book* (1650), offers picturesque variation to
the phonic approach and had probably been used much earlier. At
least, the author acknowledges that the idea of bringing children to
reading through play and of using objects and pictures with the
same shape as the letters had been borrowed from Lubinus.

Buno claimed that, by means of "a variety of devices and clear
examples," he could "simplify reading for ordinary people and
small children." He believed that letters originally were signs or
aids for memorizing definite things, and so he based his method on
it. As evidence, he quoted from the Hebrew alphabet: "Aleph is a
bullock from whose horns the curved lines are perhaps taken, and
his bellowing provides the tone and sound of the letter (see the

133

Phoenician alphabet in "Descent of the English Alphabet," page 5). Beth is a house and closely resembles the oriental houses, which have flat roofs and have an open fore-court. Gimel is a camel and has a long neck and a hump on its back. Lamed is a spit and is shaped just like one. Ain is an eye, which it resembles. Sade is a fork and has two prongs like a fork. Shin is a tooth, looks like a tooth and is also uttered through the teeth. . . . If it is a case that the only purpose of letters is to help us remember things, then the spelling method must be absolutely wrong, for it gives only the names of the things or objects."

He puts forward these principles:

1. Words should not be spelled or learnt at the same time but according to the ease with which they can be said.

2. Pictures should be used to illustrate the form of the letters, and the objects used must have the shape and appearance of the letter itself. Letters on their own, he argues, are sheer monsters for young children, and so illustrations are necessary to help retention. At the same time, the provision of pictures just to remind children of the initial sounds is quite insufficient and, unless the picture reminds the child of the form of the letter itself, it is pointless. For the letter *b*, for example, he suggests the picture of a strawberry printed in such a way as to have a vertical stalk on the left and the berry lower down on the right, so reminding the child of the letter *b* by its shape. Incidentally, this is a reminder of the modern practice of using the letters *b/d* as the head and tail of the bed to help children suffering from reversal difficulties.

3. The pictures must be explained by means of suitable, coherent stories. For this purpose he used "The Merry Tale of the Stupid Servant Hans," who, though wanting to learn to read, was unable to learn his letters. One day he happened to go into the kitchen where he saw the cook kill an eel which had just curled into the shape of an *a* (*aal*), Hans learnt the letter immediately. Alongside the letter *a* then, the teacher should place the picture of an eel of the same shape, and the story should act as a further reminder of its sound. While Hans was still in the kitchen, a donkey suddenly barged in and brayed *i–a*. This made him think that the donkey also wanted to study, and he was quite put out that even the donkey knew two letters. So he grabbed the donkey by his long ears to drag him out of the kitchen but in his excessive enthusiasm he pulled the donkey's ear off. As Hans looked at it in dismay, it occurred to him that the ear was not unlike the letter *e*, so he drew the letter *e* next to the ear and learnt it. So the tale continued, *i*

being illustrated by a girl standing up straight with a garland of flowers on her head and the letter *u* by an owl, etc.

Buno's device of using a story to illustrate the sounds of the different letters was widely adopted in England later. The well-known nineteenth-century "Synthetic Sounds" system of Rebecca Pollard employed the theme story of a boy named Johnny who went around discovering the sounds of the alphabet in Nature. Another favourite contemporary "Colour Story" method exploits the adventures of a Mr Nen and his friends for the same purpose.

The shape-of-the-letter approach became particularly popular in Germany in the seventeenth century, and various schemes of that sort were put on the market. One approach outlined in *The Delights of Philosophy and Mathematics,* published in Nuremberg in 1653, suggested parallels between shapes of the letters and common objects or animals, e.g. an *a* like an eel, a *w* like a worm and *g* like one's intestines.

Although Quintilian (see page 69) had stressed the importance of the actual shapes of the letters, such a shape-of-the-letter approach does not seem to have made an impact in England till well beyond the period under study. The first reference to its use in the teaching of English reading occurs in Richard Lloyd's *The Schoolmaster's Auxiliaries* (1653). As it might illustrate the type of alphabetical/sound example that could have been used by earlier works within this period, it is worthy of some quotation.

To help the children recognize the shapes of the letters more easily, Lloyd suggested these resemblances:

a the half heart
b the new moon stuck at the bottom of a stake
d the old moon
h the back of a chair
o the ring or full moon
v the little bell turned up
z the tack

To help with the sounds, he told his pupils to remember them as

a A	the deaf man's answer
b B	that does make honey
f F	the lawyer's reward
g Gagogu	the gander's call
Gheegegi	the carter's charge
ph Phy	a note of dislike and loathing
z Zee	the noise of hot iron in water

In recent years this device of using a picture alphabet, in which each letter is represented as an object beginning with the sound of that letter, has again become popular, and several have used it for the teaching of both adult illiterates[5] and young children.[6] One scheme, for instance, using the parts of objects to represent the shapes of capitals and small forms of letters, has the head of an axe to show capital *A*, the wing of a butterfly for capital *B*, the handle of a cup for capital *C* etc.[7]

The Reading–Writing Method

In his *Leyenschul* Petrus Jordan had also advised that "as soon as the pupils know and can say the five vowels, they should at once be taught to copy and write them." This approach was more fully developed later by Wolfgang Ratichius (1571–1635). He suggested that the child should begin reading by tracing, with red chalk, the letters which had been previously written on the board by his teacher and as he copied them, he should say them aloud. Later these same red letters should be re-formed into simple syllables. While this was an extension of the Quintilian method and was the precursor of the modern Reading–Writing approach, it is also the first recorded use of colour in teaching reading.

Vives would have lent his support to such a method, when he wrote: "It is a very useful practice to write down what we want to remember, for it is no less impressed on the mind than on the paper by the pen, and indeed the attention is kept fixed longer by the fact we are writing it down. Thus the time taken in writing helps the idea to stick in the mind."[8]

Yet, though writing schools were flourishing in England at this time, the English educationists were not convinced of the need to introduce writing at the same time as reading. In 1590 Peter Bales had already written his *Writing Schoolmaster*, and he himself had won a £20 gold pen in a writing contest. In 1618 Martin Billingsley had written *The Pen's Excellency or the Secretary's Delight* and by 1660 Cocker had produced some ten books on the art, including *England's Penman* and *Youth's Directions to Write without a Teacher*. But these masters of writing belonged to a different family from that of the reading teachers, in fact a group so lucrative that one practitioner about 1680 was earning more than £800 per annum from it.

Bullokar, Mulcaster and Kempe were all agreed about the need to write well but it was considered as a subsequent rather than a concomitant art with learning to read. John Hart, 1570, advised that children should "first learn to read before they should learn to write, for that is far more ready and easy." In 1582 Mulcaster gave his view that "next to reading follows writing at some reasonable distance after, because it requires some strength in the hand, which is not so steady and firm for writing as the tongue is stirring and ready for reading." By the 1587 edition of *The Petty School* Clement had added a section on the art of writing but again it followed that of reading. John Brinsley summarized the general pattern of the acquisition of basic skills thus: "This is a thing worth the diligence of all, who must be employed among little ones: to wit, to teach children how to read well and to pronounce their letters truly: as also to spell right and to know how to write true orthography."

Although the ancients had used writing to reinforce the skill of reading (see pages 68 ff.), clearly its use had not yet been accepted as a fundamental or even functional part of the teaching of reading in England.

Gimmickry in Teaching Reading

All sorts of tricks and devices were being used to help the alphabetic method along, some of them occasionally having the smack of programmed learning about them.

Brinsley in his *Ludus Literarius* suggested these tricks to "help them to spell. Let as many as are beginners or who cannot read perfectly stand together and then pose [i.e. put questions to] them without book, one by one. First, in syllables of two letters, as they are set down in their ABC and, where one misses, let his next fellow tell. If he cannot, then let some other. . . . Whatever syllable they miss, mark it with a dent with the nail or a prick with a pen or the like. When you have marked out those wherein they so much miss, pose them over oft, not forgetting due praise to them that do best."

Charles Hoole's *A New Discovery of the Old Art of Teaching School* (1660) was particularly fertile in ideas which must have been common practice in teaching reading even a century earlier:

"The greatest trouble at the first entrance of children is to teach them to know their letters from one another, when they see them in the book all together. . . . Some have therefore begun but with one single letter and, after they have shown it to the child in the alphabet, have made him . . . find the same anywhere else in the book till he knew them perfectly. Then they have gone through the rest.

"Some have contrived a piece of ivory with twenty-four flats or squares, on every one of which was engraved a several letter and, by playing with the child in throwing this upon a table and showing him only the letter which lay uppermost, have in a few days taught him the whole alphabet.

"Some have got twenty-four pieces of ivory cut in the shape of dice, with a letter engraved upon each of them. With these they have played at vacant hours with the child, till he has known them all distinctly. . . . Now, this kind of letter sport may be profitably permitted among young beginners in a school and, instead of ivory, they may have bits of wood or small shreds of paper or paste-board or parchment with a letter written upon each to play withal among themselves.

"Some may have pictures in a little book or upon a scroll of paper wrapped upon two sticks within a box of ising-glass, and by each picture have made three sorts of that letter, with which its name begins. But these, being too many at once for a child to take notice of, have proved not so useful as was intended. Some likewise have had pictures and letters printed . . . on the back . . . of a pack of cards, to entice children, that naturally love that sport, to the love of learning their book.

"Some have written a letter in great character upon a card or chalked it out upon a trencher and, by telling a child what it was and letting him strive to make the like, have imprinted it quickly upon his memory.

"One, having a son of two years that could but go . . . about the house and [was only able to utter] some few gibberish words in a broken manner . . . became very desirous to make experiment what that child might presently attain to in point of learning. Thereupon he devised a little wheel, with all the capital Roman letters made upon a paper to wrap round about it. [This] had a hole so made in the side of it that only one letter might be seen to peep out at once. This he brought to the child and showed him only the letter O and told him what it was. The child, being overjoyed with his new gambol, catches the ball out of his father's hand and runs with it to his playfellow, a year younger than himself, and in his broken language tells him there was an O, an O. . . . When the other asked him where, he said, 'In a hole, in a hole,' and showed it him. Which the lesser child then took such notice of, as to know it again ever after from all the other letters. . . . Thus, by playing with the box

. . . the child learnt all the letters of the alphabet in eleven days."

Sir Hugh Plat in his *Jewel House of Art and Nature* (1635) also mentioned "A ready way for children to learn their A.B.C." The teacher should "cause four large dice of bone or wood to be made, and upon every square one of the small letters of the cross row to be graven, but in some bigger shape, and the child [getting used to

A ready way for children to learn their A.B.C.

CAuſe 4 large dice of bone or wood to be made, and upon every ſquare, one of the ſmal letters of the croſs row to be graven, but in ſome bigger ſhape, and the child uſing to play much with them,

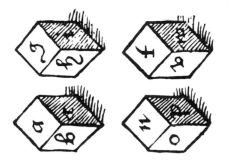

and being alwayes told what letter chanceth, will ſoon gain his Alphabet, as it were by the way of ſport or paſtime. I have heard of a pair of cards, whereon moſt of the principall Grammer rules have been printed, and the School-Maſter hath found good ſport thereat with his ſchollers.

16 *Learning the ABC with dice.* (*From Sir Hugh Plat's* Jewel House of Art and Nature, *London, 1653*)

playing] much with them, and being always told what letter chances, will soon gain his alphabet, as it were by the way of sport or pastime."

According to a German historian, Kehr,[9] the English used to organize archery contests in which whoever happened to hit, and then name, a particular letter was awarded a cherry or some similar prize for his skill as a bowman and as a reader.

The Use of English instead of Latin

Today we might underestimate the place and extent of Latin in
the life and business of this country in the Middle Ages. Though
the English peasant conducted the affairs of his everyday life in
his own vernacular, he could not escape being exposed to Latin.
Every man had to attend church, and every man from childhood
had to participate in prayers and religious formulae, join in the
singing of the psalms and often listen to sermons, all in Latin.
According to Giraldus Cambrensis, when Archbishop Baldwin was
journeying through Wales c. 1200, he found he was best understood
when he was using Latin as his preaching medium. Towards the
end of the fourteenth century John Gower, the friend of Chaucer,
was still writing his works at various times in three languages,
English, French and Latin.

Latin remained the language of international communication
throughout the whole of this period. It was the inescapable language
qualification for entry to schools of advanced learning and universities, and it was also the recording medium for most merchants,
accountants and lawyers, with tallies, charters, wills, agreements
and other documents being drawn up in it. Right into the sixteenth
century traders and shopkeepers kept their accounts in it, and most
of the entries in the *Day Book of John Dorne* (1520), a sort of
catalogue of books of the period, were written in Latin.

But for centuries after the Conquest English had to contend with
another linguistic rival, French, which had been brought here by
the invaders. Over two hundred years later (c. 1297) Robert of
Gloucester in his *Chronicle* (II. lines 7537 ff.) reported that the
Normans of England were speaking "nothing but their own language, that is, French, just as if they were at home, and they also
taught their own children. The high-born who came of their blood
kept wholly to the same language that they had taken with them,
for unless a man knew French, people thought little of him." Only
forty years later a statute decreed that "all lords, barons, knights
and honourable men of good towns should be careful and diligent
to teach and instruct their children in the French tongue."[10] In
1350, according to John of Trevisa, "children in schools, against
the usage and manner of all other nations, be compelled . . . to
leave their own language and . . . to construe things in French.
Also, gentlemen's children be taught to speak French from the
time that they be rocked in their cradle."[11]

Despite the administrative, ecclesiastical and academic odds against it, English had not been submerged and the same Robert of Gloucester had been forced to add that "the lowly-born still clung to their language of English and their way of speech." From early in the fourteenth century the English were growing much more conscious of the potential and scope of their native tongue, and the authorities were beginning to recognize the language for official purposes. From 1360 literary works in English were appearing more frequently, and the second half of that century was dominated by the works of Geoffrey Chaucer. "The poet's own works register the greatest modern fact of all, the birth and general acceptance of our language, the Saxon and French works happily blended at last into 'English tongue,' which 'all understanden' and which is therefore coming into use as the vehicle of school teaching and of legal proceedings."[12] 1362 was a memorable year for English. In that year the Lord Chancellor first opened Parliament in English, and a statute was passed making English, instead of French, the language of pleading in the law courts. To cap it all, again according to John of Trevisa, "in the year of our Lord a thousand three hundred four score and five . . . in all the grammar schools of England, children leave French and construe and learn in English."

From now on reading in the vernacular was more and more widely practised by the ordinary folk but English was by no means firmly established and was far from being accepted as the ideal vehicle for educated men. The language had not yet settled down and it was still a veritable thicket of dialects. An incident narrated by Caxton in his Prologue to the fifteenth-century version of the *Aeneid* demonstrates the linguistic confusion. "That common English . . . spoken in one shire varies from another so much that in my days [it] happened that certain merchants were in a ship in [the] Thames, [intending to sail] over the sea into Seeland. For lack of wind they tarried at the Foreland [i.e. Kent] and went to land . . . to refresh them[selves]. One of them named Sheffield, a mercer, came to a house and asked for meat and especially . . . 'eggys.' The good wife answered that she could speak no French. The merchant was angry, for he also could speak no French but would have 'eggs' and she understood him not. Then at last another said that he would have 'eyren.' Then the good wife said that she understood him well."

Even so the influence of the Lutheran movement abroad, the demand for their own English Bible and the recognition that their own language was no mean linguistic tool but one that was well able to satisfy their needs, all such factors were causing educated Englishmen to revise their opinion about its use both in church and school. Abroad the most influential of educational thinkers, Vives, had urged that every teacher should know the mother tongue of his boys so exactly that "through the vernacular he might render his instructions both easier and more pleasant for them."

This was the frame of mind in which several English educationists were beginning to examine the exciting developments both in education and in the teaching of reading in Tudor times. Yet, with all their enthusiasm, the weapons in favour of a universal vernacular literacy could not change the position overnight, and Latin was strongly entrenched as the most desirable language medium. English, it is true, was being used in the petty schools but it had not yet attained an unimpeachable position of respectability. The attitude of the grammar-school masters was rather like that of Edward I, who addressed Parliament in French but preferred to resort to the native English when he wanted to relieve himself by swearing. John Palsgrave, a chaplain to Henry VIII, in his dedication to *The Comedy of Acolastus* (1541), placed his finger firmly on the linguistic pulse when he declared frankly that schoolmasters were "not able to express in their vulgar tongue . . . perfectly to show the diversities of phrases between our tongue and Latin." Ascham too in his dedication to the *Toxophilus* (1545), confessed that though he was writing "this English matter in the English tongue for Englishmen," it would have been "more easy and fit for my trade in study "to have written it in Latin and Greek.

The next half century witnessed a dramatic change in the attitude of the educated towards the use of English. In 1570 Roger Ascham published *The Schoolmaster* in English without tendering any apology for his choice of medium. Its title-page stated his object quite clearly: "The Schoolmaster or plain and perfect way of teaching children to understand, write and speak the Latin tongue but specially purposed for the private bringing up of youth in gentlemen's and noblemen's houses." The chief objective, however, was unequivocally stated — the ultimate better acquisition of Latin. As late as 1653 Richard Lloyd was equally candid in his views. His purpose was to teach children to "read and write English dexterously," so that they might assert "the Latin tongue in prose and verse to its just enlargement, splendour and elegance." Charles Hoole adopted a patronizing attitude. "For this learning to read English perfectly I allow two or three years' time, so that at seven or eight years of age a child may begin Latin."

Which language then should be taught first, Latin or English? Like many others, Richard Mulcaster had made up his mind about this problem. "Whether English or Latin should first be learned, hitherto there may seem to have been reasonable doubt, although the nature of the two tongues ought to decide the matter. . . . While our religion was expressed only in Latin, the single rule of learning was to learn that language, as tending to the knowledge valued by the Church. But now that we have returned to our English tongue, as being proper to the soil and to the faith, this restraint is removed." We should learn "to read first that which we speak first, to take most care over that which we use most, and [to begin] our studies where we have the best chance of good progress owing to the natural familiarity with our ordinary language, as spoken by those around us in the affairs of everyday life." Latin, he considered, "had been purified to a definite form in which it has been fixed and preserved."[13] On the other hand, English possessed certain difficulties which were not present in Latin, and these could be best mastered by the children before their minds were cluttered up with the impediments of other learning

Mulcaster was no mean figure in the struggle for the recognition of English as the language of teaching and learning in England. The fact that he had to deal, as Headmaster of Merchant Taylors' and later St Paul's, with parents and friends who were "no Latinists" might have had something to do with his attitude. In the *Elementary*, which "treats chiefly of the right writing of our English tongue," he briefly summed up his personal position with these now-famous words: "I love Rome, but London better . . . I honour the Latin, but I worship the English."

His book, *Elementary*, probably more than any other, prodded others to spare more thought for the status of English at the primary level of education and prompted them to write books on the teaching of reading, and in English. Kempe, Clement, Coote and Brinsley were in no doubt about the position and value of English. The most convincing evidence of all about the victory of English over Latin at the primary level lies in the very absence of evidence. That is, from the last quarter of the sixteenth century when things were stirring in the world of pedagogy, not a single book on the teaching of Latin in the petty school, written in Latin, has come down to us. English was the pre-eminent queen of the petty-school realm.

As to whether English had yet won the esteem of the grammar school masters and others was another question. The upper classes were not easily convinced, and James Cleland in his *Institution of a Young Noble* (1607) observed that "others [i.e. parents] are so conceited that they have caused their sons to be brought up only in speaking of Latin with their tutor, as we learn English and, for that cause, have suffered none to speak any other thing but Latin in their hearing." All well and good at that stage but "when they come to man's estate," they must "go to school to learn their mother tongue."

Mulcaster, in his observations about the priority of English over Latin for initial instruction, had pinpointed one real difficulty where the vernacular was concerned. "English," he wrote, "though it is progressing very fairly, is still wanting in refinement, the spelling being harder." This is what some people had been wanting to reform long before and have been eager to modify long since.

Spelling Reform and the Teaching of Reading

Although in the English of the days of King Alfred there might have been a close relationship between its spelling and contemporary pronunciation, much had happened in the intervening centuries to lend weight to Mulcaster's strictures.

Changes are inevitable in, and are natural to, any language and, apart from the vicissitudes of vocabulary deterioration and expansion, the alphabet itself had changed from Anglo-Saxon times. Their two forms for our *th*, though clearly defined as ð and þ, were being used indiscriminately in mediaeval times. Sometimes yet another form, *y*, was being employed for þ, its relic being still found in "ye olde shoppe." Other letters, such as *k*, *q*, and *z* had been adopted, the letter *j* was blithely taking the place of an *i*, and the letter *v* was being interchanged with the *f* of "olive"/"olife" or the more normal *u*, as in "universal"/"vniversal."

The situation was further aggravated by the introduction of printing. At a vital stage when an agreed uniformity of representation of sounds and letters was urgently desirable, there was neither reliable precedent nor contemporary practice that could be employed. There were few, if any, printers in England, and so they had to recruit from foreign parts, like Germany, the Netherlands and France, skilled men, whose own command of English utterance was often alien and frequently misleading. These foreign printers could not rely on the example of current or former scribes, for they too were distinguished for their remarkable inconsistency. Where the spelling of the simplest English words was concerned, absolute licence was their principal rule, e.g. fredom, freedome, fredome, fredom: betwene, betweene, between. The name of the great Caxton himself was variously entered in the records of the Mercers' Company as Cacston, Cawston, Cauxton, Caston, Causton, Catston and Kaxum. In these circumstances further damage to English spelling was unavoidable. No sooner had these printers tried to fix the spelling than the various changes brought into train by what has been called "the great vowel shift" caused more linguistic ravage. By the Elizabethan period the desired correspondence between symbol and sound had degenerated to such an extent that John Hart (1570) dismissed it as "such confusion and disorder . . . as may be accounted rather a kind of ciphering or . . . a dark kind of writing."

The first recorded instance of a spelling reformer in English, however unconscious he might have been of such a label, was the Augustinian monk, Orm. About the year 1200 he composed a 10,000-line poem, now called the *Ormulum*, in which he used his own private system of orthography to ensure greater uniformity. For example, he doubled the consonant after every short vowel and he used three separate symbols for the various sounds of *g*, e.g. hard *g* in "goddspelle"; breathed *g* in "maʒ"; and the double *gg* (*dzh* sound) in "seggen."

For centuries after Orm little attention seems to have been paid to the inconsistencies of English spelling but in the sixteenth century, with a wider reading audience and the more popular use of English as the medium of instruction, even sharper criticism was levelled at the eccentricities of the vernacular, For example, as soon as reading teachers began to incline to the use of phonic methods, their enthusiasm was quickly doused by the nature of the linguistic code they were required to use.

So commenced a succession of books on spelling reform. One of the first was a Latin book entitled *Concerning the Correct and Amended Spelling of the English Language*, a dialogue between the Elizabethan courtier, Sir Thomas Smith, and a young man called Quintas, published in 1568. Smith proposed the "Alphabeticum Anglicum," consisting of thirty-four letters, which could be further extended by the use of accents and other signs. For instance, the varying values of the letter *a* were represented by ɑ, â, ä and ɑ–. Some new consonantal symbols were also added to the traditional code, e.g. soft *th* was represented by the Saxon ð, the hard *th* by the Greek θ or the Saxon þ, the soft *g* by the Saxon ʒ and the soft *c* by *s*.

Paierʒ of letterʒ.   Aa:Bb:C'c':Cc: ᴁʒh:Do: Eeæ: E'e': Ff: GȝIȝg: Gg:Hh:Iȝip:Kk: Ll: Ɫ:Mm:ıñ: Nn: ń: Do: ω:Pp: Ƥhꝑf: Qq: Krʒ:.ꞃ: Sſʒ:Hh: Tt: Thth:Thth: Uʋʋ: Uꝑ ꝗꝍꝙꝟ:U'ʋu:Ww: Hh:Xr: Pꝝ:Zʒ. ad tω thæʒ, ꞓ.

rrʋiij.cõsonantʒ with theiʒ paierʒ.   Of the rl. letterʒ befóʒ hewed, rrʋiij. of them, and their paierʒ ár caɫed consonantʒ, thich ár thæʒ: b. c'.c.ch.d.f.g.g.h.k.l.m.n. p.ꝑh.q.ꞃ.ſ.h.t.th.th.ʋ.w.th.r.ꝝ.ʒ.

ʋiij.ʋoꞏwoelʒ.   Other,ʋiij. a.e.e'.i.o.ω. ʋ.ꝑ. ár caɫed ʋoꞏwelʒ,with their paierʒ.

iij.haɫf ʋoꞏwelʒ.   Other,iij. Ɫ.m̃. ń. ár caɫed haɫf ʋoꞏwelʒ: ad tω thæʒ:ꞃ: and sounded aʒ this ſillabɫ: er; and so námed aɫſo.

ꞃ.thærꝑntω aded.   Thæʒ ʋoꞏwelʒ: a. e. i. p. o. ꝑ. u. ꝗ. ꝙ. ꝍ: ár aɫway of hoʒt sound: ercept: a.e.i. be dobɫd thus: aa.ee.ip.pi: oʒ that ón of thæʒ accent pointʒ:´:¨:ꞈ: be sett oúer:a:e:p:o: foʒ then be thæʒ of longer sound,wʒytñ thus: á:â:ã: and so of the reɫf, foʒ help in eqiuocꝟ.

ʋoꞏwelʒ of hoʒt sound,ercept,ꞓc.   I caɫ the firɫt, á:a, with accent: the second,â:a,with dobɫ accent: the third,ã: a, with foʒked accent: and so of other ʋoꞏwelʒ ſo nóted, bicauʒ it may help much in eqiuocꝟ.

The námʒ of thæʒ accentʒ.   And thæʒ,e'.ω.b.u. ár aɫway of long sound,ad tω thæʒ,æ, and aɫso the haɫf ʋoꞏwelʒ,Ɫ.m̃.ń.ꞃ. ár of longer sound,then anꝝ ʋoꞏwel of hoʒt sound.

ʋoꞏwelʒ of long sound.   When tωo ʋoꞏwelʒ(oʒ haɫf ʋoꞏwelʒ)com tωgether in ón ſillabɫ,they ár caɫed a diphthong, thær-of thér be ín number,ʋij.ai.ay.ei.eu.oi. ow.ωꝝ: ading hær-ꝑntω: ui: seɫdom in ʋe'.

ʋij.diphthongʒ.   So ading thæʒ seuñ mirt soundʒ (caɫed diphthongʒ) befóʒ wʒytñ, thér ár in engliſh speꞓh,rliiij. seueraɫ soundʒ in ʋoiꞓ, ꝝnder thωın aɫ engliſh woʒdʒ and ſillabɫʒ ár soundçd and spókñ: ading hær-ꝑntω

rliiij diuiʒionʒ in ʋoiꞓ, foʒ engliſh speꞓh.   the rár diphthong: uꝝ.

Thæʒ diphthongʒ hau paierʒ in sound, and thér be aɫso other diphthongʒ, but they hau the sound of ón of the ʋoꞏwelʒ befóʒ said, aɫ thich haɫ be wʒytñ tωgether in sqárʒ nert bnder: but foʒ the tým in aɫ thæʒ, nót that euerꝝ diphthong iʒ of aʒ long tým oʒ longer, then anꝝ long ʋoꞏwel: ad hær-ꝑntω that haɫf ʋoꞏwelʒ maꝝ mák a diphthong after,a,oʒ o,ꞏ ár paierʒ tω the ſillabɫ'ʒ in their sqárʒ folowing.

And hær-in iʒ tω be nóted,that foʒ lærñoʒʒ,thér iʒ ꞓ haɫ be a Pamphlct impʒinted, conteining bʒeflꝝ the effect of this book,seruing aɫso foʒ conferenꞓ with the old oʒtograꝑhꝝ hér-after.

                       Diph

---

17   *A page showing the proposed alphabet. (From William Bullokar's* Book at Large for the Amendment of Orthography for English Speech, *London, 1580)*

This was followed in 1569 by *An Orthography containing the due order and reason, how to write or paint the image of man's voice, most like to the life or nature. Composed by I. H. Chester Heralt*, that is, John Hart, whom we have frequently met already. It was, Hart claimed, rather like the action of a painter who, invited to depict a person's body, used all sorts of biographical detail to denote physical marks or inserted such items as double eyebrows or put ears in the place of his eyes. This had happened with language, one letter having been falsified for another "because the painters of this country for time out of mind have used the like."

In 1580 William Bullokar, a schoolmaster, published *Bullokar's book at large for the Amendment of Orthography for English Speech*. Quoting the irrelevance of the *o* in "people" and the *b* in "doubt" by way of example, he judged that from our spelling "grew quarrels in the teacher and loathesómeness in the learner." "In English speech," he wrote, "are more distinctions and divisions in voice than these four and twenty letters can generally signify." To improve its condition he proposed certain consonantal combinations of his own devising, a system of marks, strikes and accents which are now called diacritics, and some ligatures such as œ and ω, both of which have counterparts in our contemporary Initial Teaching Alphabet. In addition he produced in 1585 in his own orthography the Psalter, *Aesopz Fablz in tru Ortŏgraphy with Grammar-notz. Her-untoo ɋr also jooined the short sentencez of the wýz Cato . . . transláted out-of Latin in-too English,* and *Most Easy Instructions for Reading, specially penned for the good of those who are come to years.*

Though Mulcaster was perturbed about the state of English spelling, he also conceded that the "soundest people" thought our language was "in most well appointed, though in particular to be helped." Only reasonable modifications were needed, he thought, to overcome the deficiencies. We should "use all our four and twenty letters, seeing the characters being known be more familiar and easier to be discerned than any new device." To assist the letters in their functions, he recommended the introduction of accents indicating length and quality.

There were many others in the field of spelling reform in the seventeenth century: Alexander Gill's *Linguae Anglicae Logonomia* (1621); Charles Butler's *The English Grammar or the Institution of Letters, Syllables and Words in the English Tongue* (1634); Simon Daines' *Orthoepia Anglicana* (1640); and Richard Hodges' *The English Primrose* (1644). As these lie slightly outside our period and add little to the picture of spelling reform, a closer scrutiny of them would be unnecessary. Instead, more detailed consideration must be given to one specific Elizabethan work, because it combined advocacy of both spelling reform and a particular method of teaching children to read. This was John Hart's *A Method or comfortable beginning for all unlearned whereby they may be taught to read* (1570).

After listing several examples to demonstrate how "we have been taught to misname our letters to the hindrance of all those willing to learn," John Hart makes the usual claim about the efficacy of his teaching method. By using his system he had learnt Welsh "from a Welshman's mouth," though Hart had not understood a single word of the language itself. Moreover, when he proceeded to read a passage in Welsh back to a group of Welshmen, he did it so well that a complete stranger assured the others that Hart "could speak Welsh as well as he. But the rest, knowing the contrary, laughingly told Hart what the stranger had said." Though his system could be used most effectively with non-readers, he had purposely written it as a "treatise for the learned sort to consider [and] prove what they would like or mislike" of it. But, sad to say, "few have thought it their labour to read" it and fewer still have really gone deeply into it. Again, it has been argued that "no private man or any one profession of men [can suddenly] change a people's manner of writing any more than of their speaking" but there is little doubt, according to Hart, that it had actually happened several times in the previous centuries. If only he could convince people of the certainty of success from its use, the logical order underlying its structure and the sound commonsense behind its adoption, he was sure that it would soon be used everywhere. The whole secret of its success lay in the simple principle that "the effect of writing consists not in the letter, but . . . what is meant by that letter."

The continued reliance on traditional spelling, he argued, was rather like a nurse teaching a child to balance first on stilts or on a rope or on his hands in the belief that any ability he might acquire in that particular art would guarantee him greater surety of foot in later life. All that people needed to do was to adopt his system of spelling, and then even "the desirous Welsh and Irish [would be much advanced] to the true pronunciation of our [English] speech, which was never before this time presented to them."

Some potential users of his method, he realized, might delay adopting it because they were afraid that it had not been sanctioned by authority. They could rest assured that it was authorized, as "all books in the former manner [i.e. traditional orthography] might also be printed in this manner." Hart also had his eye on the most profitable corner of the Elizabethan book-market, when he forecast that if "the Psalter, with the order of morning and evening prayer, and the New Testament [were allowed to be printed in it, there would be] many a thousand well disposed creatures in England [who] would be most glad to learn it."

He was equally ingenious in the way in which he advocated the propagation of his new alphabetic system. "If the figures with their letters were drawn on the walls, pillars and posts of churches, towns and houses, they might much help and further the ignorant of letters to attain to read." In this way "parents and patrons should be able to teach their family and nurses their children, [just as well as they had taught them] to walk and speak. And some [in a house] may be able to teach it to all the rest of the house, even while their hands may be otherwise well occupied in working for their living or otherwise being idle or sitting by the fire, without any further let or cost."

To use the Hart system, the teacher had first to refer to the alphabet (see pages 130 ff.) where the initial sound of the object shown in each picture represented the first letter of the word printed below and the single letter above it. These words were to be pronounced in the same way as they would be at Court or in London "where the general flower of all English country speeches are chosen and used," for "to these two places do daily resort from all towns and countries . . . the best of all professions, as well of the landsmen as of aliens and strangers." In this Hart was anticipating the use of a Standard English or Received Pronunciation, as we now know it, and so may have been the first to nominate in print the capital as the source of the best speech.

The pupil must learn the letters "by the names of the portraitures, first the vowels forth and back" and then "downwards and upwards." When the pupil thought he knew the letter in isolation, the teacher was expected to cover the drawing of the letter with paper or his finger to make him pay more attention "to the shapes of the letters." As a further aid Hart also added marks to letters. For example, "the prick which I write under every vowel as *ạ* is worth *aa:* *ẹ* is *ee* etc. In teaching the letter or naming it you must sound no more of the portraiture . . . than the very sound of the letter. Of 'apple' *ạ*, of 'ear' *ẹ* . . . and of 'woodcock' *u̯* and so on of the rest." For a word like "lion," you should "not name the *l*,

m, n or *r*, as you have been taught, calling them el, em, en, er.
[You should] give them the same sound [which you would] find in
their portraitures without sounding any vowel before them, as in
'l—ion,' 'm—oul.' [These consonants] ought not to have the name
stayed with any of them, for that is to the learner's hindrance. It is
as reasonable to name the consonant by the help of any one or
other vowel." How often the impurity of consonantal sounds has
been uttered in contemporary conferences and methodology books
on reading as if it were a recent discovery!

Other rules follow.

i. The vowels should be set out in this order:

a   e
   i
o   u

and practised in various sequences such as:

a e i o u
e u o a i
i a u e o
o e a i u
u i e o a

ii. These six consonants should be similarly arranged:

l   m
   h ʃ
   n   r

and practised also in various sequences:

l r ʃ m h n
m h l n ʃ r
n ʃ m r l h etc.

iii. The diphthongs must now be introduced:

ae ai ao au
ea ei eo eu
ia ie io iu
oa oe oi ou etc.

iv. These eleven letters must now be put in tabular form and said
perfectly in every way

a l r o e m u i n ʃ h
e m h u i n l o r a ʃ
i n ʃ l o r m u h e a etc.

Whenever an error is committed, the learners should refer again
to the drawings to see if they can identify their own mistakes.
"If not readily, it is best to help them to lose no time."

v. Practice must be done with the syllables, set out in this order:

$$\left.\begin{matrix}a\\e\\i\\o\\u\end{matrix}\right\}\left\{\begin{matrix}h,\ h\\\int\ \int\\l,\ l\\m,\ m\\n,\ n\\r,\ r\end{matrix}\right\}\left\{\begin{matrix}a\\e\\i\\o\\u\end{matrix}\right\}\left\{\begin{matrix}r\\n\\m\\l\\\int\\h\end{matrix}\right\}\left\{\begin{matrix}a\\e\\i\\o\\u\end{matrix}\right.$$

Letters should be taken from two or more groups so as to form
words, e.g. an, ann, anna, arm, en-ne-mi, etc. The learner must also
"read the syllables [forwards well] yet, for his better exercise,
though it signify nothing, let him also name every letter backwards. . . .

"Now I will give you examples of divers words and sentences
which may be written with the eleven letters [so] that your scholar
may be comforted with them until he has learned the rest hereafter. [These] are for his encouragement to be able to read:

"oh mein ōun lam, hou ar iu? o mein ōun man, mei mār ran
ruʃ-ʃin meī hīl on a naul, and lē mi in a mei-ër. Hēr mi, uil iu hiēl
mei hīl? . . . and so on till the pupil can read: 'In God's name,
as follows: In ðe nām ov ðe fāðr and ov ðe sun, and ov ðe hol-li
gōst, so bī it, ðe lords prēr, bi-līf, and ten kom-maund-ments. Our
fāðr huitʃ art in hēvn, hal-lu-ëd bī ðei nām. ðei king-dum kum. ðei
uil bī dun in ērþ, az it iz in hēvn. Giv-uz ðiz-dē our dē-li bred.
And for-giv-uz our tres-pas-ses, az uī for-giv ðem ðat tres-pas
a-gēnst us. And lēd uz not in-tu tem-tā-si-on. But de-livr-us from
ivl. So bī it.'"

Before concluding this chapter it would assuredly be salutary
for any contemporary teacher of reading to pause awhile and re-
examine the catalogue of progressive principles which were already
being practised in England and Germany by the early part of the
seventeenth century. These significant items would include: the
use of graded and familiar vocabulary in a realistic setting; the
reinforcement of pictorial illustrations; the variety of the Look-
and-Say and Sentence approaches; the emergence of phonics as a
viable teaching method; the quasi-linguistic systems of the shape-
of-the-letter and the patterns of sounds in a coherent story; the
regularization of spelling codes; and a hint of the use of colour. Nor
can the Elizabethan reappraisal of the principle of reading readiness
be disregarded. All in all, an impressive list. One also realizes that
apart from our modern tape-recorders, electric typewriters and

electronic language-masters, very little of a totally new character has been introduced into the teaching of reading since then. As one commentator has aptly put it, much of what has been hailed as new in basic methods is reheated cabbage trying to pass itself off as freshly cooked fish.

Now that the young child of early England has progressed through his well-defined programme of horn-book, catechism, primers and books of courtesy and has mastered the mechanics of reading, one would imagine that he would next graduate to a reading of the Bible. We must now consider the special position of that work in the educational prospectus for the apprentice and adult reader.

Rewards for the Successful Learner

7 Competence in Reading as a Means of Salvation

The Vernacular Bible: to Save One's Soul

From the earliest days the Christian Fathers had urged their flock to read the Bible. St John Chrysostom (347–407), the Archbishop of Constantinople, who was famous both for his preaching and writings, in his homily "On Lazarus" had advised: "It is for this reason that we frequently acquaint you of the topic of our discourse a few days ahead so that, by taking up your Bible in the meantime and going over the whole passage, your minds will be better prepared to hear what is to be uttered. I have always urged you to do this and I shall keep on pressing you to do so — not only that you should listen here to our sermon but that you should give of your time at home to reading the Holy Scriptures."

Despite this counsel there is little evidence that the practice was continued, if it was ever taken up, in England, by the native masses in these early centuries. Apart from the lack of reading skill on the part of the people, there was also the very real impediment of Latin. Parts of the Bible, it is true, had been translated into English by Bede (see page 26) and Caedmon, but there was no complete version of the Bible in English and available to the masses till the fourteenth century. Some monasteries had copies of the gospels in the vernacular as early as 1100 but these were probably intended for internal use or personal solace rather than for external encouragement. Royal personages too might have possessed their own copies. In consequence, however surprising it might seem, there was very little reading of the Bible by the ordinary people.

Various reasons have been suggested to explain this absence of a vernacular version of the whole Bible, especially at a time when other works in the vernacular were becoming more freely available (see Chapter 8). Whereas Latin was the native language of the readers in the days of the Christian Fathers, it was a foreign language when it came to be read by the peoples of Northern Europe. In time Latin had come to be regarded as a sort of holy speech, a unique language that was almost divinely appropriate and necessary to express the word of God. From the point of view of the priests, the loss of intelligibility on the part of the people merely served to enhance their own clerical value as interpretative media. That the priests themselves might not understand or read Latin was of less significance.

Over the centuries yet another reason for the retention of the Bible in the Latin language had arisen, and this was stated quite plainly, for example, in a letter from Pope Gregory VII (1073–85) to a king of Bohemia: "It has pleased Almighty God that Holy Scripture should be a secret in certain places, lest if it were plainly apparent to all men, perchance it would be little esteemed and both subject to disrespect; or it might be falsely understood by those of mediocre learning and lead to error."[1] This line of argument was to be hotly pursued later.

In the second half of the twelfth century, for example, a heretical Christian sect in the south of France, called the Waldenses after the name of their leader, Peter Waldo of Lyons, had been responsible for the translation of the New Testament into their native Provençal. Not only had rigorous persecution followed but the Synod of Toulouse (1229) narrowly defined the viewpoint of the ecclesiastical authorities. Lay people would not be allowed to have books of the Old or New Testament in their vulgar tongue, though they might be permitted for the sake of devotion to have a psalter or a breviary for divine office or the *Horae Beatae*. In Aragon in Spain too in 1233 James I ordered all copies of the Testaments in the Romance language to be burnt and the owner, lay or cleric, to be held suspect of heresy. As similar bans were being imposed in other countries in the Middle Ages, one can conclude that, through the fear that an inability to understand properly might lead to heresy or deviation from the official teachings of the Church, a similar attitude to versions in English was held by the ecclesiastical authorities in this country. Indeed it had become a matter of keen controversy as to whether it was lawful or otherwise to translate the Bible into English, as the discussion between the Lord and the Clerk in the preface to John of Trevisa's version of the *Polychronicon* (1387) shows.

It would seem that the authorities were more concerned about the dangerous effects on the ordinary folk rather than on the clergy or the upper classes. A complete French version of the Bible was available in French as early as 1361, while several versions of the psalter had already appeared in the same language. The result of this official attitude was that acquaintance with the Bible on the part of the masses was possible only through Latin or French, and no English version was available for general lay circulation or school instruction. Although books were owned by lay people before the days of Wycliffe, not a single reference has been found to a private person owning a complete copy of the Bible in English in that period. Nor can any record be quoted of any urging by the authorities in England that the people should take to the reading of their Bible. It has been suggested that the illiterate masses learnt about the Bible instead through attendance at Church services, watching religious plays and gazing at the coloured scenes in the windows of their churches. This was to change.

By the fourteenth century an increasing number of religious or liturgical books in English were becoming available for the layman. For example, about 1300, the *Lay Folk's Mass-Book*, which had been originally composed in French *c*.1180, explaining the Creed and outlining the conduct of behaviour, was rendered into English. About 1340 the *Ayenbit of Inwit* ("The Remorse of Conscience"), a prose translation from the French, containing the Ten Commandments, the Creed and the Lord's Prayer, was issued in English, while the preface of the *Memoriale Credentum* declared frankly that it had been composed deliberately in English for men who could not understand Latin. These books were designed as easy guides, as it were, to the basic principles and prayers of the Christian religion.

More daring steps were to follow. About 1370 Walter Hilton in his *Epistle on Mixed Life* openly recommended that people who were able to read the Gospels for themselves should proceed to do so. A few years later John Purvey, a faithful Oxford friend of John Wycliffe, in his series of twelve Gospels in English (1382—95), went straight to the point. While some "good clerks and well lettered men" could read the sacred books in Hebrew, Greek or Latin, there were others who "could read but little or nought understand." Books in their mother tongue should be provided for these people, books in French for the French, in Italian for the Italians and in English for the English, "in which book they may read to know God and his Law."[2] "No one," exhorted Wycliffe, "was so poor a scholar that he is unable to learn the words of the Gospel." All men of simple wit should be stirred to read God's law. A version of the Bible in the vernacular would be one way of encouraging people to understand the holy word for themselves and so help rid the Church of abuses that were defiling her name.

The first version of this so-called Wycliffe or Lollard Bible was issued in 1382 and was followed by another in 1388. It was like a spark setting fire to the dry African bush. "You could not," it was said, "meet two persons on the highway without one of them being Wycliff's desciple." From then on references to people possessing copies of Biblical works occurred regularly. In 1394 a chantry priest at York left "a book of Gospels in English," in 1397 the Duke of Gloucester bequeathed another and in 1404 John Blount, a Bristol burgess, also left a book of Gospels in English.

So widespread had the habit of reading the Bible in English become that official steps were taken to combat it. In 1401 Henry IV's Parliament passed the Statute de Haeretico Comburendo, whereby heretics refusing to abjure were to be handed over to the secular authorities and publicly burned. It directed that "none from henceforth should preach, teach, hold or instruct anything, openly or privily, or make or write any book contrary to the Catholic faith or determination of the Holy Church . . . and that all and singular having such books or any writings of such wicked doctrine and opinions shall really, with effect, deliver or cause to be delivered all such books and writings to the diocesan of the same place within forty days."[3] The Oxford Synod of Clergy (1407) decreed that in future no one should translate any text of the Holy Scriptures into English "by way of book, booklet or treatise" without Church authority and no one could read any such book, booklet or treatise "now lately composed." Any translation of the Bible had first to be approved by the bishop. In 1426–7 the Abbot of St Albans had even ordained at a synod that everyone should do their utmost to remove any books in the vernacular from the homes of people who were known to possess them.

But people went on reading the Bible, and people went on being punished. In 1415 John Claydon was declared a Lollard because he admitted owning English books, including the *Lantern of Light*,[4] and in 1429 John Baker was convicted of having a book with the Lord's Prayer and other prayers in English.[5] A few years later John

Baron of Lincoln came under suspicion for having "certain books," one on the life of Our Lady, another about Adam and Eve, a book of the *Canterbury Tales* and a book of plays about St Dionysus.[6] As late as 1514, when Richard Hunne was imprisoned and hanged, one of his crimes was listed as the possession of "divers books prohibit[ed] and damned by the law, as the Bible in English."

Meanwhile a more favourable climate was arising on the Continent. Helped immeasurably by the invention of printing, more Bibles were being produced and eighteen editions of the Bible in the German vernacular were published between 1466 and 1522. No less a scholar than Erasmus had declared in the preface to the 1516 and 1522 editions of his New Testament in Greek that he dissented from those who were unwilling for the Scriptures to be read in their native tongue. It was, he maintained, as if Christ had wanted his works to be understood only by theologians or as if the strength of Christianity lay in men's ignorance of it.

Amid the spread of Lutheranism such matters did not pass unnoticed in England (see page 102). In 1526 William Tyndale, who had been forced to move to Germany to pursue his project of translating the Scriptures into the vernacular, despatched copies of his New Testament in English to London, where they were sold at two shillings to four shillings each. "It was," wrote the historian Froude in a colourful description, "seen how copies were carried over secretly to London and circulated in thousands by Christian Brothers. The council threatened; the bishops anathematized. They opened subscriptions to buy up the hated and dreaded volumes. They burnt them publicly in St Paul's. The whip, the goal, the stake did their worst; and their worst was nothing. The high dignitaries of the earth were fighting against Heaven and met the success which ever attends such contests. Three editions were sold before 1530,"[7] and as many as thirty editions were sold before the end of Edward VI's reign. This in itself was proof sufficient of the enthusiasm to procure the Bible in English and also of the size of the reading audience in England fairly early in the sixteenth century. In *An Abridgement of the Statutes* (1527) Sir Thomas Rastell commented in general terms that "the universal people of this realm had greater pleasure and gave themselves greatly to the reading of the vulgar English tongue." Only a few years later Sir Thomas More in his *Apology* estimated the number of readers at more than half the population, that is, some 2½ millions of an estimated 4—5 millions.

Though the fear of heresy still persisted, the plaintive utterances of the Church leaders also emphasized the hopelessness of the war of official religion against increasing mass literacy. In 1530, for example, Bishop Nix of Norwich complained that he was "encumbered with such as keep and read these erroneous books in English." and Bishop Stokesley of London (see page 28) marvelled what his Lord of Canterbury meant by giving the people "liberty to read the Scriptures, which does nothing else but infect them with heresy." In the same year Henry VIII issued a proclamation condemning "erroneous books and heresies and prohibiting the having of Holy Scripture translations in the vulgar tongue."

Then the official attitude changed. Henry VIII decided to have a Bible rendered into English and he directed the preparation of an appropriate version without delay. In 1533 Archbishop Thomas Cranmer, appointed to Canterbury, had a resolution for such a translation approved by a convocation of bishops, and in 1535 Miles Coverdale's own folio version of the Bible, with a dedication to the monarch himself, was published. Thus the vernacular book which had been scorned for centuries as the tool of the agitator received royal approval.

It is said that as the initial copy was being severely criticized by sundry people, Henry VIII ordered several bishops to submit it to rigorous examination. When he asked them for their report, the bishops informed him that they were hesitant about recommending it for universal usage, as they had found many faults in it.

" 'But,' asked the King, did you find any heresies in it?'

" 'None,' they replied.

" 'Then in the name of God,' directed Henry, 'let it go abroad among my people."

In 1538 Thomas Cromwell, who had been the principal figure behind the dissolution of the monasteries, issued the famous royal injunctions to Archbishop Cranmer: "You shall provide on this side of the feast of Easter next coming one book of the whole Bible of the largest volume, in English, and the same set up in some convenient place within the said church . . . where your parishioners may most commodiously resort to the same and read it. . . . You shall discourage no man privily or apertly [i.e. openly] from the reading or hearing of the said Bible but shall expressly provoke, stir and exhort every person to read the same."[8]

In 1539 appeared Cranmer's "Great Bible," a recension of the 1535 version, and another was issued in 1540 "appointed by the commandment of our most redoubted Prince and sovereign Lord, King Henry VIII." A Royal Proclamation (1541) instructed this "Bible of the largest and greatest volume to be had in every

Church." Further, it was to be sold unbound for ten shillings a copy but "for every one of the said Bibles well and sufficiently bound, trimmed and clasped, not above twelve shillings."

A contemporary account of an incident involving William Maldon vividly illustrates the inspiration it provided for the people. When Henry "had allowed the Bible to be set forth to be read in all churches, immediately several poor men in the town of Chelmsford in Essex, where his father lived and where he was born, bought the New Testament and on Sundays sat reading it in the lower end of the Church. Many would flock about them to hear the reading and he, among the rest, being but fifteen years old, came every Sunday to hear the glad and sweet tidings of the Gospel. But his father, observing it once, angrily fetched him away and would have him say the Latin Matins with him, which grieved him much. And, as he returned at other times to hear the Scripture read, his father still would fetch him away. This put him upon the thoughts of learning to read English so that he might read the New Testament himself. Which, when he had by diligence effected, he and his father's apprentice bought the New Testament, joining their stocks together, and, to conceal it, laid it under the bed-straw and read it at convenient times."[9]

By 1543, for political and religious reasons, Henry felt that the pendulum had swung too far, and the Act for the Advancement of True Religion was passed. This again condemned the reading of unorthodox translations of the Bible and forbade the reading of an English Bible by women, artificers, apprentices, journeymen, serving-men of rank, husbandmen and labourers. The higher grades of noblemen, merchants and gentlemen were considered less likely to be infected and were allowed to read it privately but even they were forbidden to read it to others.

Such impediments were but temporary and an intense period of Bible production followed. In 1557 William Whittingham's version of the New Testament in English was issued in Geneva, with his version of the full Bible in 1560. In 1568 the Bishops' Bible was produced at Canterbury, and later in the century an official translation of the New Testament was issued at Rheims and the Old Testament at Douai in 1609, both for the use of Catholics. In 1611 the famous Authorized Version was published.

The fact that over a hundred editions of the Whittingham version were issued by 1605 and some twenty of the Bishops' Bible by 1606 not only illustrates the huge demand for this one book but also the incalculable influence it must have had on the growth of

English literacy. It also helps to explain why the second half of the sixteenth century saw a profusion of reading teachers, the struggle about the teaching of the petties, the compilation of so many books on the pedagogy of reading and the emergence of new methods of introducing the child to the printed word. As further testimony to its popularity, all sorts of manuals, giving guidance or instruction in the reading of the Bible, were being published, e.g. *A method or brief instruction for the reading of the Old and New Testaments* (1590) and John Waymouth's *A plain and easy table, whereby any man may be directed how to read over the whole Bible in a year. First framed for the use of a private family and now made public for the benefit of God*. The author declared that he had been "earnestly entreated by divers well affected gentlemen (some of no small note) to publish it for the common good" (see page 115). In fact, all the book did was to list the various portions of the Bible to be read throughout the year, e.g.

January

1	Genesis	i	ii	Matthew	i
2		iii	iv		ii
3		v	vi		vi, etc.

The desire for spiritual solace was not, however, the single motivating force behind this mass movement towards literacy. Many people also wanted to learn to read, and to read parts of the Bible, so that they could enjoy *privilegium clericale* or "benefit of clergy."

Ability to Read the Bible: to Save One's Neck

In straightforward terms, benefit of clergy was the principle or means whereby an ordained priest could gain exemption from trial or punishment by lay people or in a lay court. Once a man could prove his undoubted clerical status, then he could be tried and punished, if this was necessary, only by his ecclesiastical brethren in an ecclesiastical court. If he could do this, his salvation in law could on occasion mean the saving of his own life.

The enjoyment of this narrow privilege had grown up only in mediaeval times, for under the Anglo-Saxons the court included both the bishop and ealdormen sitting together, and no nice distinction between lay and spiritual offenders was required. Seeds of trouble had been sown when William the Conqueror separated the joint court into two, civil and ecclesiastical. Naturally, when the Norman kings were still striving to ensure their own absolute powers, they were suspicious of any body that might infringe or threaten to undermine their position. On the other hand, the spiritual or ecclesiastical courts were convinced that they, the representatives of the Church, were the senior partners in the eyes of God and so, if anyone tried to punish clerical offenders in the lay court, the clerical authorities regarded this as an infringement of their rightful spiritual powers.

The struggle between the two courts was finally brought to a head with the assassination of Thomas à Becket in 1170. Shortly afterwards Henry II yielded to the Church courts their persistent claim that they alone could exercise jurisdiction over criminous clerks in either sphere of offence.

For us, where this study of reading is concerned, the interest lies in the evolution of the definition of a *clerus* or clerk. Originally the *clerici* were those who *ad sacros ordines pertinent et eis qui sacris ordinibus promoti sunt*, i.e. who were in Holy Orders, ordained clerks, monks and possibly nuns. Production of the Bishop's authority or letter of ordination usually sufficed as proof of rank. By the reign of Henry III (1216–72) the definition had grown so loose that those who had had the first tonsure, that is, undergone the rite of having part of the hair of the head so cut or shaved as to leave a circular patch on the crown, were included in the clerical ranks. But the tonsure could be achieved by anyone and so the statute *pro clero* officially extended it to embrace other officials assisting in church duties, such as door-keepers or readers. Probably due to pressure of numbers claiming the privilege in court, a more rigorous definition was urgently needed to curb the abuse, and reference to the use of a reading test in the accounts of several trials is first found in the reign of Edward III (1327–77). A thief, Thomas le Blake, for example, was described in Latin as "that scoundrel who is not literate." At the same time another, William of Asshendene, who claimed the clerical privilege, was handed a book to demonstrate his reading prowess but as he could not read his claim was turned down and he was duly hanged.[10]

At first the test was used as a supplementary piece of evidence to support the traditional means of identification but "literacy as proof of clerkship was in time to take precedence of, and in the end to supplant, the other modes of proof. . . . The reading test became the outstanding characteristic of the privilege in the fourteenth and fifteenth centuries."[11] Although it did not apply to offences such as treason directly concerning the king or those involving forest law, it still offered a very desirable avenue of escape to those, other than genuine clerks, who had become entangled with the law in other ways.

The accepted procedure was that the accused could pray or plead clergy either before or after conviction in the civil court to which he had been taken. If his clerkship was proved beyond doubt, the process was routine. If not, then the bishop's official, the ordinary, examined his claim in the court, requesting his letters of ordination and checking if he had committed bigamy. There followed an examination of the claimant's literacy by means of a short reading test in Latin, based on the assumption that, if anyone could read, then he was certainly a clerk. While any passage from the Bible might be chosen at random by the ordinary, like most streamlining processes, the text popularly employed was Verse i of the fifty-first Psalm: "Have mercy upon me, O God, according to thy loving kindness; according unto the multitude of thy tender mercies blot out my transgressions." In time this came to be known as the "neck-verse." If the ordinary was satisfied the accused could read, he pronounced *Legit* (he can read) but if not, then he pronounced *Non legit*. The offender was left to the civil authorities to undergo the processes of law. If he was deemed to be a clerk, he was removed from the jurisdiction of that court and handed over to the church court.

This was the particular area in which the clerical privilege lay, for the punishment usually apportioned here was comparatively mild, either degradation and/or some period of penance or, what might seem harsh at first sight, commission to the bishop's prison. From there the prisoner enjoyed a real chance of escape! When one considers the lawlessness of those days and the prevalence of capital punishment for the most trivial offence, it will be appreciated how important it was to "prove clergy" to escape being hanged. Reading, however superficial, had become an enviable skill.

In consequence more and more tried to claim clergy under shelter of the reading test. For example, one robber, William Pernill, was unable to read and was sentenced to be hanged. Before sentence could be carried out, the ordinary claimed that he had learnt to read. Another, named John, charged with murder *c.* 1366, was examined in his claim to literacy. After he was given a psalter, the ordinary declared that the accused could not *sillibicare*, i.e. break up into syllables, but had learnt the passage by heart. The judges now took it into their own hands to examine his reading skill by giving him the psalter once more but this time with the book turned upside down! John read it exactly as before. It transpired that though he had been illiterate when first brought to the prison, two boys from Appleby had been secreted into the prison by the gaoler to teach him.[12] The extent of the injustice of clerical privilege is also demonstrated in the case of Thomas Gurney, quoted in the *Paston Letters* (1464), who had tried to kill "my lord of Norwich's cousin." Though both were tried and convicted, Thomas Gurney pleaded clergy and was granted mercy as "a clerk convict," while his wretched servant accomplice who was unable to read was hanged.

The actual effect of this privilege on literacy in England cannot be assessed because the test itself was so superficial that even success in it could not be taken as proof of real or strong literacy on the reader's part. Gabel,[10] after scrutinizing gaol records for the reigns of the first three Edwards (1272–1377), found civil occupations mentioned in only twenty-five instances of the 1,635 criminous clerks involved. After 1377 she found frequent references to the occupational status of such clerks, including those of butcher, cooper, labourer and *vacabund* (vagabond), and all were able to read. The Rolls too from Richard II onwards (1377 ff.), showed the occupations of mercer, servant, tailor, spicer, fishmonger, mason and labourer as possessing the necessary skill. The *Paston Letters*, in the account of the litigation involving the will of Sir John Fastolf in 1466, also reveal that of the twenty witnesses called six were literate, and these included husbandmen and a tailor. A Book of Depositions of the Consistory Court of London (1467–76), providing facts about various court witnesses, reveals that half the witnesses were literate. Many, of course, might have taken the priest's test and then stayed in their occupation but still holding the clerical privilege for possible hazardous times ahead.

Though the privilege continued for several centuries, further changes were effected in the reign of Henry VII, when a preamble to a measure of 1489 recognized the abuse to which the privilege was being put. Through it "divers persons lettered have been the more bold to commit murder, rape, robbery, theft and all other mischievous deeds, because they have been continually admitted to the benefice of clergy." To improve things the statute attempted to distinguish between those who were in Holy Orders and those who were not. Benefit was allowed only once to offenders but thereafter it was confined only to those who were actually in Holy Orders. Offenders who were not in Holy Orders were also to be branded. The necessity for the reading test, however, was not finally abolished till 1705 in the reign of Queen Anne.

Let us now consider the availability of books for the general reader in this period and look in particular at the nature of some of the supplementary books that might have appealed to the taste of the young reader for further practice or as a leisure pursuit.

8 Supplementary Books for Leisure Reading

Availability of Books for the Prospective Reader

Evidence for the existence of books in Britain from the time of the Roman departure (*c.* 410) till the middle of the seventh century is sparse. An eleventh-century tradition claims that while some workmen were excavating at St Albans, they unearthed a hoard of rolls and books which dated from the fifth century.[1] Another Gaulish tradition of the sixth century maintains that at the time of the attacks of the barbarians learned men fled with their manuscripts to Britain and Ireland.[2] If one reads the work *De Excidio et Conquestu Britanniae*, by the British historian, Gildas (*c.* 545), one is soon aware of the broad literary and historical knowledge that he must have derived from "the large mass of volumes" he was supposed to have owned.[3] Apart from such scraps as these almost nothing is known of the book situation in these early centuries, and the statement of Ammianus Marcellinus in his *Historia* (xiv) that "the libraries were shut for ever like tombs" would seem to be true of Britain.

The Celtic and Roman missionaries had probably compensated for this deficiency by carrying with them their own supply of religious works not only for the urgent task of Christianization but also for their personal comfort. St Patrick certainly had his own supply and made others for his converts (see page 16). We also read that once, when he was returning from Rome, he gave six young clerics a hide of seal- or cow-skin to make a wallet for the books they were carrying "at their girdles." On another occasion the Saint's own books fell into the River Suir and were "drowned." This must have been a bitter loss to him, for they had probably been given him by Pope Celestine (422—32), when he first set out for Ireland.[4] In his *Life of St Columba* too the biographer Adamnan (624—704) tells us that Columba used to carry his books around with him in a watertight bag. St Augustine also brought his own library of books with him to England. It has long been a popular pastime for scholars to argue about their identity but they are usually considered to have included a Bible, the apocryphal *Lives of the Saints* and various commentaries which had been given him by Pope Gregory.

The rare value of such religious books is colourfully illustrated in the story of St Finnian (497—579) and the well-born abbot and missionary, St Columba (521—97). The story goes that Finnian had once returned from one of his visits to Rome with a copy of the complete Bible that had been translated and corrected by St Jerome himself. As it was so valuable, he guarded it very closely and so, when Columba asked Finnian's permission to make a copy of it, Finnian refused lest his treasure of "pure red gold" might be damaged or lost. Secretly Columba began making a copy of it but he was caught in the act in his cell by Finnian. Finnian demanded the return of both the original and the copy but Columba claimed that the copy was his personal property. The disagreement was referred to arbitration by King Diarmaid. The king ruled that "the calf goes with the cow, and the son-book or copy should go with the mother-book or original." This so incensed Columba that when another wrong occurred, he and all his kinsmen flew to arms to avenge the insults. A bloody battle was fought at Cull-Dreimhe, where the forces of King Diarmaid were overwhelmed. The book became the property of the victors.[5]

As time went on, we find an increasing number of references to the owning of books and, in particular, to the accumulation of books for library and educational purposes. In 669 Theodore of Tarsus, who had come to fill the see of Canterbury, brought with him "a noble library" of some half dozen volumes including "a splendid Homer," and only two years later Aldhelm hints at a number of books being available at the school in Canterbury.[6] Benedict Biscop, who had founded Bede's own monastery at Wearmouth (674), was also pre-eminent as a library-builder. He made five journeys to Rome for books[7] and, according to Bede, he was constantly bringing back "many books on all sorts of subjects on divine learning, which had either been bought at a price or had been given him as gifts by his friends."[8] Others too joined in this work of accumulation. Ceolfrid, the seventh-century Abbot of Wearmouth and Jarrow, brought back with him from Rome not merely the Codex Grandior of Cassiodorus, from which he had three copies of the Vulgate made, but also Italian scribes to help the monastery develop and extend its own copying of books. Bede provides a list of forty-five works of which he himself was the author, and the content of his writings which have come down to us indicates a personal knowledge of a wide variety of books, including the Bible, the Fathers, the histories of Pliny the Younger, Josephus and Orosius, and the scientific work of Isidore of Seville. All these must have been available in the Wearmouth library. By 712 too the Archbishop of York had also established at his school in York a library which enjoyed the greatest fame till unhappily it was burnt down in 1069.

A brisk exchange of books began to flourish between the Continent and England, one of the foremost figures being the Englishman, Boniface, who had been appointed to a German archbishopric and who was endeavouring to set up various monastic libraries throughout his see. His *Letters*[9] frequently show him pestering his friends in England for books. For instance, in 725 he took a copy of the *Passions of the Martyrs* as a gift to Rome from Eadburga, the English Abbess of Thanet. One letter thanks the same lady for "the gifts of sacred books" and asks her for a copy of the Epistles of St Paul, another asks Nothelm, the Archbishop of Canterbury, for some works of St Augustine and another begs Egbert of York to send him more works of Bede. Lullus, the Bishop of Mainz who had been educated at Malmesbury and who died in 786, followed Boniface's practice of seeking books from England and approached Cuthbert of Wearmouth for works of Bede.[10] One writer believes that the drain of English libraries on continental sources, the reverse process to that of Boniface and Lullus, was so great around this time that "it was becoming increasingly difficult to find in the libraries of Western Europe books which the Anglo-Saxons did not already have."[11] This is borne out by the fact that Charlemagne had sent scribes to York at the instigation of Alcuin to copy books which were then lacking in his own country. No wonder Alfred recalled in his preface to the *Pastoral Care* that in former times "the churches throughout all England were standing full of precious things and books."

Though great damage was suffered by these libraries and churches in the terrible years of the Danish upheaval, the foundations had been laid. The fashion of owning one's personal library had also begun, Leofric, the Bishop of Exeter, who died in 1072 and who bequeathed the now-famous "Exeter Book," a collection of Old English poems, to Exeter Cathedral, being the most distinguished owner. About 1077 Abbot Paul left twenty-eight of his personal books to the monastery at St Albans, and Henry of Winchester (*c.* 1150) left some fifty to Glastonbury. According to William of Malmesbury, who died *c.* 1143, old and wonderful books were still plentiful in his days, and by 1200 several monasteries boasted libraries of some size — Rochester had 300 and Durham 400. It was being commonly accepted that "a cloister without books is like a fortress without an arsenal." All in all, it may well be that we have underestimated the number of books that were available to the readers of this country by the middle of the fifteenth century. For instance, more books were written between 1400 and 1450 in this country than in any previous century.

As a further indication of the improving book situation one might turn to one of the more flamboyant figures of the literary world of the fourteenth century, Richard de Bury or Richard Angervyle. He was a bishop who was "mightily carried away" with a passion for book-collecting but whose usual means of acquiring his treasures were so unscrupulous as to leave a sour taste in the mouth of the modern reader of his *Philobiblon*. So successful had he been in his looting and scrounging that visitors to his palace had the greatest difficulty in getting past the volumes that were crammed everywhere. Once obtained, de Bury took special care of them, even directing students how to open and shut them and cautioning readers not to mark them with their finger nails or scribble alphabets in the margin. He complains, for instance, about "some stiff-necked youth sluggishly seating himself to study and, while the frost is sharp in the winter time, his nose, all watery with the biting cold, begins to drip."[12] He is most severe on children: "Let no crying child admire the pictures in the capital letters, lest he defile the parchment with his wet hand, for he touches instantly whatever he sees. . . . Again, a becoming cleanness of hand would add much both to books and scholars, if it were not that the itch and pimples are marks of the clergy."

In addition to the habit of collecting books, that of borrowing books and not returning them had also started. Henry V was one of the most eminent people who had developed this irritating practice. After his death several people, including the Countess of

Westmorland and the Prior of Christchurch, had to request the return of volumes borrowed. The Vatican Library also suffered in this respect, and Pope Sixtus IV (1471—84) issued a bill against "certain ecclesiastical and secular persons, having no fear of God," who had borrowed sundry volumes in theology and other faculties . . . from the library." Unless the volumes were returned within forty days, the offenders would be excommunicated.

They were also being stolen, and the strictest measures had to be taken against potential biblioklepts, for, with the books being so scarce and costly, hardly any keen reader could be above suspicion. For example, in 1130 the great scholar, Peter of Blois, while on business in Paris for the King of England, chanced upon a set of books on jurisprudence, which he decided to buy for his nephew. He gave the bookseller the necessary cash and left the books with him, while he went to finish some other business. Meanwhile the Provost of Saxeburgh, entering the shop, was filled with an overwhelming desire to own the set and being told they had already been sold, he offered a much larger sum for them. When he still could not get his way, he stole them.[13]

Where the mediaeval monasteries were concerned, the loss of books was a serious matter and they had to take meticulous care of their treasures. Most of them had an armarian, who apart from superintending the scribes issued the parchment, catalogued all the books, cared for them, stored them properly and administered a lending scheme. As early as 1212 the Council of Paris had forbidden monks to give an oath, often requested in some monasteries, that they would not lend their books to the poor. Instead, the books were arranged in two groups: those for the use of monks alone and those for "lending to the poor." In England the care of books was so rigorous that a book was rarely lent even to another monastery without a large bond or deposit as security.

The loss of books continued. Sometimes the owner of a book wrote a terrifying anathema on the inside cover of the book, and one twelfth-century Bible had these fearsome words inscribed on the cover to scare off thieves or jog the memory of tardy borrowers: "The Book of St Mary and St Nicholas in Arrinstein. If anyone steals it, let him die the death, be boiled in a cauldron, let epilepsy and fever come upon him, let him be broken on the wheel and be hanged. Amen."[14]

Later more obvious means were devised against the book-thief and books were kept "locked in a box" or in "a glass-covered case, also locked," or "chained in public places for the vulgar to read."

In 1481, when a book was bequeathed to the Convent at Halesowen, the directive was given that it had to be "laid and bound with an iron chain in some convenient part within the said church, at my cost, so that all priests and others may see and read it when it pleases them."[15]

Although the technical production of books does not directly concern this study, a few general points might be helpfully mentioned. Early in the sixth century Cassiodorus had established in his monastery at Vivarium in Italy a scriptorium for the copying of old works and the creation of new literature. His example had been eagerly imitated by most monasteries of the West. This book production for many centuries was in the hands of the regular clergy, monks were allocated and trained for the specific purposes of transcribing and copying (see page 19) and so they also directly controlled the output and the type of work to be issued. It was, wrote Alcuin in his *On Orthography*, "a noble task to transcribe holy books, nor shall that scribe fail to have the reward that will be awaiting him for his work. The writing of books is superior to the cultivating of vines, for the man who tends a vine is taking care of his own belly, whereas he who writes a book is serving his own soul."

Not everyone regarded the work as highly as Alcuin, and one chronicler, Richard of Cirencester, wrote centuries later that "the negligence and inattention of our ancestors in omitting to collect and preserve such documents [were] not deserving of censure, for scarcely any but those in holy orders employed themselves in writing books, and such even esteemed it inconsistent with their sacred office to engage in such profane labours."[16]

Nor must we forget the rigorous working and climatic conditions under which the scribes often toiled in their monasteries in the north. When Lullus, for instance, begged for copies of Bede's works to be sent to him, Cuthbert, the Abbot of Wearmouth, in reply asked for a little patience because "this winter the frost in our island has been so severe, with such terrible winds, that the fingers of our transcribers have been unable to do any more books." Heartrending too are the lines that a monk of St Gall once inserted on the corner of one of his manuscripts: "The one who us unable to write thinks this is no hard work but, while three fingers do the writing, the whole body is full of toil." Or the words of the mediaeval monk, Louis of Wissobrunn: "Good readers who may use this work, do not, I pray you, forget the one who did the copying. It was a poor brother named Louis, who while he transcribed this volume, was brought from a foreign country, endured the cold and was obliged to finish in the night what he was not able to write by daylight."[17]

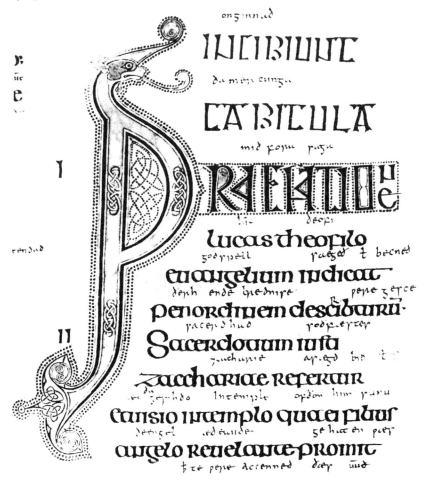

18   *A passage from the Lindisfarne Gospels, written by Bishop Eadfrid*
      (early eighth century)
      (From E. G. Millar's The Lindisfarne Gospels, 1923)
      (By permission of the Trustees of the British Museum)

Yet, however painful the process of production and however costly the books might have been, exquisite beauty was often the result of their devoted worksmanship. Bede, for example, tells us in his *Ecclesiastical History* (IV. 29) that Wilfred, the Bishop of

York, ordered a copy of the four Gospels "in the purest golden letters set on purple illuminated parchment." Boniface too in his letter to Eadburga asked her to send him a copy of St Paul's Epistles in letters of gold, so that his neophytes might be filled with greater reverence for the Scriptures.[9] The failure of ageing eyesight was not forgotten. In 742—6 Boniface wrote to Bishop Daniel of Winchester, requesting him to send the Book of the Prophets, "which the Abbot Winbert, my master, left at his death. It is written in large and very distinct letters. I could have no greater consolation in my old age, for there is no book like it in this country and, as my sight grows weak, I cannot distinguish the small letters which run together in the volumes I now have."[18]

With the increasing demand for books, professional scribes were being employed to help, or in place of, the devoted monk. This had been permitted by the Westminster Consuetudinary (1266) but the professionalizing process had been in operation in the St Albans monastery two hundred years earlier. "In the days of Abbot Paul (1077—93) one warlike noble gave over tithes to help in the making of books for the Abbey; for he was himself a man of letters, a keen listener to and lover of the Scriptures. Other tithes in Redbourne were also added to this work and the Abbot decreed that some daily allowances should be allocated to the scribes from the charities of the brethren and of the cellarers . . . so that the scribes should not be hindered in their work."[19] Such arrangements as these must have accelerated tremendously the production of books. Further, such scribal work continued to be executed so competently that the art of book production in England was one of real excellence as early as the fourteenth century. All sorts of books, liturgies, religious and devotional manuals, grammar and rhetoric books, and patristic works were turned out in numbers.

Let us now look more closely at some of the books that the young readers themselves might have been attracted to peruse without the promptings of ecclesiastical sanction as had been found necessary with respect to the Catechism, the Primer, etc., of Chapter 5.

Books Suitable for Children or Apprentice Readers

The traditional curriculum pattern of the classicals, the Liberal Arts (see page 40), presented the early Christians with a complex, and often disquieting, problem, as the masses of pagan material of classical origin were entirely unsuitable for their religious purposes. In the eyes of the early Christians most of these writings were degrading in spirit, and the practices they exhorted were obnoxious to Christian morality. These pagan writers, wrote Lactantius (*c.* 240 −320), "destroy our lives," while Augustine contemptuously dismissed them on another occasion as "croaking frogs."

At first, then, they were frankly antagonistic to such works. "Refrain," ordered the authoritative voice of the Church of this period, "from all the writings of the heathen, for what hast thou to do with strange discourses, laws or false prophets, which in truth turn aside from the faith those that are weak in understanding? For if thou wilt explore history, thou hast the Books of the Kings; or seekest thou for words of wisdom and eloquence, thou hast the Prophets, Job and the Book of Proverbs, wherein thou shalt find a more perfect knowledge of all eloquence and wisdom."[20]

The Christian teacher and scholar found themselves in a dilemma. If, suggested Tertullian (*c.* 160−220), they used the pagan writers, then they themselves would be accused of accepting the beliefs and ways of life of the heathen. St Jerome himself, who had once been a pupil of Donatus, the famous grammarian, in Rome and who had therefore been immersed in classical learning, vividly illustrates his personal quandary in his "Letter to Eustochium."

"Very many years ago," he wrote, "for the sake of the kingdom of heaven, I had cut myself off from my home and my parents. . . . Despite the fact that I was on my way to Jerusalem, intending to conduct myself as if I was on a military campaign, I just could not give up the library, which I had amassed for myself with such great care and labour in Rome. In my uncertainty, I used to fast so that I could later read Cicero; and, after frequent night-vigils and floods of tears, induced by the memory of my past sins, my hands used to grasp Plautus; but, when I had recovered my mental equilibrium and started reading the Prophets again. I discovered that I was put off by their uncouth style. . . .

"Towards the middle of Lent, however, it happened that my exhausted body fell victim to a virulent fever [which] so wasted my unhappy frame that I was no more than skin and bones. As a result, preparations for my funeral were put in hand. Then, as my body was growing cold, my spirit was suddenly caught up and haled before the tribunal of the Great Judge. There issued such exuberance of light . . . that I hurled myself to the ground and dared not raise my gaze. I was interrogated about my identity and I informed Him that I was a Christian.

"'You lie,' he shouted. 'You are not a Christian. You are a Ciceronian, for *where your treasure is, there will your heart be also.*'

"I instantly lost the power of speech and, along with the strokes of the scourging, which he had also ordered for me, I was tortured still more by the fire of my conscience. . . . I began to cry aloud, 'Have mercy on me, O Lord, have mercy on me!' My voice re-echoed to the lashes, till at last those nearby . . . implored the Lord to take pity on my youth . . . and to torture me anew, if I read the works of the Gentiles ever again. In such straits, I myself would have been content to make still stronger promises . . . and so, calling upon His name, I swore 'if ever again I read or even take up a secular book, I have denied You.' As the words of this oath liberated me from my predicament, I returned to the world above. To the amazement of all present, when I opened my eyes, they were so drenched in tears that the reality of my grief convinced even the incredulous. . . . Moreover, I assure you that my shoulders were black and blue and my bruises were paining me long after my dream. From that time onwards I read Divine works with as much enthusiasm as I had previously read the books of men. . . ."

The problem generally was not solved as easily as in St Jerome's own case. The early Christians also realized that the works of classical antiquity remained the unrivalled source of accumulated knowledge and that divine studies were not possible without secular studies. So they had already begun to look around for any reason to justify their employment, however partial. St Augustine of Hippo (354–430), in his work *On Christian Instruction*, argued that the Liberal Arts were necessary for an understanding of the Scriptures but, he went on to add, teachers should use only those parts that did not clash directly with the Christian faith. After all, every sincere Christian knew that truth was truth wherever it might appear and the liberal disciplines also contained many moral truths and precepts concerning the worship of one God

So it was that the monasteries could amass rare treasures of classical authors with no great twinge of conscience; and so it was that gradually the classics and the works of new pagan writers of the early Christian period itself came to be regarded as acceptable sources of knowledge and instruction, together with the Bible and other Christian compilations. *The Consolation of Philosophy* of Boethius (*c*. 481–525) and the *History of the Goths* of Cassiodorus (*c*. 480–575) were to play a substantial part in Christian education, and the encyclopaedic collection of classical and patristic writings, the *Sources* of Isidore of Seville (*c*. 570–636), remained a trusted treasure-house for many centuries.

Naturally, works such as these were hard fare for any youngster on the threshold of reading. Fortunately other more agreeable books were being written by the English themselves both in Latin and, even from the Anglo-Saxon period, in English but it would be rather tiresome to consider them in bulk. Instead, it might be more fitting to review briefly only a few works that would have formed a pleasurable part of the learner's leisure reading and, where necessary, to quote appropriate passages by way of illustration for the modern reader.

Certainly the works of Bede were well known but one book in particular, *About the Nature of Things*, was the sort of book that might well appear in a children's book-corner today. This work offered a wealth of information for the beginner about the formation of the world, the heavens, the stars, the planets, the clouds, the ocean, etc., however quaint some of the entries might now seem to us. For example, Bede believed that "lightning is caused when clouds rub together, just as when flints are struck together," and that disease was caused by dry or hot air and an excess of rain, which infected man through the act of eating or breathing.

His lives of various saints must also have fascinated the young Christian. That of the seventh-century Cuthbert covered most of the events of his life, including an adventure with an eagle, a miracle involving a burning house, and his own retirement to a hermitage Ending dutifully with a prayer, as all traditional lives of the saints did, it was a typical reader that might have been confidently recommended as further reading for any Anglo-Saxon child.

His most important work was the *Ecclesiastical History of the English Nation* (731), which began with an accidennt of the British Isles and then recounted the story of Christianization. Undoubtedly this would have offered rare delight for both young and old, for it dealt with people and events that were still on the lips of their descendants. What person, for example, would not have been thrilled by the stories of the Pope and the Angles, or the poetical stirrings of Caedmon? This extract might remind us of this fine story:

"In the monastery of this abbess," wrote Bede, "there was a certain brother whom God had blessed with a remarkable talent. He had the gift of being able to compose poetry of exceeding melody and simplicity, and in his native English, out of anything that was interpreted to him from the Scriptures. As a result of his poetic renderings, the minds of many were often excited to despise the world around them and aspire to heaven." Bede now describes how Caedmon, for that was his name, discovered his gift for poetry:

"It was usually agreed that to entertain themselves every person present should sing a song in turn. But whenever Caedmon noticed that the musical instrument was approaching his place, he used to arise from the table and slip off home. One evening, just as this was happening, he left the house where the entertainment was being held and he made his way to the stable to look after the horses for the night. As he was settling down to sleep at his normal time, a figure appeared to him and, calling him by name, said, 'Caedmon, sing me something.'

" 'I can't sing,' he muttered. 'That was why I left the festivities and came here. I just can't sing.'

" 'But you are going to sing,' the other insisted.

" 'What shall I sing then?' Caedmon asked.

" 'Sing the Song of Creation.'

"Immediately he began to sing verses in praise of the Almighty . . . and in the morning he approached the steward, his superior, and after telling him all about the gift he had been given, he was taken before the abbess. In the presence of many learned men, he was ordered by her to recount his dream and sing the verses again." (IV. 24 ff.)

King Alfred also made a significant contribution to literature suitable for the apprentice reader, chiefly because his works were in English (see pages 26–7). Apart from his translation of Bede's Latin version of the *Ecclesiastical History*, he produced *The History of the World*, which had been originally written by Orosius in 418. To the account of Orosius Alfred added the personal narrative of two other voyagers, Ohthere and Wulfstan, in the Baltic. What a mine of eye-opening information this must have been! Here is a short extract:

"The Estonians have a custom that when a man dies, his body is left unburnt with his relatives or friends for as long as a month or more. Sometimes kings and men of high rank are not burnt for as long as six months, the length of the period being determined according to their wealth, and their bodies are left in that state in their houses. During the whole of this time there must be drinking and sports right up to the day on which the body is actually burnt.

"The day on which they have agreed to remove his body to the funeral-pile they divide his property, which has been left over after the cost of all the drinking and sports, into five or six shares or perhaps more, according to the amount of property he owned. They put the largest share within a mile of the town and the smallest nearest the town where the deceased used to live. Then all the men who own the fastest horses in the land are assembled about five or six miles from the property and they all have to gallop towards it. Of course, the one with the fastest horse makes for the largest share and so on, each after the other, till all the shares have been claimed. The one who arrives at the property nearest the town is awarded the smallest share. . . . "

He also produced an English version of *The Consolation of Philosophy* of Boethius, and this was used as a standard text-book

† ÐEOS BOC SCEAL TO WIOGORA CEASTRE

19 A passage from King Alfred's translation of Gregory's Pastoral Care *(From W. W. Skeat's* Twelve Facsimiles of Old English Manuscripts *(Oxford, 1892, by permission of the Bodleian Library, Oxford)*

both in schools and universities for many centuries well down the Middle Ages. In it occurred the captivating story of Orpheus and Eurydice, which is worthy of quotation.

"Once upon a time a harper lived in the country of Thrace in the kingdom of Cracas. The harper was so skilled that he had no equal in the art. His name was Orpheus, and the name of his wonderful wife was Eurydice. People used to say that he could play his harp so brilliantly and sweetly that the trees of the forest used to sway, the rocks to tremble and the wild beasts to stand so still that men on horseback could go right up to them without their stirring. It is said that the harper's wife died and her soul was transported to Hell. At this Orpheus grew so sad that he could no

longer stand the company of other men but he betook himself to
the forest or sat on the hills day and night, weeping and so playing
on his harp that the woods trembled, the rivers stood still and the
hart neither shunned the lion nor the hare the hound. Out of sheer
joy for the music no beast felt rage or fear for any other. When it
seemed to Orpheus that nothing in this world could bring him
contentment, he decided to seek out the gods of Hell and try to
win them over by his music and so implore them to return his wife
to him. . . . " Then followed a description of his journey to Hell,
where he played his harp till "the king of Hell's folk cried out, 'Let
us give the good man his wife, for he has won her with his harping.'
But the king of the nether regions bade her not to look back even
once on their journey homewards. If he glanced back, he said, he
would forfeit his wife. . . . Orpheus kept his wife close behind him
all the way till he reached the margin of light and darkness. He had
almost stepped into the light when he took a glance back at his
wife. At once she was lost to him." Then followed the moral.
"These fables teach every one who wishes to flee from the darkness
of Hell and come to the light of the True Goodness not to look
back upon his old sins, so as to want to indulge in them fully as
once he did." Surely this is a story that still fascinates all readers,
both young and old, over a thousand years later.

As the Anglo-Saxon period progressed, so more works, prose and
poetry, in English and Latin, were available. There was *The Physio-
logus*, a description of the panther, the whale and the partridge;
and there were the vernacular *Lives of the Saints* of the tenth-
century Aelfric (see pages 73 ff. and 91), many religious books
including the Gospels and the Psalms, a variety of books on herbs
and medicine, and biographies of the martyrs and Fathers. An
abundance of sermons had also been sparked off by the common
belief that the end of the world was imminent in the year 1000!
There were also importations from abroad that were to be the
forerunners of mediaeval romance, e.g. *Letters of Alexander to
Aristotle from India* and *Wonders of the East,* which dealt with all
sorts of fabulosities, eight-footed animals with Valkyrie eyes,
creatures with fiery breath, two-headed serpents and men with hair
on their heels. Another great favourite was *Apollonius of Tyre,*
which had been translated into English out of a Latin version of
a Greek original. The opening section dealing with the shipwreck
illustrates the character of the direct narrative couched in simple
but vigorous language. Some of the early sentences have been set
out in both the original Anglo-Saxon and a parallel version in

Modern English so as to demonstrate the huge differences between the two languages with a gap of some 900 years between them.

"Apollonius hīe bǣd ealle grētan and on scip āstāh. Midðy-ðe hīe ongunnon ða rōwan, and hīe forðweard wǣron on hiera weg, ða wearð ðǣre sǣ smyltnes āwend fǣringa betweox twām tīdum, and wearð miclu hrēohnes āweaht, swā ðæt sēo sǣ cnysede ða heofonlican tunglu, and ðæt gewealc ðǣra yða hwaðerode mid windum."

"Apollonius bade them all good-bye and went on board ship. When they began to row, and they were advanced on their way, then was the calm of that sea changed suddenly within two hours and a great storm was aroused, so that the sea smote the stars of heaven, and the welter of those waves raged with the winds.

"Moreover, north-easterly winds came and the violent south-westerly wind fought against them and the whole ship broke to pieces in this dreadful storm. Apollonius's companions all perished, and Apollonius alone came in safety to Pentapolis in the land of Cyrene and there came upon the shore. Then he stood naked on the shore and looked at the sea and said, 'O Neptune, god of the sea, despoiler of men and deceiver of the innocent! You are more cruel than King Antioch. You have so persisted in your spite against me that through you the cruel King might all the more easily destroy me, destitute and poor. Where can I go now? Whom can I ask for help? Who will give sustenance to this unknown man?'

"While he was saying these things, he suddenly saw a fisherman approach. He turned and in his dejection uttered these words: 'Have pity on me, an old man, whoever you may be. Have pity on me, naked and shipwrecked. I am not of humble birth. To let you know whom you are pitying — I am Apollonius, prince of Tyre.'

"Then as soon as the fisherman saw the young man lying at his feet, he lifted him up with compassion and took him to his own house and put before him such food as he had to offer. He wanted to show still more kindness, as much as he could. He tore his cloak in two and gave half of it to Apollonius, saying, 'Take what I have to give you and go into the town. You may meet some-one who will pity you. If you do not find anyone to do so, come back here, and my few belongings will be enough for the two of us and you can go fishing with me. Still, I beg you, if with God's help you return to your former dignity, not to forget my poor garments. . . .'"

"So in the greatest church of London . . . all the estates were long before day in the church to pray. When matins and the first mass were done, there was seen in the churchyard against the high altar a great stone four square, like a marble stone. In the midst thereof was an anvil of steel a foot high and therein stuck a fair sword naked at the point, and letters were written in gold about the sword that said thus: 'Whoso pulls out this sword of the stone and anvil is rightwise king born of all England.' Then the people marvelled and told it to the archbishop.

"'I command,' said the archbishop, 'that you keep within the church and pray to God . . . that no man touch the sword till the high mass be all done.'

"When all masses were done, all the lords went to behold the stone and the sword. When they saw the scripture, some — such as would have been king — essayed but none might stir the sword or move it.

"'He is not here,' said the archbishop, 'that shall achieve the sword. Doubt not God will make him known. But this is my counsel . . . that we purvey [i.e. provide] ten knights, men of good fame to keep this sword.'

"So it was ordained. . . .

"When he came to the churchyard, Sir Arthur alighted and tied his horse to the stile. . . . He went to the tent and found no knights there, for they were at the jousting. So he handled the sword by its handles and lightly and fiercely pulled it out of the stone and took his horse and rode away. . . ."

"Chansons de Geste," stories which had originally centred around the exploits of Charlemagne, were also attracting readers of all ages. Large numbers were produced in the eleventh and twelfth centuries but the later appearance of this type of work in English indicated a reading audience with reading tastes similar to those of the French. By 1300 the English too were turning out such favourites as *Sir Tristram*, *King Horn* and *Havelok the Dane*. This last romance had as hero and heroine two young people from different countries who had been cheated of their rights by wicked guardians. Havelok is brought to England where he works in a kitchen and, through his feats of strength, Goldborough is made to marry him. Ultimately they both recover their kingdoms of England and Denmark. Others dealt with Bevis of Hampton, who had been sold to the Saracens but who became King of England after an amazing series of adventures, while the most popular of all told of the exploits of Guy of Warwick. Others were *Merlin and Arthur*,

21   A passage from Havelok the Dane (written before 1300)
(From W. W. Skeat's Twelve Facsimiles of Old English Manuscripts, by permission
of the Bodleian Library, Oxford)

King Alisander, *The Seven Sages of Rome*, *Sir Isumbras* and *Sir Gawain and the Green Knight*. How avidly they were read is evident from the words of this Anglican apologia of 1535: "Englishmen have now in hand, every Church and place, and almost every man, the Holy Bible and the New Testament in their mother tongue instead of the old fabulous and fantastic books of the Round Table, Lancelot du Lac and such order, whose impure filth and vain fabulosity the light of God has abolished utterly."[21]

Another popular type was the *Gesta Romanorum* or *The Tales or Deeds of the Romans*. These were large collections of tales, full of marvel and adventure, which had been derived from a variety of sources including the East. Seemingly intended for the education or recreation of monks, each tale, which had been written in the late thirteenth century by an unknown hand, had a moral or Christian interpretation appended, and this was regarded as being as important as the tale itself. As a children's book it held its appeal down to the eighteenth century. One such tale is entitled "Of an Eternal Recompense."

"A king once prepared a great feast and sent out messengers with invitations in which the guests were promised not only magnificent entertainment but also considerable wealth. When the messengers had gone throughout town and country, executing everywhere the commands of their king, it happened that there dwelt in a certain city two men, one of whom was valiant and robustly made, but blind. The other was lame and feeble, but his sight was excellent. The blind man said to the lame, 'My friend, ours is a hard case, for it is spread far and near that the king gives a great feast, at which every man will receive not only an abundance of food but much wealth. You are lame, while I am blind. How can we get to the feast?'

"'Take my advice,' replied the lame man, 'and we shall obtain a share of both the dinner and wealth.'

"'Truly,' answered the other, 'I will follow any advice that could benefit me.'

"'Well then,' replied the lame man. 'You are strong of heart and robust of body and so you shall carry me, lame and weak, on your back. My eyes shall be as yours and so, in exchange for your legs, I will lend you my eyes. By this means we shall reach the festival and secure the reward.'

"'Just as you say,' answered the one with the legs. 'Get on my back immediately.'

"He did so. The lame man pointed the way and the other carried him. They arrived at the feast and received the same recompense as the rest.

"*Application:* My beloved, the king is our Lord Jesus Christ, who prepares the feast of eternal life. The blind man is the powerful of this world, who are blind to their future safety. The lame man is any devout person, who has nothing in common with the man of the world but sees the kingdom which is to come."[22]

Impact of the Invention of Printing on Leisure Reading

The introduction of printing was momentous in the progress of English literacy, for it made a variety of books, particularly in the vernacular, more easily available for the native reader and, by making the cost an estimated hundred times cheaper, rendered the purchase of books possible for an immensely larger circle of people. More important, Caxton had an eye to the tastes not only of the readers at Court but also of the merchants of the middle classes with their consequent influence on other trading, craft and apprentice classes.

Between 1477 and his death in 1491 nearly a hundred different books were turned out by his press. One was the *Aeneid* of Virgil and another was *Reynard the Fox*, his translation from the Flemish of a story that was widely popular in Europe, telling the story of a clever fox outwitting the other animals. Of great delight too was his translation of Jacobus de Voragine's treasure, the *Golden Legend* (1483), with seventeen pages of woodcuts and fifty stories from the Old Testament, a book that was cherished by young and old for many centuries. In 1487 he published his version of *Aesop's Fables*, which according to a critic in 1932 still remained "with infinitely little modernization . . . the best text for children [at that time]. A proof that it was 'read to pieces' is given by the survival of only one perfect and two imperfect copies at the present day."[23] He also saw to it that the ever-popular romances were published in numbers, such as *Godfrey of Bologna*, *Charles the Great* and *The Knight Paris and the fair Vienne . . . who suffered many adversities because of their true love, ere they could enjoy thereof each other.*

Caxton also showed zeal for useful books "in our English language," one of which was the *Mirror of the World*, a sort of encyclopaedia translated from the French, and various manuals on manners and devotions. One of the books recommended for the use of children was in the form of a catechism, "This little treatise, entitled or named *The Lucidarie*, is good and profitable for every well-disposed person, who has the will and affection to know of noblesse spiritual." The child put questions of this kind to the teacher:

> "Master, tell me what thing is God?"
> "My child, he is a thing spiritual in you, which is all dignity and perfection."
> "Master, may he be no more but only one God?" etc.

After Caxton's death his work was continued by his foreman, Wynkyn de Worde, who by 1534 produced more than 800 books. Meanwhile, foreigners, encouraged by the 1484 Act, migrated here in such numbers that between 1476 and 1553 some two-thirds of the printing force were aliens. In 1478 Theodoric Rood set up his press in Oxford, in 1480 John Lettou started one in London where he was later joined by William de Machlinia, and in the same year another press was established by the "schoolmaster of St Albans," his output including popular English chronicles and works on hawking, hunting and coat-armour. By 1500 others had been put into production at York, Cambridge, Canterbury and Abingdon.

An interesting feature of the printed works from now on was the appearance of large numbers of popular poems and tracts, which must have come into the hands of young readers. For example, in addition to prose abridgements of popular traditional tales of men like Richard Cœur de Lion, chap-books printed before 1520 included such titles as *A Merry "Gest" of a Sergeant and Friar*, *A Hundred Tales* and *The Pastime of the People*. The variety of reading matter can also be judged from the *Day-Book of John Dorne* (1520), which contains 1,850 entries for books in the space of just ten months, embracing such saleable works as almanacks, *Robin Hood*, *Nutbrown Maid*, *The Squire of Low Degree*, *Sir Isumbras* and *Robert the Devil*, in addition to the usual instructional books (see page 101).

To our certain knowledge, the fifty-four books printed in England in 1500 had jumped to 214 in 1550, and by 1557 a total of over 5,000 different works had been published in England. As an observer of the times wrote, "a number of books there be abroad in every man's hand of divers and sundry matters which are greedily devoured of a great sort."[24] These included educational books, legal works, herbals, medicine, first-aid manuals, hints for recipes, information, popular science, geography and history. Nor was there any shortage of books implied in this passage from *The Description of the Sphere or Frame of the World* by William Salisbury (1550): "I walked myself round about all Paul's Churchyard from shop to shop, inquiring of such a treatise. . . . I asked again for the same works in Latin, whereof there were iii or iv of sundry authors brought and shown me." In fact, St Paul's had become an important centre for the book trade as early as 1500, as indicated by one book that was for sale, according to its title-page, *apud bibliopolas in cimiterio sancti Pauli*, 1514 (i.e. among the booksellers in the cemetery of St Paul's).

There were also small Bible tracts known as ballets or ballads, mostly in verse, such as "A Brief Sum of the Bible" (1560) or "Four Stories of the Scripture in Metre" or "A Brief of the Bible, drawn first into English Poetry" (1596). Ballads about the popular heroes of oral tale were also being produced and Robin Hood, who had been mentioned in *Piers Plowman* as early as the fourteenth century, was making his bow in tales like "Robin Hood and the Monk," "Robin Hood and Guy of Gisborne" and "The Little 'Gest' of Robin Hood." Another ballad that appeared in 1595 used the babes in the wood as its theme. All these must have been eagerly snapped up by the young or apprentice reader.

To satisfy the popular thirst for contemporary news or unusual happenings, all sorts of sheets were issued, e.g. "The true description of two monstrous children born at Herne in Kent. Ballad. 1565"; "The description of a rare or rather monstrous fish taken on the east coast of Holland" (1566); "A notable and prodigious history of a maiden (C. Cooper) who for sundry years neither eats, drinks nor sleeps" (1589); and "John Chapman: A most true report of the moving and sinking of ground at Westram in Kent, December 18 to 29, 1596." As Giovanni Florio commented in *Second Fruits* (1591), "every man is busily working to feed his own fancy: some by delivering to the press the occurrences and accidents of the world, news from the mart or from the mint, and news are the credit of a traveller and the first question of an Englishman."

Prior to printing, the very cost of books had been a formidable barrier to the prospective buyer. The wardrobe accounts of Edward IV show that Piers Baudwyn was paid twenty shillings for "binding, gilding and dressing" two books and, though this may have referred to rather lavish copies, just one-hundredth of that price placed their purchase beyond the pocket of the common man. The invention of printing substantially reduced the cost of books. Further, an Act of 1533 declared that if a printer or bookseller charged an unreasonable price for his books, the Lord Chancellor and others could prescribe the maximum price for its sale and were empowered to fine offenders. Books therefore appeared with the caution that they were "not to be sold above xvi d" on the title-page and so they became cheaper than ever. *The ABC and Little Catechism* cost a penny in paper and twopence in vellum in 1520, ballads were sold for a halfpenny each and a *Book of Cookery* was fourpence. To put these prices in perspective, one might note that two pounds of butter at that time cost a penny, a one-pound cheese could be obtained for a halfpenny, two hens were worth four- and a pair of shoes could be bought for sixpence. Later in the century a whole sheep at nine shillings was still cheaper than an unbound copy of the Bible, while an entire pig was no more than one shilling and twopence. Books came within reach of an appreciable number of the population and, to help the ordinary man select his purchases, Bishop William Alley published a book entitled *The Poor Man's Library*. The giving of books at New Year had come to be a favourite practice, as confirmed by titles such as *A New Year's Gift, entitled "A Crystal Glass for all Estates to look into"* (1568) and *My troth's New Year's gift being Robin Goodfellow's News* (1592).

Books had already been established in places outside London like Lichfield and Shrewsbury, and the Stationers Company (1558), recorded that they had fined Walley and Smythe because "they did keep the shops open festival day and sold books." Fairs also flourished at places like Oxford, Cambridge, Ely and Bristol, where the book trade thrived, judging from the complaint of the Stationers' Company against John Wolfe, who "runs up and down to all the fairs and markets through a great part of the realm and makes sale of them."[25]

Pedlars too, pack on back, were busy. They were offering the bookshops such severe competition that in 1521 they had been forbidden "certain books in French and English, which were taken . . . hawking about the streets, which is contrary to the orders of the City of London."[26] An Act of 1553 ordered that pedlars should be licensed but they still went around hawking almanacks, religious tracts or "whatsoever things they have to sell . . . as 'News out of India' or 'The Original of the Turkish Empire' or 'A Powder to kill worms' or 'Merry Tales' or 'Songs and Ballets' or 'A Preservative against the Plague' or 'A Water to make the skin fair' " — so wrote Rastell in *The Third Book* (1566). By the end of the century too Chettle in his *Kind Heart's Dream* (1592) was made to comment that "chapmen are able to spread more pamphlets . . . than all the booksellers in town." As such they must have played a vital part in bringing the printed word to those living in remote rural areas and in extending literacy among the urban masses.

In fact, by the late sixteenth century the conditions for the acquisition and enjoyment of the skills of literacy in England were exceptionally propitious. Books, pamphlets and sheets were in good supply and more reasonably priced, the public were being constantly urged — and were themselves eager — to learn to read, and there were both schools and teachers sufficiently skilled to help them to the coveted skill. Early in the century (see page 157) Sir Thomas More had estimated that more than half the population were able to read. In view of the favourable factors subsequently prevailing, the number of literates might well have risen to three-quarters of the population, if not more, by the turn of the century.

However, despite the production of literature of varying sorts and quality, it remains extremely difficult in the absence of direct evidence to identify confidently those books to which the young learners definitely turned for their supplementary reading, apart of course from those prescribed by the religious authorities. That many of the publications of Caxton, such as *Aesop's Fables* and *Golden Legend*, were being popularly used can be taken as granted because these books were still being recommended as suitable for youngsters nearly four hundred years later. Of the other books produced in the sixteenth century one can only assume that some of them were considered appropriate for the apprentice reader because they too were being prescribed for use in school by later generations. Such a book might have been the "Chronicles" of the Frenchman, Jean Froissart, who had travelled extensively in Scotland, Italy and Belgium. His work, which provided a fascinating picture of the courts and wars of Europe in the fourteenth century, was admirably translated into English by Lord Berners in 1523—5. In 1539 he also translated from the Spanish another work which he called *The Golden Book of Marcus Aurelius* but which proved to be one of the most influential books of the century and went through no less than seven editions by 1586. This short extract will illustrate its nature.

"There was an ancient law that nothing might be taken and received from a citizen in Rome unless he were first examined by the Censor. In the time of Cato Censorius, when anyone would wish to become a citizen of Rome, this examination was made of him. He was not demanded . . . whence he was or what he was or whence he came or wherefore he came. They only took his hands between theirs and, if they felt them soft and smooth, forthwith as an idle vagabond they dispatched and sent him away. If they found his hands hard and full of knots, by and by they admitted him as a citizen and dweller in Rome. Also, when any officers took ill-doers and put them in prison (that was called Marmotine), instead of information, the first thing they took heed of was their hands. If they were as a labourer's and a workman's hands, though his crime was grievous, yet his chastisement was mitigated and made easier. If the unhappy prisoner chanced to have idle hands, he would have sharp punishment, even for a little fault. It has been an old saying: 'He that has good hands must needs have good customs.' I say that I never chastised a labouring man without being sorry for it. No, I never caused a vagabond to be whipped but I was glad of it. I will tell you more about this Cato Censorius, who was greatly feared. For, even as children in school run to their books when they hear their master is coming, so when Cato went through the streets of Rome, everybody went to their work. . . . "

Another influential book which must have been placed in the hands of the Protestant children of the period was *Acts and Monuments*, popularly known as the *Book of Martyrs*, of John Foxe. The English version was first issued in 1563, with three further editions in 1570, 1576 and 1583 during the author's lifetime. This illustrative passage tells the story of William Hunter, an apprentice, who had been martyred at the age of nineteen:

"In the meantime William's father and mother came to him and heartily desired of God that he might continue to the end in that good way in which he had begun. His mother said to him that she was glad that she had ever been so happy to bear such a child who could find [it possible] in his heart to lose his life for the sake of Christ's name. Then William said to his mother: 'For the little pain which I shall suffer, which is but a short breath, Christ has promised me, mother, a crown of joy. May you not be glad of that, mother?'

"With that his mother kneeled down on her knees, saying, 'I pray God [will] strengthen you, my son, to the end. Yea, I think you as well bestowed [i.e. behaved] as any child that ever I bore.'

". . . Now, when it was day, the sheriff, M. Brockett, called to set forward the burning of William Hunter. . . . Then there was a gentleman who said, 'I pray God have mercy on his soul.' The people said, 'Amen, Amen.'

"Then William cast his psalter right into the hand of his brother, who said, 'Think, William, on the holy passion of Christ and be not afraid of death.'

"William answered, 'I am not afraid.' Then he lifted his hands to heaven and said, 'Lord, Lord, Lord, receive my spirit!' And, casting his head again into the smothering smoke, he yielded up his life for the truth, sealing it with his blood to the praise of God. . . ."

Another popular book of the time was *The Lives of the Noble Grecians and Romans*, originally written by Plutarch but translated into English by Sir Thomas North in 1579. Written in vivid and magnificently idiomatic English, this book was largely Shakespeare's encyclopaedia of classical knowledge. This passage on ostracism might be an appropriate sample:

"But briefly to let you know what ostracism was and after what sort they used it. You are to know that at a certain day appointed, every citizen carried a great shell in his hand, whereupon he wrote the name of him he would have banished, and he brought it to a . . . place railed about with wooden bars in the market-place. Then, when every man had brought in his shell, the magistrates and officers of the city did count and tell the number of them. If there were less than 6,000 citizens, they proclaimed him by sound of trumpet a banished man for ten years, during which time . . . the party did enjoy all his goods. . . . Now it is reported there was a plain man of the country, very simple, who could neither write nor read. He came to Aristides, being the first man he met . . ., and gave him his shell, praying him to write Aristides' name upon it. He, being abashed by this, did ask the countryman if Aristides had ever done him any displeasure.

" 'No,' said the countryman, 'he never did me any hurt. I know him not but it grieves me to hear every man call him a just man.'

"Aristides, hearing him say so, gave him no answer but wrote his own name on the shell and delivered it again to the countryman. But as he went his way out of the city, he lifted up his hands to heaven and made a prayer, contrary to that of Achilles in Homer, beseeching the gods that the Athenians might never have such troubles in hand as they should be compelled to call for Aristides again. . . ."

If such stuff were considered too tame or possibly claustrophobic by the adventure-seeking young reader of the spacious days of Elizabeth I, he could turn to the more daring material of Richard Hakluyt. He published several books about the activities of English explorers, and in 1589 he produced his *Principal Navigations, Voyages and Discoveries of the English Nation*, which was reissued in a much-enlarged edition between 1598 and 1600. Here is one short action-packed extract:

"The 26th July, 1592, on my return from Barbary in the ship called the 'Amity' of London . . . at four o'clock in the morning we had sight of two ships, one being about three or four leagues distant from us. Their boldness in having the King of Spain's arms displayed made us judge them ships of war rather than laden with merchandise. As it later appeared from their own talk, they had full intention to take us but it was a question among them as to whether it would be better to take us to St Lucia or Lisbon. Each of us carried a mainsail. They had placed themselves in warlike order, one a cable's length in front of the other, and we began the fight. We continued in this as fast as we were able to charge and discharge for five hours, with neither of us being more than a cable's length from the other. During this time we received divers shot both in the hull of our ship, masts and sail, to a total of thirty-two great shots, besides 500 musket and heavy harquebus shots at least. Because we perceived them to be stout foes, we thought it good to board the 'Biscaine,' which was ahead of the other. We lay aboard an hour, plying our ordnance and small shot, and in the end we stowed his men. Now the others in the fly-boat, thinking we had put our men into his fellow vessel, made room for us, meaning to leave us aboard and so entrap us between the both of them. By this means they fell away from us. Then we immediately held our luff, hoisted our topsails and weathered them and came hard aboard the fly-boat with our ordnance prepared. We gave her the whole of our broadside, with which we slew divers of their men so that we could see the blood run out at the scupper holes. After that we cast about, newly charged all our ordnance and came upon them again, willing them to yield or we would sink them. Whereupon the one would have yielded . . . but the other called him a traitor. To him we made answer that, if he would not yield immediately as well, we would sink him first. Thereupon, understanding our determination, he immediately put out a white flag and yielded."

This was indeed rip-roaring stuff but very soon the comparative freedom of access to literature, which seemed to be enjoyed by the young reader of the sixteenth century, was to be denied him. With the emergence of Puritanism, the pursuit of intellectual culture and the pleasure of reading for its own sake were far less important in the educational programme for the young pupil. Whereas religion had been honoured for the glory of God and desired for the enhancement of one's own soul, it now became the means of emphasizing the wretchedness of man. The child was born to a weight of sin, he struggled through a world enmeshed in wickedness and he had only the most meagre chance of escape. The near-hopelessness of man's existence was summed up in these lines of James Janeway (1636—74):

> When by spectators I am told
> What beauty doth adorn me,
> Or in a glass when I behold
> How sweetly God did form me;
> That God such comeliness bestowed
> And on me made to dwell —
> What pity such a pretty maid
> As I should go to Hell.

In the sixth century the art of reading had been taken up as an indispensable weapon for evangelization; but by the end of the sixteenth century it would seem that the battle for mass literacy had been almost won, chiefly through the endeavours of servants of the Church. Ironically, as we have seen in Chapter 7, it was that same Church which had for long periods in the intervening thousand years disapproved of the skill being applied to a vernacular Bible. By the early seventeenth century the new servants of the Church saw a fresh battle ahead — to rescue the Christian child from the horrible fate to which he seemed predestined. Determined efforts had to be made for his salvation, and again reading and books were conscripted for that specific purpose. Children's books, both their instructional primers and supplementary readers, were subjected to rigorous censorship.

For all that, the stern policy adopted by the Puritans to control and mould reading tastes was in itself an unequivocal sign not only of the power of books but also of the remarkable expansion of literacy among people of all estates. Where reading was concerned, these were stirring times. Schools were prospering both in town and village; tutors, schoolmasters and teachers of reading were plying their brisk trade; the bases of structured reading instruction had been competently and firmly laid; and, "according to the complaint" of 1635, there were "too many books abroad already."[27]

Such a surfeit of printed works was a further token that there were numbers of people who were both willing to buy books and able to read them. The existence of a sizeable reading public too can be safely deduced from the calculated efforts of authors to capture the market of the common reader. In *The Plain Man's Pathway to Heaven* (1605) Arthur Dent advertised that his work was for "the ignorant and vulgar sort"; in his *Oppositions of the Word of God* (1610) Pierre du Moulin asserted that there was "nothing here but for the simple"; and in *The Grounds of Divorce*

(1614) Elnathan Parr claimed that his book was "for the stomachs of the unlearned." Certainly, all the various pieces of evidence, when accumulated, present a picture of far more extensive literacy in early seventeenth-century England than we might now realize.

Annotation

Chapter 1

1 Kendrick, T. D. *The Druids.* 2nd ed. Methuen, 1928 (p. 60)
2 Richmond, I. A. *Roman Britain.* Penguin Books, 1955 (p. 28)
3 Bodmer, F., ed., and Hogben, L. *The Loom of Language.* Allen & Unwin, 1944 (p. 73)
4 Rivet, A. L. F. *Town and Country in Roman Britain.* Hutchinson University Library, 1966 (p. 61)
5 Haverfield, F. *The Romanization of Roman Britain.* 4th ed. revised by G. Macdonald. Oxford, 1923 (p. 3)
6 Jackson, K. *Language and History in Early Britain.* Oliver & Boyd, 1953 (p. 100)
7 Boyd, W. *The History of Western Education.* 5th ed. A. & C. Black, 1950 (p. 107)

Chapter 2

1 Parry, A. W. *Education in England in the Middle Ages.* U.T.P., 1920
2 Bede. *Ecclesiastical History of England* (II.xv)
3 Ibid. (IV.xviii)
4 Ibid. (V.vi)
5 Ibid. (V.xx)
6 Ibid. (V.xxiv)
7 Ibid. (III.xviii)
8 Ibid. (III.xxvii)
9 Mullinger, J. B. *The Schools of Charles the Great.* London, 1877 (p. 98)
10 Ibid. (p. 102)
11 Ibid. (p. 103)
12 Coulton, G. C. *Mediaeval Panorama.* Cambridge, 1938 (p. 386)

13   Asser. *Life of King Alfred.* Trans. L. C. Jane. Chatto & Windus, 1908
      (p. 53)
14   Wilkins, D. *Concilia Magnae Britanniae et Hiberniae.* 1737
15   Frere, W. H. *Visitation Articles and Injunctions.* Alcuin Club, 1910
      (XIV.ii. ¶ 17)
16   *Injunctions . . . of Richard Barnes, Bishop of Durham, 1575—87.*
      Surtees Society (XXII, 1850)
17   Leach, A. F. *English Schools at the Reformation.* Constable, 1896
      (ii. 317)
18   Ibid. (ii. 200)
19   Ibid (ii. 92)
20   Heath, P. *English Clergy on the Eve of the Reformation.* Routledge &
      Kegan Paul, 1969 (p. 84)
21   Carlisle, N. *A Concise Description of the Endowed Grammar Schools in
      England and Wales.* 1818 (II. 578)
22   Thompson, A. H. "Song Schools in the Middle Ages." No. 14. Church
      Music Society Occasional Paper. S.P.C.K., 1942 (p. 76)
23   Giraud, F. A. *Archaeologia Cantiana* (XX. 203—10)
24   Grindal, E. *Remains.* Parker Society, 1843 (p. 142)
25   *English Schools at the Reformation.* (ii. 31)
26   Ibid. (ii. 41)
27   Ibid. (ii. 34)
28   Heath (p. 85)
29   Coulton, G. C. *"Monastic Schools in the Middle Ages."* From the
      Contemporary Review. June, 1913 (pp. 818—28)
30   Coulton, G. C. *Mediaeval Panorama* (p. 388)
31   Trevelyan, G. M. *English Social History.* Longmans, 1948 (p. 108)
32   Bede (IV.i)
33   Bede (IV.ii)
34   Deanesly, M. *The Lollard Bible.* Cambridge, 1920 (p. 172)
35   *Historiae Dunelmensis Scriptores Tres.* Surtees Society, 1839 (p. 118)
36   Thompson, J. W. *The Literacy of the Laity in the Middle Ages.* Burt
      Franklin, 1960 (p. 182)
37   Stenton, D. M. *English Society in the Early Middle Ages.* Penguin Books,
      1965 (p. 219)
38   *Opera.* Rolls Society. (I. 90; II. 341—6)
39   Coulton, G. C. *Mediaeval Panorama* (p. 157)
40   *Sermo Exhortatorius Cancellarii Eboracensis.* Sigla A (iii—ix)
41   Campbell, W. E. and Reed, A. W., ed. *English Works.* London (II. 219)
42   GLC Record Office. MS DL/C/330 (fos. 265r—266r)
43   Price, F. D. *Gloucester Diocese under Bishop Hooper.* Transactions
      Bristol and Gloucester Archaeological Society (IX. 51—151)
44   Heath (pp. 111—12)
45   London Guildhall MS 9164 (iv) (fos. 18v, 21v)
46   Bury, Richard de. *The Philobiblon.* California University, 1948 (p. 94)
47   British Museum MSS. Arundel (f. 69)
48   Knowles, D. *The Religious Orders in England.* Cambridge (III. 291)
49   *Dialogues of Heresies.* (Dialogue iii. 12)
50   *Letters and Papers of Henry VIII.* 1509—47
51   *Chronicle of Florence of Worcester.* Ed. Forester, T. Bohns, 1854 (p. 72)

52   Coulton, G. C. *Europe's Apprenticeship*. London, 1940 (p. 67)
53   Capgrave: *Lives of St Augustine and St Gilbert of Sempringham*. Ed. Munro. Early English Text Society, 1910 (p. 63)
54   Rashdall, H. *Universities of Europe in the Middle Ages*. Ed. Powicke, F. M., and Emden, A. B. Oxford, 1936 (II. 602)

Chapter 3

1   *King Horn, Floriz and Blaunchefleur*. Ed. Lumby, J. Early English Text Society (Original Series), 1866 (p. 71)
2   Whiston, R. *Cathedral Trusts and their Fulfilment*. 2nd ed. London, 1849 (pp. 10—12)
3   Leach, A. F. *Early Yorkshire Schools*. Yorks. Archaeological Society Series, 1899—1903.
4   Leach, A. F. *The Schools of Mediaeval England*. Methuen, 1915 (p. 198)
5   Ibid. (p. 275)
6   Leach, A. F. *A History of Warwick School*. Constable, 1906 (pp. 65—66)
7   *The Schools of Mediaeval England* (p. 210)
8   *English Schools at the Reformation* (II. 200)
9   Ibid. (ii. p. 98)
10   Leach, A. F. *Educational Charters*. London, 1911 (p. 312)
11   Ibid. (p. 252)
12   Trevelyan (p. 15)
13   *The Schools of Mediaeval England* (p. 241)
14   Watson, Foster. *The English Grammar Schools*. Revised edition Cass & Co., 1968 (p. 187)
15   *Educational Charters* (p. 417)
16   *English Schools at the Reformation* (ii. 201)
17   Chambers, R. W., and Daunt, M. *A Book of London English*, 1384—1425. Oxford, 1931
18   Charlton, K. *Education in Renaissance England*. Routledge & Kegan Paul, 1965 (p. 254)
19   Thrupp, S. L. *The Merchant Class of Mediaeval London*. Chicago, 1948 (p. 158)
20   *The Schools of Mediaeval England* (p. 326)
21   *English Schools at the Reformation* (II. 89)
22   Ibid. (ii. 66)
23   *The Schools of Mediaeval England* (p. 267)
24   *Educational Charters* (p. 435)
25   Clay, R. M. *The Mediaeval Hospitals of England*. Antiquary's Books, London, 1909 (p. 27)
26   *The Schools of Mediaeval England* (p. 272)
27   Fitzstephen, William. "A Picture of London." From Kendall, E. K. *Source Book of English History*. Macmillan & Co., 1909 (p. 67)
28   Victoria History of the Counties of England: Lancashire, 1908 (ii. 605)
29   Charlton (p. 98)
30   *Educational Charters* (p. 501)
31   Ibid (p. 123)

32   Carlisle (I. 157)
33   Ibid. (I. 517)
34   Concilia (III. 722)
35   Charlton (p. 99)
36   Schools Inquiry Commission (XII. 217)
37   Savage and Fripp. *Minutes and Accounts* (III. 9)
38   *Educational Charters* (pp. 139—41)
39   De Montmorency, J. E. G. *State Intervention in English Education.*
      Cambridge, 1902 (pp. 19, 31—32)
40   *The Schools of Mediaeval England (p.* 206)
41   *Early English Meals and Manners.* Ed. Furnivall, F. J. Early English Text
      Society, 1868 (p.xlv)
42   *Rotuli Parliamentorum* (III. 294)
43   *Statutes of the Realm.* Ed. 1816 (II. 157)
44   *Educational Charters* (p. 107)
45   Bacon, Roger. *Opera Inedita.* Rolls Series, 1904
46   *Educational Charters* (p. 37)
47   *The Schools of Mediaeval England* (p. 111)
48   *Educational Charters* (p. 235)
49   Ibid. (p. 417)
50   *The Schools of Mediaeval England* (p. 285)
51   Woodruff, C. E. and Cape, H. S. *A History of the King's School,*
      Canterbury. Hughes & Clarke, 1908 (pp. 28—30)
52   Watson, Foster (p. 138)
53   *Educational Charters* (p. 431)
54   De Montmorency (p. 19)
55   Watson, Foster (p. 154)
56   Ibid. (p. 153)
57   Lawson, J. *A Town Grammar School through Six Centuries.* Oxford,
      1963 (pp. 17—19)
58   *Educational Charters* (p. 423)
59   *The Schools of Mediaeval England* (p. 267)
60   Percival, E. F. *The Foundation Statutes of Merton College, Oxford.*
      William Pickering, 1847 (p. 65)
61   Watson, Foster (p. 18)
62   Stowe, A. R. M. *English Grammar Schools in the Reign of Queen*
      Elizabeth. New York, 1908 (p. 178)
63   Frere, W. H. (p. 322)
64   Power, Eileen. *Mediaeval English Nunneries.* Cambridge, 1922 (p. 238)
65   Gardiner, D. *English Girlhood at School.* Oxford, 1929 (p. 46)
66   Ibid. (p. 89). From Foxe's *Acts and Monuments*
67   Ibid. Foxe
68   *The Fifty Earliest English Wills.* Ed. Furnivall, F. J. Early English Text
      Society, 1822
69   Curtis (p. 54)
70   *Stonor Letters.* Camden Society Series (III.xxix)
71   *Sandwich Book of Orphans* (pp. 22 ff.)
72   *Early Chancery Proceedings* (II. 167, 188)
73   Calendar of State Papers. Elizabeth (XVIII. 264)
74   *Italian Relation of the Island of England.* Camden Soc., 1847

75 Montalembert, Count de. *The Monks of the West.* Nimmo, 1896
   (V. 104)
76 Gardiner (p. 15)
77 Curtis (p. 52)
78 Power (p. 578)
79 Ibid. (p. 577)
80 Strype, John. *Life and Acts of John Whitgift.* Oxford, 1812 (III. 383)
81 *Story of the Wars.* Ed. Dewing. Loeb. Heinemann, 1914—28 (III. xiv)
82 Richardson, H. G. and Sayles, G. C. *The Governance of Mediaeval
   England.* Edinburgh, 1963 (pp. 277—8)
83 Quoted in *Early English Meals.* (Introduction, p. xviii)
84 *Early English Meals.* (Introduction, p. xiii)

Chapter 4

1 Specht, F. A. *History of Education in Germany from the Earliest Times
  to the Middle of the Thirteenth Century.* Stuttgart, 1885
2 See life by Kruch in *Scriptores Rerum Merovingicarum* (V) 1910
  (pp. 249—362). Monumenta Germaniae Historica.
3 See crit. ed. of life by Waitz, G. in *Scriptores Rerum Germanicarum*,
  1884
4 Asser (p. 19)
5 Quoted by Baldwin, T. W. *Shakespeare's Petty School.* Urbana, 1943
6 Milne, J. G. Relics of Graeco-Egyptian Schools." *Journal of Hellenic
  Studies*, 1908 (pp. 121 ff.)
7 Athenaeus. *Deipnosophistae* (X.cccclix) Ed. Gulick, C. B. Loeb:
  Heinemann, 1929
8 Fries, C. G. *Linguistics and Reading.* Holt, Rinehart & Winston Inc.,
  1963 (pp. 191 ff.)
9 Morris, Joyce. *Reading in the Primary School.* Newnes, 1959 (p. 56)
10 Laurie. S. S. *Historical Survey of Pre-Christian Education.* Longmans,
   Green & Co., 1895
11 Stubbs, W. *Tractatus de Inventione Sanctae Crucis Nostrae*, 1861
12 Hendrickson, G. L. "Ancient Reading." *Classical Journal*, XXV. 1929—
   30 (pp. 183—93)
13 Lucian. Ed. Harmon, A. M. Loebe: Heinemann, 1947 (III, p. 177)
14 Ed. Pusey, E. B. Everyman: Dent, 1907 (VI.iii ¶3)
15 *Rule of Saint Benedict.* Ed. Cardinal Gasquet. Chatto & Windus, 1936
   §48
16 Merryweather, F. S. *Bibliomania in the Middle Ages.* 1849 (pp. 14—15)
17 Healy, John. *Ireland's Ancient Schools and Scholars.* Dublin, 1890
   (pp. 406—7)
18 *Chronicle of Florence of Worcester.* Ed. Forester. T. Bohns Library,
   1854 (p. 183)
19 Marrou, H. I. Trans. Lamb, G. *A History of Education in Antiquity.*
   Sheed & Ward, 1956 (p. 159)
20 See also *Fun with Phonics.* Muriel Reis. Cambridge Art Publishers, 1962
21 Marrou (p. 143)
22 Asser (p. 70)
23 Ibid. (p. 18)
24 Ibid. (p. 69)

25 Jackson, Holbrook. *The Anatomy of Bibliomania*. Faber & Faber, 1950 (p. 72)
26 *The Schools of Mediaeval England* (p. 289)
27 See Chapter 2, Note 16

Chapter 5

1 *Proceedings of the Society of Antiquaries of London* (XXIII)
2 Tuer, A. W. *A History of the Horn-book*. London, 1897 (p. 105)
3 Gibbon, A. M. *A History of the Ancient Free Grammar School of Skipton-in-Craven*. Liverpool, 1947 (Appendix C)
4 *The Schools of Mediaeval England* (p. 300)
5 Birchenough, E. *The Prymer in English*. Library. 4th Series (XVIII) 1937–8 (p. 177)
6 Arber, E. Ed. *A Transcript of the Registers of the Company of Stationers of London, A.D. 1554–1640*. 1875
7 Judge, C. E. *Elizabethan Book Pirates*. Harvard Studies. VIII. 1934 (p. 34)
8 Kehr, C. *Geschichte d. Methodik d. deutschen Volksschulunterrichts*. 4 Bde in 2. Gotha, 1879–82 (p. 19)

Chapter 6

1 Kehr (p. 19)
2 Ibid. (pp. 28–9)
3 Wright, T. *Anglo-Saxon and Old English Vocabularies*. Ed. Wülcker. London, reprinted 1884
4 Reprinted in Fechner, H. *Vier seltene Schriften des sechzehnten Jahrhunderts*. Wiegandt und Grechen. Berlin, 1882
5 Lauback, F. C. *Teaching the World to Read*. Friendship Press, New York, 1947
6 McKee, P. *A Primer for Parents*. Houghton Mifflin & Co. Boston, 1957
7 Allen, R. L. and Allen, V. F. *Read Along with Me*. Columbia, 1964
8 *On Education. Cambridge*, 1913
9 Kehr (p. 65)
10 Froissart, Jean. *Works*. Ed. Luce. (I. 359, 402)
11 Higden, Ranulf. *Polychronicon*. Rolls Series (41.ii.157)
12 Trevelyan (p. 1)
13 Oliphant, J. *The Educational Writings of Richard Mulcaster*. James Macklehose & Sons. Glasgow, 1903

Chapter 7

1 Deanesly (p. 30)
2 Ibid. (p. 272)
3 Gee, H. and Hardy, W. J. *Documents Illustrative of Church History*. Macmillan, 1896 (p. xlii)
4 Kingsford, C. L. *Chronicles of London*. Oxford, 1905 (p. 69)
5 Foxe, John. *The Acts and Monuments*. London, 1843
6 Chedworth's Register. London (f. 62b)
7 Froude, J. A. *History of England: Henry the Eighth*. Everyman: Dent, 1909–12 (II)

8   Gee & Hardy (p. 1xiii)
9   Strype, John. *Memorials of Archbishop Cranmer*. Oxford, 1848 (I.xiii)
10 Gabel, L. *Benefit of Clergy in England in the Later Middle Ages*. Northampton, Mass., 1929 (p. 66)
11 Ibid. (p. 64)
12 Gaol Delivery Rolls. 145 m.56 d (39 ed. III). Quoted by Gabel

Chapter 8

1   *Gesta abbatum monasterii Sancti Albani a Thomas Walsingham Compilata*. Ed. H. T. Riley. Rolls Series No. 28. i.24 f.
2   Kenney, J. F. *The Sources for the Early History of Ireland:* I Eccles. Columbia, 1929
3   *Gildae de Excidio Britanniae*. Ed. with trans. by H. Williams (Cymmrodorion Record Series. No.3). Including "Life of Gildas" by Caradoc of Llancarfan (p. 394)
4   Healy, John. *Ireland's Ancient Schools and Scholars*. Dublin, 1890 (p. 63)
5   Ibid. (p. 250)
6   Thompson, J. W. *The Mediaeval Library*. Hafner. New York, 1957 (pp. 114—15)
7   Ibid. (p. 25)
8   Ibid. (p. 109)
9   *S. Bonifati et Lulli Epistolae:* MGH Epistolae Merowingici et Karolini aevi (I)
10 Thompson, J. W. (p. 50)
11 Ogilvie, J. D. A. *Books in England from Aldhelm to Alcuin*. Harvard Summaries of Theses. 1933 (pp. 293—6)
12 Bury, Richard de (p. 94)
13 Merryweather (pp. 30—1)
14 Jackson, Holbrook (p. 370)
15 Ibid. (p. 367)
16 *Six Old English Chronicles*. The Chronicle of Richard of Cirencester. Ed. Giles, J. A. Bohns, 1882 (I.viii.455)
17 Montalembert. (V. 151—2)
18 Thompson, J. W. (p. 50)
19 *Gesta abbatum . . . Sancti Albani*. (p. 57)
20 Mullinger (p. 8)
21 Westcott, B. F. *A General View of the History of the English Bible*. 2nd ed. Cambridge, 1872
22 Modernized version from original in *Gesta Romanorum* by Chas. Swan. New ed. T. Wright. London, 1871 (pp. 248—50)
23 Darton, F. J. Harvey. *Children's Books in England*. C.U.P. 1958 (p. 10)
24 Pollard, A. W., and Redgrave, G. R., *et al. A Short-Title Catalogue of Books printed in England, Scotland and Ireland*, etc. Bibliographical Society, Oxford, 1946
25 State Domestic Papers. Elizabeth. 33. Art. 38.
26 Stationers' Register (I. 184)
27 STC.19570. Sig. A2.

Index